Space, the City and Social Theory

For Phillip

Space, the City and Social Theory

Social Relations and Urban Forms

FRAN TONKISS

polity

First published in 2005 by Polity Press

Polity Press
65 Bridge Street
Cambridge CB2 1UR, UK

Polity Press
350 Main Street
Malden, MA 02148, USA

ISBN: 0-7456-2825-7
ISBN: 0-7456-2826-5 (pb)

A catalogue record for this book is available from the British Library.

Typeset in 9.5 on 12 pt Utopia
by Servis Filmsetting Ltd, Manchester
Printed and bound in Great Britain by TJ International, Padstow, Cornwall

For further information on Polity, visit our website: www.polity.co.uk

Contents

Acknowledgements

I would like to express my thanks to my friends Caroline Butler-Bowdon, Anne-Marie Fortier, Monica Greco, David Hansen-Miller, Clare Hemmings, Michael Keith, Belinda McClory, Kate Nash, and Steve Pile. Emma Longstaff at Polity has been a very helpful and sympathetic editor. I am especially grateful to my former students at Goldsmiths College, whose enthusiasm and imagination have, more than anything else, helped my thinking about cities. My greatest debt of thanks is to my friend and colleague Les Back, for his generosity, encouragement and support.

This book is dedicated to my cousin Phillip Kent (1958–2003), in memory of our times together in different cities.

Parts of chapter 1 first appeared in 'The ethics of indifference: community and solitude in the city', *International Journal of Cultural Studies* 6/3 (2003): 297–311.

Figures 1 and 3 in chapter 2 are taken from E. W. Burgess, 'The growth of the city: an introduction to a research project', in R. E. Park et al., (eds), *The City* (Chicago: University of Chicago Press, 1967).

Figure 2 in chapter 2 is taken from M. Davis, *Ecology of Fear: Los Angeles and the Imagination of Disaster* (New York: Metropolitan Books, 1998). Copyright © 1998 by Mike Davis. Reprinted by permission of Henry Holt and Company, LLC.

Parts of chapter 4 first appeared in 'Inner City Living', in J. Barrett and C. Butler-Bowdon (eds), *Debating the City* (Sydney: Historic Houses Trust, 2001), pp. 3–10.

An earlier version of chapter 7 appeared in C. Jenks (ed.), *Urban Cultures: Critical Concepts in Literary and Cultural Studies* (London and New York: Routledge, 2004).

All reproduced with permission.

Every effort has been made to contact all the copyright holders, but if any have been inadvertently omitted the publisher will be pleased to make the necessary arrangements at the earliest opportunity.

Introduction

This book examines the relations between social processes and spatial forms in the modern city. How are key social categories – such as community, class, race, gender or sexuality – constituted and reproduced in urban contexts? How do broader social processes – such as political mobilization or economic change – take shape in the city? Rather than viewing the urban as a fixed space within which various social processes are worked out, the discussion here draws on perspectives in social theory to open up different versions of the city: as a site of social encounter and social division, as a field of politics and power, as a symbolic and material landscape, as an embodied space, as a realm of everyday experience. In these ways, it aims to relate issues in urban studies to wider debates within social theory and analysis.

The text does not provide an overview of the development of urban sociology or urban studies as disciplines (for a valuable survey, see Savage et al. 2003; see also Saunders 1995; Smith 1980; Soja 2000). Rather, it examines particular ways in which the city has found its place in the sociological imagination. It does so by starting with two key literatures in urban sociology and social theory. The first contains the founding arguments of a specifically urban sociology, developed by the researchers of the Chicago School in the 1920s and after. The second is based on work in European social theory, particularly that of Georg Simmel and Walter Benjamin, which has greatly influenced conceptual approaches to urban space and urban experience. My aim in returning to these US and European foundations – the former analysing urban spatial and social organization, the latter highlighting movements in urban social theory – is to examine how contemporary issues in urban social life relate to different traditions of thought that have shaped the understanding of the modern city.

This framework organizes the discussions which follow in particular ways. First, it directs attention to questions of social interaction, community formation and subjectivity in the city. The primary focus is therefore on these modes of urban 'sociation', to borrow Simmel's term, rather than larger-scale economic and political processes in the city (see, instead, Judge et al. 1995; Logan and Molotch 1987; Smith and Feagin 1987). Second, it means the text is largely concerned with social relations and urban forms in liberal capitalist cities, especially in North America and Western Europe (see, in contrast, Gufler 1997; Knox and Taylor 1995; Pile et al. 1999; Potter and Lloyd-Evans

1998; Robinson 2005; Sassen 2002). These founding perspectives in urban sociology and social theory were concerned with specific cities in specific contexts, even as they aimed to develop general accounts of urban form and urban experience. The Chicago School project, as Louis Wirth (1995: 58) put it, was to create a distinctively sociological approach to the study of the city, one focused on 'the peculiar characteristics of the city as a particular form of human association'. Such an analysis was meant to provide an alternative to the insights of geographers, economists, historians or political scientists. For the early urban sociologists, cities were excellent laboratories in which to observe social relations (Park 1967a), but also could be seen to constitute definite forms of sociality in themselves (Wirth 1995). While the Chicago approaches fell out of favour in the latter half of the twentieth century, they continue to underpin thinking about urban sociality and remain the precedent for social analysis that takes space seriously. As Soja (2000: 93) writes, 'The Chicago School and its followers must be duly recognized as the first successful attempt to develop and sustain an explicitly spatial theorization of the city.'

Urban sociology, of course, hardly has had the last word on cities, and a broader approach to urban studies cuts across the work of sociologists, geographers, architectural and cultural theorists, political theorists and other urban critics. No single discipline can lay claim to the city. The discussions that follow therefore take critical arguments from writers working across the fields of urban sociology and geography, social and cultural theory. Each chapter draws on relevant approaches to the city within social theory and analysis and explores these ideas in contemporary urban contexts. The discussion develops via a thematic approach to issues in urban life: community; difference and division; politics and public space; gentrification, consumption and urban cultures; the embodied experience of the city; and urban subjectivity. In each case, urban spaces can be seen as structuring social relations and processes, and in turn as shaped by social action and meanings. 'Spatial relations', as Simmel (2004: 73) asserted, 'are only the condition, on one hand, and the symbol, on the other, of human relations.' The organization of space both provides the basis for social relations, and offers a reflection of them.

Cities in this sense are one of the best examples of the idea that things which are real are also imagined. Social structures, relations and practices are linked in sometimes complicated ways to symbolic urban forms. Cities, after all, are dense material realities which also take their shape in memory and perception. While the experience of the city may be over-determined by structural relations, material inequalities and social circumstance, it is not simply the case that critics must choose between the hard news of urban social facts and the vagaries of subjective or symbolic analysis, between studying cities as 'distinct spatial formations or imaginaries' (Amin and Thrift 2002: 2). The lines drawn between the material and the ideal, the objective and the subjective, the physical and the perceptual, tend to blur when you look at how they work out in the spaces of the city. One critical way of integrating these different modes of conceiving space is via Henri Lefebvre's (1991) treatment of space as a social product. Lefebvre argues that the social production of space operates on three levels, which – if they are separated in his account – do not always appear as distinct moments in reality. The first and most obvious sense in which space is produced is as an effect of spatial practice. The geography of social practice is based on relations and locations of production and repro- duction; it also includes the routine forms of spatial 'competence' and 'performance' which are required of social actors (1991: 38). The second level on which to think about the production of space is in terms of 'representations of space'. These are ordering conceptions of space, abstract designs related to formal 'knowledge, to signs, to codes', and are typical of a scientific, architec- tural or governmental ordering of space (1991: 33). Such representations of space are the stuff of maps, of plans, of systems and projects. They are templates of power that rationalize the spaces of the city and the normal conduct of bodies and things within them. Lefebvre's third level is that of 'representational space' – the most evocative and also the least defined cat- egory. Representational spaces are spaces of imagination, embodiment and desire. They are tied to symbolic and artistic practices, subversive or clan- destine designs, but are also the inhabited spaces of ordinary 'users'. Representational spaces refer to 'space as directly *lived* through its associated images and symbols . . . the dominated – and hence passively experienced – space which the imagination seeks to change and appropriate' (1991: 39). This typology treats space as the product of practice, perception and imagination, so that the same spaces may be reproduced, represented and experienced in different ways. In outlining these three modes of spatial production, Lefebvre tests the oppositions between objective and subjective spaces, structure and symbolism, real and discursive space (see also Soja 1995).

The spaces of social life are social products. This statement has the hollow ring of truism, of course, but it reminds us how solid, how concrete, how sheerly *objective* the effects of social action – cities, streets, buildings – can be. Lefebvre's argument points to how these practical spaces are overlaid by the work of thought; suggesting that urban forms are made not only out of mater- ials and things but out of meanings, language and symbols. It can be rela- tively easy to knock down a building, but it is much harder to demolish a space which is composed around memory, experience or imagination. There is no such thing, in a social sense, as empty space. Space is always and only produced as a complex of relationships and separations, presences and absences. 'Haunted places', as de Certeau (1984) has it, 'are the only ones people can live in'.

Different cities haunt the accounts that follow. Chicago is like a hometown to urban sociologists, and it frames the discussions of community and soli- tude in chapter 1, and of difference and division in chapter 2. Berlin is the backdrop to Simmel's and Benjamin's reflections on urban consciousness, discussed in chapter 6. Paris animates the arguments in chapter 7, lying behind Foucault's, Barthes's and de Certeau's speculations on 'other' spaces, on the erotics of the city, and on the kinds of spatial tactics which undo urban rationality. In each case, these authors are writing about particular cities, but also speak to the experience of being in other urban spaces. The early studies of Chicago, of course, do not simply explain contemporary Los Angeles, or Hong Kong or Johannesburg – they didn't really explain Chicago. Rather, they offer a framework for thinking about broader urban processes, forms and relations that can help make sense of specific places: and where they don't make this kind of wider sense, the differences can be even more instructive. Urban identities are always constituted in part through the exchange of meanings, ideas, images and people between different cities. It is this that makes for the jolt of recognition one hundred years later, when we read Simmel on a Berlin street-scene in the first decade of the twentieth century as the stream of pedestrians takes on the city, their nerves steeled and their faces hardened. It is not so far away from Elijah Anderson's street in Philadelphia in the 1980s, where people blank each other through various postures of inattention or evasion as a tactic for dealing with urban space and social strangers.

The chapters that follow take up different social questions which can be set in the spaces of the city. The first of these concerns the way social relations are shaped by urban spaces. In chapter 1 this problem is posed in terms of a tension between community and solitude in the city. Can a sense of 'community' exist in modern cities? Some of the central arguments in urban social theory and urban sociology are based on the social fragmentation and anonymity of the modern city. These approaches have continually been challenged, however, by accounts which stress the endurance of community in the city, and the role of urban networks in producing alternative forms of solidarity or community life. The discussion outlines key perspectives in these debates – from the early contributions of the Chicago School to the community studies of the post-war period to more recent critiques of community thinking – and advances an argument which sits somewhere between the poles of community and anonymity. It suggests that solitude in the modern city can be read not simply in terms of estrangement from others, but in terms of an ethics of indifference which creates its own forms of freedom and a broad space for tolerance. The choice is not merely between alienation and familiarity; rather, there exist ways of being with others in the city which preserve difference and maintain separateness while recognizing shared claims to social space.

Chapter 2 considers how social differences and divisions are reinforced by the spatial organization of cities. It examines the manner in which spatial borders reproduce economic, social and cultural divisions. The carving-up of the city into spatial and social zones was central to the Chicago School's ecology of urban areas, which sought to depict patterns of urban growth and decline as well as patterns of social segregation. This linking of spatial and social factors was reflected in later approaches to urban problems and policies. From the 1960s, constructions of an urban problem in different national contexts gave a range of social issues – poverty, crime, disorganization – a distinctly spatial character. It also gave them a racial character. The language of an 'urban problem' emerged at a point when social and government research, public debate and moral panic came together. Concerns over poverty and racial justice were twin spurs to an inner city debate in the 1960s, and to the subsequent development of various urban policy programmes. The first issue, poverty, provided a clear impetus for government action. The second, race, was a highly charged but often unspoken element of how urban problems came to be understood. In this sense, the notion of the 'inner city' worked as both a spatial and a social category. A similar complex of meaning is apparent in the contemporary study of urban neighbourhoods which links issues of urban poverty and inequality to the social pathology of certain local spaces.

These demarcations in urban space help to make legible the workings of power in the city. Chapter 3 addresses the city as a site of political agency and contested power. The focus here is less on dominant landscapes of power in the city – the architecture of authority and privilege – than on how cities frame more informal political movements. Urban spaces provide spatial and social resources for political mobilization, and are also constituted as objects of political struggle in their own right. The politics of urban space, that is, concerns not only contests staged *in* the city, but contests over competing rights *to* the city. One of the primary rights to the city is the claim to common public space. A division between 'public' and 'private' has been a key device used by social theorists in analysing social relations, but it is not always clear how this critical dualism relates to actual public spaces in the city. The discussion explores public spaces on three levels – as sites of collectivity, social exchange, and informal encounter – and examines how social relations and behaviours are organized within these different orders of public space. While the idea of public space is founded on principles of equality and access, the exclusions which operate in real public spaces point to the limits of belonging in the city. Dynamics of control in public, and the ways in which certain individuals and groups (whether homeless people, beggars or youths) come to be perceived as a problem, suggest that access to public space is not simply a matter of exercising one's 'rights' to the city, but is organized through forms of regulation and exclusion.

The politics of urban space is also played out through economic and symbolic claims to the city. Chapter 4 is concerned with how economic processes in urban spaces are reflected at the levels of meaning and representation. It considers the way socio-economic change can be read through changes in the organization of urban space. The focus here is on the gentrification of the inner city as a shift in both material forms and cultural meanings. The inner city has always been as much a social label as a spatial fact. Where once it connoted a site of acute deprivation, however, more recently the inner city has come to represent a space of development. As a real and figurative place, the inner city offers narratives of economic and cultural change in the remaking of urban spaces. Recent shifts at the level of class and capital – the accelerated gentrification of certain parts of the late capitalist city – in this sense produce new patterns of spatial stratification and also alter urban meanings and identities.

The relation between material and symbolic spaces is central to the discussion in chapter 5, which concentrates on the gendering and 'sexing' of urban spaces. A number of critics have suggested that modes of conceiving the body are often run together with ways of picturing space (Brown 2000; Duncan 1996; Grosz 1992; McDowell 1999a; Nast and Pile 1998; Pile 1996; Sennett 1994; Stallybrass and White 1986). The discussion here considers the place of the gendered or sexualized body in the city on three different levels: the meaning, the use, and the shape of urban spaces. It suggests that bodies make a difference in terms of the symbolic, the practical, and the formal ordering of space. In looking at questions of meaning, first, the argument draws on perspectives in cultural and social history on the representation of women in the modern city. It goes on to examine the gendered use of urban space – taking up recent work within geography and criminology on how women's spatial practice is constrained by spatial perceptions of violence and fear. The final part of the discussion explores the impact of sexuality on the shaping of urban space – examining patterns of lesbian and gay residential and community formation in contemporary cities. Taken together, these arguments address the roles of cultural meaning, spatial practice and physical forms in placing bodies in the city.

Chapter 5, on issues of gender and sexuality in the city, forms a bridge between the earlier discussions of the social and spatial order of cities, and the final two chapters which are more closely concerned with questions of subjectivity and meaning. Cities can be thought of not simply as built forms or complex social systems, but also as modes of consciousness and experience. Chapter 6 focuses on the intersection between the subject and the city. It engages with the city as a perceptual as well as a physical space: how individuals experience the city is not only or always determined by larger social or economic structures, but is organized by their own mental maps and particular spatial practices (see de Certeau 1984; Lynch 1960). The argument here draws on the work of three major theorists of the subject in the city: Georg Simmel, Walter Benjamin, and Michel de Certeau. Each thinker offers insights into how subjects encounter the city – the peculiar psychology of urban life; the city's relation to memory, dream and perception; the ways in which people's routine practices tell different 'spatial stories' of the city.

Chapter 7 extends this concern with how people make space for themselves through everyday practice and imaginative spatial tactics. It looks to places and practices in the city that resist a conventional order of space and conduct. The discussion begins with Michel Foucault's treatment of 'hetero-topias' – or 'other spaces' – which work according to their own logics of design and use. It goes on to draw on the work of Roland Barthes and Michel de Certeau to consider how urban spaces can be signified and practised so as to alter conventional meanings or ignore official uses. In thinking about places of expression in the city, my concern is not with organized spectacle, valorized sites of consumption or privileged fields of culture, but with every-day distractions and subcultural practices. Finding different ways of being in the city can be a question of thinking tactically and moving quickly. And some of the best diversions to be had in the city can be the most ordinary. The little 'spatial tactics' through which users defy the order of maps, upset the plan, slip between the lines on the grid, suggest that the city is not merely a labora-tory for studying the organization of social life, nor a machine for engineer-ing social order, but a site of agency, a space 'in use' (Thrift 2000: 234), which is never wholly captured by efforts either to model or to manage it.

1 Community and Solitude: Social Relations in the City

Appeals to community are usually anti-urban.

(I. M. Young, *Justice and the Politics of Difference*)

'On any person who desires such queer prizes', E.B. White once wrote, the city 'will bestow the gift of loneliness and the gift of privacy' (1999: 19). White was thinking of New York, but solitude is a more general urban reality. Writers on the city have often noted the peculiar kind of loneliness that one finds in the middle of a crowd. It is as if the press of strange bodies makes the point of otherness in a way that simple physical isolation does not. This special capacity for solitude, though, stands in an interesting relation with another way of thinking about the city – that is, as a primary site for community. Approaches to the modern city frequently have described urban life as isolating, anonymous, degrading of social ties, hostile to community. Almost as often, it seems, these accounts are offset by efforts to find new and different bases for community in the city. In some versions, the size, density and diversity of urban populations serve to insulate and alienate individuals from each other; in different readings these same factors provide the setting for subcultural formations, for imaginative and voluntary social ties, for remaking community.

The tension between anonymity and community in the city underpins the discussion in this chapter. Such a tension appears in early debates in urban sociology, most notably in the work of the Chicago School theorists in the 1920s and 1930s. Their accounts of the modernizing and rationalizing push of urban processes appeared to sit at odds with the continued existence of community in contemporary American cities, especially on the part of immigrant and minority ethnic groups. One response was to treat such community forms as a 'non-urban' residue in the city, a social adaptation to new urban environments which mimicked familiar spatial and cultural arrangements, and transplanted older social and economic ties. On the other side of this impulse for community stood the pull of assimilation, understood as the erasure of both cultural difference and spatial divisions between groups. To be 'assimilated' in the modern city, it followed, was in fact to be individualized, to be deracinated, to be just as anonymous as anybody else.

These founding arguments within urban sociology contain certain themes that have proved very durable in broader debates over community in the modern city. One is the assumption that community forms were somehow 'pre-modern' or non-urban; their persistence in contemporary cities became something to be explained, much like the survival of a threatened species in a hostile environment. If social relations in the city were characterized by anonymity and rationality, urban communities were throwbacks to other places and older kinds of sociality. They appeared like villages in the city, based on familiarity and shared cultural norms, and usually transported by rural incomers or foreign immigrants. The 'lament' for community as a disappearing social form is a standard theme within academic and political discourses, as well as in certain versions of the popular imagination (see Nisbet 1953; see also Cohen 1985; Suttles 1972). Community stands in this context for a world that has been lost, especially crushed under the wheels of urban progress. The life of community is the vanishing counterpoint to urban life, and the longing for community carries an implied critique of the city. As a social form that is always receding from view, continually at a point of crisis, community might be seen as much as the stuff of political fantasy or sociological romance as a matter of social actuality.

A second significant move within early urban sociology was to link the formation of communities with patterns of social difference. Ethnicity and class provided the twin analytical frames for an emerging sociology of community, and did so by describing both distinct social groups and segregated spaces in the city. Being part of a community, on these terms, could be seen as a badge of social disadvantage or of ethnic difference. Though the category of class (if never entirely absent) has been rather sublimated in more recent debates, 'community' still provides a very common collective term for talk about ethnicity, bringing together notions of cultural ties, social networks and local spaces. Ideas of group identity continue to hang around the language of community, especially in the way that urban minorities are constructed. The politics of group identity, of course, tends to depend on who is doing the naming. While the language of community at times underpins a collective politics of identity, it can also be used to mark out recalcitrant or inassimilable 'others' in the city. As Homi Bhabha (1994: 231) writes, an ascribed notion of racial or ethnic community has been set against the rationalizing order of the modern city: 'in the metropolitan space it is the territory of the minority, threatening the claims of civility'. Community, in this reading, is a code for 'race', a politer means of lumping people together on the basis of skin or culture, a way of identifying a problem.

The problem of community, then, is a central way in which questions of social and spatial difference have been posed in the modern city. If the rhetoric of community frequently has been a means of framing troublesome minorities in the city, it has also often been claimed for more assertive politics of difference. Recourse to the group, too, can be a crucial strategy for those who find the ambience of the city 'uncivil' or who cannot easily assume the freedoms of urban anonymity. Still, my argument below is that forms of urban *indifference* are also part of an everyday politics of difference in the city. Privacy or anonymity is not simply an index of the alienation of city life, nor is it purely one of the benefits of cultural privilege that allows certain people to make their way in the city unhindered, unremarked, unbothered. The indifference of others potentially affords wider rights to and freedoms in the city. Such relations of indifference may be fragile, grudging, uneven, but they also can be seen as *ethical* in inscribing an attitude, however minimal, of the self in respect of others. Alongside an active politics that recognizes differences, that is, there lies an ordinary urban ethics that looks straight past it.

The discussion that follows traces some key approaches to these themes of solitude, community and indifference within urban theory and sociology. It uses these categories to reflect on how different urban thinkers have understood the nature of social relations in the modern city, and how such ideas might engage with more recent and critical questions of identity and difference. The first part of the discussion focuses on the work of Louis Wirth to examine a tension which ran through early Chicago School urban sociology – the conflict between the atomizing effects of modern urbanism and the persistence of urban communities. It goes on to consider two key strands of work on local social ties in the context of post-war programmes of urban renewal: Herbert Gans's ethnographic study of 'urban villagers' in the West End of Boston, and the community studies of Michael Young and Peter Willmott in the East End of London. These studies traced the community forms which endured in urban locales, and outlined the threat they faced from the physical and social redevelopment of urban environments. Such accounts sit alongside the contemporary work of Jane Jacobs in New York, who based her version of urban sociality less on enclaves of community than in the minor everyday contacts that animated the streets and public spaces of a mixed urban scene. Against the backdrop of these debates in sociology and urban studies, the latter part of the discussion turns to more conceptual arguments regarding urban issues of community, identity and indifference. Modern cities, I suggest, are not simply inimical to community ties; nor is the anonymity of the city only to be understood in terms of the erasure of differences or the alienation of strangers. The point, then, is not to set a conception of solitude or indifference against one of community or identity in the city. While people make and remake versions of community in the city, it is also possible to see indifference as a key social relation between urban subjects – one premised less on any face-to-face ideal of community than on the 'side-by-side' relations of anonymity typical of being with others in the city (Young 1990a).

The solitude of the city

The idea of solitude or separation as a social condition is a theme we often find in urban social theory, and has its classic statement in the work of the German sociologist Georg Simmel. In his 1903 account, 'The metropolis and mental life', Simmel remarks the tendency to reserve among people in the city, a reserve that shades 'not only into indifference, but, more often than we are aware . . . a slight aversion, a mutual strangeness and repulsion'

(1997b: 179). This notion of indifference is cut through by ambivalence. For Simmel, relations of indifference or even aversion are fundamentally *social* relations in that they offer the only feasible way of being together with countless strangers in the crowded spaces of the city. Adopting such an attitude enables individuals to negotiate a teeming social space and at the same time preserve some degree of 'psychological private property' (Simmel 1997a: 163). What appears as dissociation is in fact a basic form of urban sociation, one that allows us to coexist with all these largely unknown others. Refusing interaction is not, therefore, merely a matter of social withdrawal but is instead a primary condition for urban social life, securing individual calm together with relative social peace.

For Simmel, this social effect is the expression of a larger spatial truth. The modern city, even as it presses people up close, remains subject to the 'merciless separation of space', such that 'a real unity of the diverse does not exist in spatial terms' (1997c: 170, 171). On one level this is a simple statement of material fact – two different things cannot occupy the same position in space at the same time. But it also makes a psychological point, one which underlines the fact of otherness in social life. Difference is understood here as a profoundly spatial reality, lived over and over in the glancing encounters of the street. Being in the crowded city magnifies the contradiction between the collective nature of social life and the radical solitude of the individual, between the claims of the group and that of the person. It distils that 'unity of nearness and remoteness involved in every human relation', however casual or intimate (Simmel 2004: 73). The mundane manoeuvres of everyday routine (not making eye contact on the sidewalk, ignoring the weird intimacy of the crowded subway) in this sense play out at the micro-scale a broader tension between individuality and collective life, a more general trade-off between autonomy and community. In the modern city, as elsewhere, individual freedom goes together with impersonality and anonymity. 'For here, as elsewhere', Simmel writes wonderfully, 'it is by no means necessary that the freedom of man be reflected in his emotional life as comfort' (1997b: 181).

We find similar ideas in the urban memoirs of Walter Benjamin – who remembers how on childhood walks in the city with his mother, 'solitude appeared to me as the fit state of man' (1986f: 13) – as well as in the urban sociology of Louis Wirth and his Chicago School colleagues. For the urban sociologists, cities were not merely good contexts in which to observe social relations at work; they constituted distinct forms of interaction and association in themselves. The clearest statement of such an idea is in Wirth's 1938 essay, 'Urbanism as a way of life', but this conception of the city as a social form runs through a number of contemporary accounts (see, for example, Park 1967a). At its centre stands the equation of the city with modernity. The social relations that exemplify life in the city – based on increasingly rational, instrumental, impersonal and voluntary forms of interaction – are also typically modern. In this sense, Wirth's effort to distinguish urbanism as a mode of social life takes its place within sociology's larger project to describe the anatomy of modern societies. The city is analysed as a primary site for the social experience of modernity.

Wirth starts with the proposal that 'the beginning of what is distinctively modern in our civilization is signalized by the growth of cities' (1995: 58). There is something basic to be understood about the nature of modern social forms in the study of the city, and in particular there is something to be learnt about the formal changes in social interaction that modernization has produced. Wirth's writing shows the clear influence of Simmel, and echoes those early twentieth-century thinkers (such as Durkheim or Cooley) whose analyses of modern societies traced a shift in the foundation of social order. A modern transition from shared norms to formal rules as the basis for association is captured most neatly during this period in Ferdinand Tönnies' distinction between *Gemeinschaft* and *Gesellschaft* – a distinction which can be mapped onto Wirth's concern with the special nature of urban sociality and also has informed wider debates over the conflict between city and community life (see Tönnies 1955; see also Park 1967a: 23, 28). *Gemeinschaft* (usually translated as 'community') refers to a mode of interaction where social ties are based on mutual dependence, and where individuals' relations with others take place within and derive meaning from the larger group. Such a model of sociality is exemplified by family or kinship relations but also haunts notions of community. *Gesellschaft* ('society' or 'association'), in contrast, describes a formal mode of interaction which tends to the impersonal, instrumental and voluntary. It involves social relations based on rational interest rather than on mutual identity, and is shaped by external rules rather than by shared belonging. Tönnies' distinction stands, here, for a broader concern within classical social theory with the changing bases of social solidarity, away from the primary ties of kinship or communal life and towards more indirect or impersonal modes of association. These ideal-types generally have been read in terms of a schematic difference between 'traditional' and 'modern' societies, but the work of early urban sociologists such as Park and Wirth suggested that such a distinction was not only temporal but also spatial. If the rational and impersonal were considered essentially modern forms of sociality, they also appeared as deeply urban. It was in the city that new kinds of sociality and new forms of subjectivity were most intensely and clearly lived out.

Writing in a period when positivist sociology was in the ascendant, Wirth began with three raw facts about cities: their size, density and social heterogeneity. These factors not only defined cities in empirical terms, however, they also produced typical modes of social interaction and characteristic kinds of subjective experience. At the heart of this concept of urbanism lies the tension between physical proximity and social distance. For Wirth, modern cities pushed people up close together but set degrees of subjective or social distance between them. These dual logics of social life derived from the same basic facts of urban interaction: the proliferation of social encounters together with the weakening of social ties. In the modern city people might have more frequent and numerous encounters with others, but these tend to be transitory, instrumental or incidental. Everyday urban life has the potential to bring you into contact with any number of people in any number of more or less impersonal ways – from the man who sells you a train ticket (a machine, of course, might do just as well), to the woman who shoves you on the street, to your interactions with colleagues or employers, to those nameless others you share a subway with – all of which are more or less 'freely' entered (it is usually easier to quit your job, after all, than to change your family). These are relations based either on fairly explicit forms of contract, from the employment contract to legal codes of public behaviour to the market exchange involved in buying a newspaper, or else on the minimal contacts of shared social space. Relations, that is, based on *Gesellschaft* or less. Just as it increases these formalized or anonymous interactions, urbanism as a way of life tends to undermine the power of relations based on duty or custom, on shared and strongly valued social norms, on the clannish culture of family or group.

The city in this way could be seen as remaking social interaction in terms of those sociological keynotes of modernity – instrumental reason, individuation, *anomie*. Wirth (1995: 76) glossed the logic of urban social life in terms of the 'substitution of secondary for primary contacts, the weakening of bonds of kinship, and the declining social significance of the family, the disappearance of the neighborhood, and the undermining of the traditional basis of social solidarity'. Such a litany has been repeated countless times by numerous social commentators and contains some very stock elements; it would seem that the urban neighbourhood, for instance, has always been in a state of crisis. Wirth's own arguments refer to an ideal-type city defined in terms of its basic empirical features but his analysis is backed by the demographic detail of city life traced in other Chicago School accounts, and which has preoccupied urban social research ever since: declining rates of marriage and childbirth, the mobility of urban populations, the prevalence of crime and delinquency, the numbers of people living alone (see Park et al. 1967). The symptoms may have become very familiar but the distinctive nature of urban sociality was not simply expressed as a raft of objective data, it also was seen to shape urban psychologies. In the modern city patterns of social life were linked to forms of subjective life; certain attitudes and personalities could be seen to follow from urbanism as a social form. Here the echoes of Simmel are loud: urban life, for Wirth and his colleagues, produced a social psychology of impersonality, anonymity and indifference. Strong sources of identification were eroded by the nature of social life in the city, marked as it is by impermanence, isolation and differentiation.

There is a certain melancholy in this reading of the modern city. It characterizes the urban condition in terms of the breakdown of traditional social ties, the proliferation of impersonal and instrumental contacts, the 'social void' that Durkheim foresaw in the absence of shared and binding cultural norms. Robert Park (1967d: 130) argued that in the modern city 'most of the interests and values of life have been rationalized, reduced to measurable units, and even made objects of barter and sale'. These social arrangements were expressed subjectively by a distinctive kind of solitude – the peculiar loneliness of those who 'live side by side for years without so much as a bowing acquaintance' (Park 1967a: 24). This tendency towards separation and indifference, however, does not entirely pacify social relations in the city. The constant rubbing together of different interests and bodies inevitably produces friction, and in this respect urban life also tends to require formal modes of control. Whether in the form of rational contracts or coercive crack-downs, city life is (or needs to be) extensively governed by systems of law. At the level of subjectivity, social interaction in the city requires a change in indi-vidual psychology to accommodate the proximity of many unknown others. At the collective level, it involves the increasing use of legal controls to govern behaviour, to regulate association, and to secure order.

In sum, city life is characterized by anonymity, instrumentality and atom-ization, because cities are – as social as well as physical forms – large, dense and diverse. People learn to keep their social distance, even in the press of the crowd. Wirth's seminal account, though, was sketched in broad strokes and it describes only a tendency (however marked) at work in urban social life. His analysis of the modern city was grounded in a comparison between two ideal-types of social and spatial order, 'urban industrial and rural-folk soci-eties', which are given to fall apart when you try to map them onto any real context. Closer up, the detail of social space can look rather different. Wirth's essay emphasized one major aspect of the sociological analysis of cities: as complex, dynamic and often unstable social systems. However, it under-played another strand of Chicago sociology which has strongly inflected the concerns of urban studies; one focused on local social spaces within the modern city, informal modes of urban order, and the formation of different urban subcultures (see, classically, Whyte 1943). The very size, density and diversity of urban populations that fragmented traditional bases of social order could also be seen to heighten the appeal and the value of community, or provide the context for new and inventive sources of solidarity. At a smaller scale, different kinds of urban order were at work.

Community in the city

Wirth's colleague Robert Park makes this point very well. He writes:

> processes of segregation establish moral distances which make the city a mosaic of little worlds which touch but do not interpenetrate. This makes it possible for individuals to pass quickly and easily from one moral milieu to another, and encourages the fascinating but dangerous experiment of living at the same time in several different contiguous, but otherwise highly sep-arated, worlds. (1967a: 40–1)

Urban life, then, is not simply hostile to forms of collective identification and solidarity; the choice is not between the loneliness of the urban crowd and the folksy *Gemeinschaft* of the backwater. Park's notion of the 'moral milieu' raises the question of what forms of community or identity might be possible within the larger anonymity of the modern city. His line seems strikingly contemporary now, with its emphasis on the diversity of the city and the changeable nature of identity and experience within it. The metaphor of the urban mosaic might look a little jaded – at once exotic and over-simplified – but Park's account does point to a notion of difference as a *spatial* experience. Crossing the tracks, going downtown, passing from one 'little world' to the next: different ways of belonging in the city frequently involve mobile bodies in space.

It should be noted that Park's treatment of the fascinations and dangers of urban difference assumes a segregated city. The Chicago School city is always one based on social and spatial divisions which carve up the city as a geography of difference. A key challenge for more recent urban theory has been to conceive of forms of identity, diversity and community in the city without reinforcing actual or imagined lines of segregation. In these earlier accounts identity and community invariably were tied to spatial separation and cultural differentiation. Community gave a social form to these patterns of difference. To Park, the concept of community did not merely denote a 'collection of people occupying a more or less clearly defined area' but was defined by the social, cultural, political and economic institutions that organized this group: 'Not people, but institutions, are final and decisive in distinguishing the community from other social constellations' (1967c: 115). In this respect, of course, he was advancing an impeccably sociological conception of community, based not just on shared spaces or personal ties but on the ways in which these relations were socially organized. Being drawn into the arc of community was not merely a matter of stepping across a spatial line, nor did it reduce to a simple fact of membership. 'Community' referred, rather, to the formal and informal means (meeting places, institutions, conventions, codes and values) through which social groups organized and reproduced themselves in particular spaces.

In Park's thinking we can see the cross-cutting lines of three different ways of defining 'community'. The first of these is based on a model of *locality*, where communities are mapped around place. Urban community is an effect of location. This definition is at work, for example, where 'community' is seen as co-extensive with a housing estate, neighbourhood, suburb or village. The second is a *social* model, in which communities are defined by social networks and institutions. Such a model often underlies versions of ethnic community, based not only on cultural ties but on the institutional forms (clubs and associations, religious organizations, newspapers and other media, meeting and eating places) through which these are mediated. The third, linked to Park's notion of 'moral milieux', is an *affective* model of community in which shared identities and interests provide a sense of belonging. Park's moral formations remained spatialized in specific parts of the city, but affective communities include groups that are spatially dispersed. They allow for forms of 'community without propinquity', where social networks are organized across space. This third sense is apparent on one level, for example, in contemporary friendship networks, particularly in terms of how people use internet and phone technologies to overcome spatial distance. On another level, it underpins broader invocations of a gay or lesbian community, or of diasporic communities, where 'members' may not necessarily know or meet each other. While these three modes of community may be distinguished conceptually, however, they are rarely very distinct. There is a great deal of slippage between communities imagined in terms of shared spaces, in terms of social ties or institutions, and in terms of identities of interest. These definitions – based on place, based on association, or based on affective solidarities – tend to overlap and interrupt each other. Communities of diaspora, for instance, extend across space but also cohere around neighbourhoods, social institutions and personal networks.

For the Chicago School sociologists and their contemporaries, an interest in community was spurred by the persistence of what appeared as non-urban or even pre-modern social forms in the modern city. If the logic of urbanism was to weaken and fragment traditional social ties, the endurance of such relations was in some sense a throwback; certain social spaces in the city existed almost as if in a different time. Ideas of community put very well this question of how time passes (or does not) in space. In early urban sociology the typical model of community was based on the immigrant area, a social milieu that invoked both another time and a distant place. In his study of *The Ghetto*, Wirth (1928: 290) argues that Jewish communities offered 'as near an approach to communal life as the modern city has to offer' and a model for understanding other urban minorities. Wirth treats Jewish immigrant groups in the United States as a 'cultural community' formed around common traditions and values, language and shared histories – including long and continuing histories of exclusion and persecution (1928: 289). While the Jewish population may become spatially dispersed, it remains 'welded into a community because of conflict and pressure from without and collective action within' (1928: 290). In this way the recourse to community can be understood as both a *defensive* gesture in response to prejudice, threat or discrimination, and an *assertive* gesture of identity, self-determination and mutuality. In Wirth's account, the ghetto – the enclosed space of community – functions as both a real place of origin, refuge and familiarity, and a symbolic space of belonging.

For Wirth, the communal life of the American Jew is imagined in deeply spatial terms around the real and figurative ghetto, as a social site in itself and as a place of segregation from others. In this sense the Jewish experience is exemplary of a more general marking of cultural difference across urban space. The modern American city appears as a 'patchwork of little ghettos'; as different groups settle in various parts of the city 'each group tends to repro-duce the culture to which it was accustomed in its old habitat as nearly as the new conditions will permit' (1928: 283). The work of community includes the process of making and holding space. These ethnic enclaves enclose forms of identity at the same time as they redraw lines of difference. In Wirth's account, the physical segregation of different social groups in the city (espe-cially of 'natives' and 'immigrants', as he renders it) is an expression of the social distance that exists between them and also a means of maintaining it. 'This does not,' he suggests (1928: 284), 'so much imply mutual hostility as it implies and makes possible mutual tolerance.' Again there are shades of Simmel here, as social distance and urban indifference become conditions for collective life in the city. This is no longer a matter of individual encoun-ters, however, but of coexistence between groups. In Wirth's account, spatial separation and community formation are modes of accommodation to the strange city which do not simply entail assimilation. It is, throughout, a notion of community defined through difference: cultural communities are reproduced insofar as differences are marked, valorized and localized.

Urban spaces and urban communities

In these founding stories of urban sociology, making community in an unfa-miliar city was a matter of recreating familiar conditions of social and cultural life in a new locale. The endurance of community in the modern city held out against the disintegrating and isolating currents of urban life, shoring up local spaces of identity and belonging. It is important, however, to stress that the modernizing processes Wirth and others saw as undermining commu-nity in the city were not only social but also spatial, and found acutely mater-ial expression in the physical transformation of urban environments from the middle part of the twentieth century. Local enclaves, often in low-rent inner areas, were especially vulnerable to the rationalizing impetus of urban planning and renewal. From the 1950s onwards a number of urban commen-tators analysed the changes in communal life that went with the physical redevelopment of the city. A key contribution to this field was Herbert Gans's ethnographic work in the West End of Boston during the 1950s. Gans's study was undertaken in a period when the landscape of the city was being trans-formed; even by the time he published *The Urban Villagers* in 1962, tracts of old inner Boston had disappeared in programmes of slum clearance and urban renewal. Such physical processes pointed only too clearly to the rationalizing principle of modern urbanism Wirth had described.

For Gans, the disappearing urban landscape took with it vanishing social forms. In the pocket of Boston he studied, first- or second-generation Italian immigrants sought 'to adapt their nonurban institutions and cultures to the urban milieu' (Gans 1982: 4). Here again the problem of community was seen as a translation between the 'nonurban' and the urban, as a question of remaking parts of the city in the paradoxical form of the 'urban village'. As Robert Park (1967d: 119) had written in the 1920s, '[the] immigrant colony is frequently nothing more than a transplanted village, for America actually has been colonized not by races or nationalities but by villages'. If these urban villages appeared as something of a pre-modern relic to urban sociologists such as Park or Gans, the idea that cities might be composed of different 'villages' has proved a lasting and very flexible metaphor in carving up social space – from ethnic enclaves to gay villages to the place-making fictions of urban gentrifiers. The village does not appear simply as the opposite of the city, but itself becomes an ideal for organizing urban social space. Different versions of the urban village, what is more, can support both 'authentic' and 'synthetic' readings of urban community – whether understood in terms of deep-rooted cultural ties (as in certain treatments of 'ethnic' neighbour-hoods), or seen as a product of imagination, politics and will (say, in the case of gay neighbourhoods). Indeed the idea of the urban village has had some-thing of a late modern revival. Even large cities, it seems, can be imagined as a network of urban villages, partly through strategies of 'place marketing' in a competitive urban system with its efforts to engineer new 'quarters' and 'villages' around codes of social and spatial distinction (see Neal 2003; Kearns and Philo 1993).

If the urban villagers of Gans's study have fed into more recent romances of urban *Gemeinschaft*, however, the account he offered was somewhat more complex. Boston's West End appeared to Gans as one of those sites that speak of other places and different times; on first encounter, the winding streetscape, the passing social scene, the Jewish and Italian stores, made Gans feel as if he was in Europe (1982: 11). Beyond the picturesque details, though, this 'village' in the city was a scene of physical disrepair and economic hardship. The immigrant population in the West End at this time lived in relatively impoverished circumstances, in old and overcrowded tene-ment housing. Against such a backdrop of material disadvantage, Gans traced an intact social system based on 'group and class' – the melding, that is, of cultural ties and economic position. This local culture involved its own social order, interlinking family networks with commercial relations and forms of cultural association, and mediated in various ways by such neigh-bourhood figures as the caretaker or landlord, the local political fixer or entrepreneur. Gans's account makes visible those overlapping lines through which community may be traced within bounded spaces, through social networks and institutions, and around affective ties. It captures a social space in the city at the point of its disappearance, pointing to the way that processes of urban renewal remake not only physical but social environments.

A similar linkage of class, kinship and urban space is evident in the community studies literature that emerged in Britain at the same time. Willmott and Young's classic accounts of family and community forms in

East London in the 1950s and 1960s also work through the contrast between
enduring social ties and changing spatial arrangements in the city (Young
and Willmott 1957; Willmott and Young 1960; see also Willmott 1966).
Countering ideas of the modern city as destructive of traditional bonds and
social norms, Willmott and Young depicted a white working-class community in Bethnal Green strongly integrated by extended family networks
and shared cultural codes. The family was central to making urban community: the researchers noted the frequency of contacts between family
members, and – as Gans had found in Boston – the larger role of kinship ties
in co-ordinating local social and economic life. Women were crucial to these
social networks, with the mother-daughter relation in particular serving to
anchor kinship relations in place. Such an observation, of course, tends to
reinforce the association of community with 'traditional' kinds of social
organization, and highlights the importance of conventional gender roles in
making and maintaining community. The domestic and emotional labour of
women appears as especially significant in tying communal networks
together, based on their family work and their situation within a very local
social geography. While Willmott and Young's findings in this way underpinned standard versions of community as a sort of communal hangover in
the modern city, their work also challenged the notion of familial ties as
simply enclosed, limiting or exclusive. Family and kinship networks in fact
could open onto wider contacts, notably in providing access to economic
and employment opportunities. In this respect there was a degree of continuity, rather than simply conflict, between the affective or 'irrational' ties of
family and community, and the instrumental, rational ties of economic interaction. Wirth's ideal-type distinction between folksy familiarity and urban
impersonality hid the more complicated ways in which strong and weak ties
could be interwoven (cf. Granovetter 1973).

Willmott and Young's analysis of how community forms endured in the
modern city contrasted with the disintegrating effects of urban development
and suburbanization. The accounts of their respondents in Bethnal Green
were set alongside those of former residents who had moved to a new outer
urban housing estate to the east of London. The emigrants – while they were
glad to have moved out of slum housing conditions – regretted the loss of
community, the familiarity of the old neighbourhood, and the more private
world of the new development. Their stories rehearsed that trade-off
between urban improvement and authentic locality which is such a common
theme in accounts of urban renewal. In plotting this narrative of urban
change, the British community studies can be seen to mirror the work of the
US urban sociologists in two key ways, one social and the other spatial.
Willmott and Young give us, first, another take on Gans's story of 'group and
class': a version of cultural community integrated by common histories and
social norms, and also clearly positioned in class terms. These issues of social
location, second, are tied to questions of spatial location. Physical mobility

was an expression of social and economic mobility, but also produced various forms of disorientation. This is evident in the sense of disconnection experienced by those who moved away from their inner London enclave, and is especially marked in Wirth's treatment of urban Jewish communities. For him, the path out of the ghetto both as a place and as an idea complicates issues of identity and difference without necessarily resolving them. 'When the ghetto walls do finally crumble', he writes with some drama and suspect biology, 'those that get a taste of the life in the freer world outside and are lured by its color are likely to be torn by the conflicting feeling that comes to hybrids generally, both physical and social' (Wirth 1928: 289–90).

This conflict between locality and mobility touches on a deeper spatial problematic which can dog attempts to define and chart community. Tracing the outlines of community, that is, can be a matter of holding this social form in place, even though people do not simply stay still, and physical and social space is subject to change. One effect of accounts within urban sociology and community studies is to pitch an idea of community, as a social form stuck in place, against the onward and outward rush of urban development. It is as if the modern city enclosed certain 'non-urban' spaces of communal life. We need not understand this, however, as the fragile resilience of outdated or outback kinds of sociality in the hostile environment of the modern city. Nor do alienating or rationalist modes of urban development simply realize some intrinsic logic of urbanism. With a different emphasis it is possible to speak of the forms of sociality and the distinct versions of locality for which cities themselves make space. It is not a matter, then, of city versus community, of anonymity versus familiarity, of estrangement versus belonging – let alone of development versus the slum.

A somewhat different approach to urbanism from this middle part of the twentieth century is evident in Jane Jacobs's work on US cities, and New York in particular (Jacobs 1964). While Jacobs's chief argument is for the kinds of social goods that cities can promote, she remains critical of a sentimental reading of neighbourhood life. And though she is intensely interested in local social spaces, she does not tend to use the language of community. Jacobs's principal vantage-point on the city is the window over her own street in Greenwich Village, at this time still pre-gentrification. In the local order of the street, Jacobs identifies some of the features that make cities work. These turn on the relation between the physical fabric of the city and the weave of social interaction within it. The area around Eighth and Hudson Streets is a physical and social mix. It includes houses, apartment buildings, shops and other businesses; it therefore takes in different household forms, and various residential and commercial populations. One effect of this social mix is to put people on the street at different times, workers and children going out in the morning and coming back later, shopkeepers holding their ground during the day, the leisure traffic of the evening. This changing social scene – the unchoreographed 'ballet of the city sidewalk' (1964: 60) – both gives a social shape to the street and links it into the larger circuits of city life. Jacobs prefers to think of the urban neighbourhood not as a spatial enclave but as part of the flow of city life, the 'mobility and fluidity of use' that should characterize urban space. Against a bounded notion of community she writes that the 'lack of either economic or social self-containment is natural and necessary to city neighborhoods' which are able to sustain social diversity and a mixture of uses (1964: 126).

The presence of various people on the street at different times during the day also has the critical effect of putting numerous 'eyes upon the street' (1964: 45). There is always, simply, someone around. For Jacobs this amounts to a mutual and 'informal policing' of urban space which individuals perform for each other simply by going about their everyday business. It can make the streets of big cities feel oddly safe. This is not the safety of the enclave or the shelter of community, but the spatial freedom of the well-used city street. Nor is the sense of belonging in this space some urban version of *Gemeinschaft*, based on mutual dependence or local tribalism; rather, it is the everyday matter of sharing social space with familiar strangers. Jacobs's version splits the difference between the anonymity of the modern city and the clinch of community. As in Wirth's account, urban social relations are highly dependent on the organization of urban space: the city is still big, dense and diverse, and it is the spatial expression of these factors that gives a form to urban social life. In Jacobs's treatment, however, the density and diversity of urban populations do not (or do not only) produce social distance. Rather, these features are basic to the freedoms of city life, its sociality and its degrees of safety. The notion of diversity used here is always both social and spatial. Social mix, for Jacobs, entails and requires a mix of spatial uses – the kind of urban mix she finds back on Hudson Street, with its shopkeepers and residents of different kinds, the bar with its assorted drinkers, the varied social and physical streetscape. Against this version of urbanism, Jacobs sets the 'decontaminated sortings' of modern urban planning which seek to separate out different uses, and consequently segregates different users (1964: 35). Such an effect is especially evident in the rationalized architecture of urban renewal, particularly in the total environments of housing projects that remove social life from the street and enclose it within the precinct, striate the city by income group, separate out housing from places of work and leisure, and close off spaces of incidental encounter. These designs militate against any 'mobility and fluidity of use' in urban space; they carve out tracts of the city from the run of everyday social traffic; they create dull and unsafe spaces that are not visible to the social eye of the street. Jacobs's especial grievance is with the mass housing projects of mid-century urban planning, but she sees a similar deadening logic at work in the way the middle-class apartment building on her street insulates its more affluent residents from the scene outside. Both serve to 'undiversify' the city (Jacobs 1964: 256) through strategies which effectively are those of social and spatial segregation.

These forms of enclosure, the spatial organization of sameness (typically along class or ethnic lines), do less to produce forms of community within the city than to entrench alienation and distrust. Jacobs, too, is less interested in the possible claims of community than in a different and more minimal kind of sociality which she sees as deeply urban. This is a low-level trust in the tolerance or indifference of the people with whom one must share the city. It is there in the improvised ballet of the streets that allows so many strangers and near-strangers, with something like grace, to negotiate common spaces. It depends on different users being on the same streets at different times, in pursuit of different (and usually private) ends. It is a nice image, this urban dance, which doesn't always square with the open combat of the subway station or the railway concourse, where at peak hours vast numbers of people, all with the same individual purpose (getting to work, getting home – getting, simply, on *that* train), take each other on in unyielding flow and contra-flow. Even less does it account for the kinds of mundane spatial dominance that are everyday expressions of sexual and racial privilege, or the ways in which certain social actors have to 'choreograph' their own movement to accommodate others' spatial prerogative and to protect themselves from harassment or violence. There is more riding on the dance of the streets for some people than for others. Still, one can recognize in Jacobs's metaphor the bare social order that underlies the apparent disorder of the city street. It is one built up through the many exchanges of the everyday, the 'small change' or mundane trust of city life without which little could function. Jacobs writes of a trust relation that is peculiarly urban: the 'trust of a city street is formed over time from many, many little public sidewalk contacts'. Such trust is trivial, reasonably impersonal, and crucially 'it implies no private commitment' (1964: 66–7).

The ethics of indifference

This raises the question of urban sociality in a different way: not in terms of whether communal ties can withstand the wider impersonality of city life, but of the value of the impersonal as a social stance in itself. Impersonality, that is, might be seen as an urban good, as a social form proper to the city as a 'world of strangers' (Lofland 1973). It involves a certain kind of freedom in the city, the lonely liberty of knowing that no one is looking, nobody really is listening. Solitude should be understood here as a social relation, as a way of being with others, rather than simply as the absence of sociality (Levinas 1987; see also Riley 2002: 9). It involves an ethics of indifference as a tacit relation between urban subjects, the implicit exchange between strangers of what White called 'the gift of loneliness and the gift of privacy'.

For Wirth, as we have seen, being with others in the city is characterized by close – sometimes unsettlingly close – physical proximity, twinned with social distance (1938: 70). Keeping your distance in the press of bodies is a special urban art. People, especially women, manage it all the time in the face of accidental or unwanted physical contact in public. The weird intimacy that is the touch of strangers is only the most immediate version of the physical nearness and social distance that are typical of urban life. As the passing scene orients the individual to a succession of images, others become just so many things in a general field of objects. You learn to look past a face. Such an attitude is at once an inuring against and an acceptance of difference. It tends to 'produce a relativistic perspective and a sense of toleration of differences which may be regarded as prerequisites for rationality and which lead toward the secularization of life' (Wirth 1938: 71). This is indifference as a politics of tolerance, even if only by default. In Wirth's account, while urban individuals are not objects of duty or especial concern to one another, neither are they objects of antipathy or even (very much) of curiosity. Though the disaffected or disconnected nature of urban sociality might fragment strong loyalties, interests or solidarities, it should also weaken strong antagonisms, animosities or grudges. Lefebvre (1991: 56) described this unspoken urban settlement in terms of a 'non-aggression pact, a contract, as it were, of non-violence' which 'imposes reciprocity, and a communality of use'. Such a *pax urbana* obtains in the city 'as that urban universe of life among strangers; among those one does not know and those who do not know you; among those who, if unknown, are nevertheless not dangerous' (Seligman 2000: 17).

This last point, about danger, is an important one. An ethics of indifference or dissociation could be seen as the projection of a particular masculine subjectivity onto urban sidewalks, based on detachment, self-sufficiency and certain assumptions about one's own spatial claims. However anonymity, the ability to go unnoticed in the streets of the city, has particular resonance for women as well as for men whose bodies are marked in terms of racial, sexual or cultural difference. One version of freedom in the city for women is tied to not being seen (Wilson 1991, 1992; see also chapter 5); one form of passing is as a private individual whose claim to public space is usual, unprovoking. This is a difficult moment in thinking about difference – the room to move afforded at times by erasure, by taking the stance of the abstract subject, unregarded in terms of skin, sexual signs, gendered bodies. It is a precarious freedom, one based on a fragile trust in the indifference of others. Indifference appears here as a minimal ethical relation, involving less any recognition of identity than the assumption of non-identity. Its limits are the limits of anonymity. On the street, in the park or on the subway, different people continually are recalled to their bodies, and to various ascriptions of their selves, in more or less violent ways (see Bowling 1999; Gardner 1995; Herek and Berrill 1992; Moran 2000). Individuals' relations to the possibilities and the security of indifference are unequal, as is the power to grant to others the 'right' of being left alone. As Michael Walzer (1997: 52) has put it: 'To tolerate someone else is an act of power; to be tolerated is an acceptance of weakness.' To be the subject of indifference is a different matter from being its object, and here one crucial if paradoxical effect of a politics of recognition might be to enlarge the scope of anonymity, to insist on the ordinariness of difference. On the other side of claims to visibility and to voice is the every-day politics simply of being there and staying there.

It is hard to make claims for rights that are flawed, contingent or partial (Riley 2002). A right to be anonymous, to be left alone, *not* to be looked at, seems minimal indeed. The right not to be assaulted, menaced or harassed is a different, although related, matter. It makes a stronger claim for the integrity of the person, it appeals to law. There is no law to say that you should not be subject to hostile gazes, to startling insults, to degrading comments, to the small change of social violence: here our freedom relies in some way on the minimal social contract of the street, and on the indifference of others. The fact this is not always reliable confuses the classical distinction between positive and negative types of freedom. Where certain subjects cannot take for granted their right to be left alone by others, negative liberty comes to represent a positive, assertive claim.

The politics of community

Recourse to community – via defences of space or forms of group identifica-tion – can make sense when public spaces seem forbidding, when strangers appear hostile or potentially threatening (see Bauman 2000; Sennett 1974). Wirth (1995: 79) noted the tendency of urbanites to 'create fictional kinship groups', to form affective and voluntary bonds, given the weakening of 'actual' family ties in modern urban contexts. If gestures of community in the city are seen in this way as synthetic and often strategic, this is not to suggest that they are not real (see Cohen 1985; Suttles 1972). These affective ties – formed around shared politics, sexual identities, common experience, force of circumstance, accidents of locality or the coincidence of origins – can be objects of intense attachment. They rely on the imaginative, emotional and political work of maintaining the fiction; on people honouring for itself a bond they have in fact invented. There can be a great deal riding on the 'fictional' ties of urban community, even if there may be relatively little underpinning them.

Community is one of the shiftier concepts in contemporary social and political theory (see Ahmed and Fortier 2003). Difficult to define, harder to observe and unvirtuous to reject, the idea of community opens itself to conservative or progressive uses even as it confuses the distinction between them. Depending on how you put it, the language of community can provide an idiom for the gathering together of identity, for fantasies of collective personality, or for the marking of difference. Setting analysis of community in an urban context, shifting the emphasis from the social to the spatial, does not clarify matters much. In framing community, the spatial and the social are continually overlaid, as if particular spaces might produce definite social ties or vice versa. Notions of community, in this context, can both enfold forms of diversity in the city and outline pockets of relative homogeneity along class, ethnic or cultural lines.

Perhaps the most familiar theme in recent debates over community is its use to sugar the pill of new political orthodoxies that claim to go 'beyond left and right'. Talk of community can be a proxy for speaking about social issues when the language of 'society' sounds a bit too Old Left. At other times the idea of community takes in various anxious majorities, disquieted by the claims or even the simple presence of those unlike themselves in a shared (or vaguely nearby) social space. Here the community denotes a supposed mainstream, a beleaguered majority which is defined against certain strange or dangerous others. This is the stuff of everyday moral panic, and is especially common in the politics of race and immigration. At other points again the term sets up particular groups – often defined ethnically or spatially – as constituencies or objects of government, tracing a boundary around what then are produced as common interests or problems. This mutable politics of community also runs the other way. In tension with the unifying or dividing practices of government, the language of community can provide a vehicle for mobilization, for opposition, for a positioning of and claim to voice. Here, discourses of community frame an assertive rather than a defensive politics of difference, a collective agent in arguments for social and cultural recognition and the pressing of group or minority rights (see Benhabib 1996; Gutman 1994; Taylor 1992). Such critical strategies of community seek to mark and valorize differences in ways that might make a political difference.

The true fictions of community in the modern city in this sense cut through a logic of anonymity, obviate the fact of otherness in social life (see Abrahamson 1996). Or from another standpoint, the impersonality of cities offers an escape from the clasp of community, an alternative to compulsory familiarity. Such an idea is to be found in Richard Sennett's treatment of the 'urban' as a certain cast of mind, an ethical disposition towards others which takes difference for granted. The 'essence of urbanity', for Sennett (1974: 255), is that different people 'can act together, without the compulsion to be the same'. This ethics of city life finds its spatial expression in a public geography which makes room for impersonal encounter and general anonymity. It reinforces the idea that life in public is not the same as private life; that one takes up different roles in the public sphere and in the domain of private concerns. In the latter part of the twentieth century, however, Sennett writes of a city which has become the stage for a particular drama of the late modern psyche – the acting out of a psychology of privacy and a craving for familiarity. Private anxieties increasingly displace public or collective issues as objects of social and political concern, and the spaces of private life are valorized over those of public belonging (see also Bauman 1999).

Such a turn to the private within political and ethical life, Sennett suggests, affects both the perception and the organization of social space. The erosion of public life degrades the city as a social and imaginative space which is shared by strangers. As privacy and interiority are valorized, 'the world outside, the impersonal world, seems to fail us, seems to be stale and empty' (1974: 5). And as we become stranger and stranger to each other, the risks of interaction, of dealing with the unfamiliar, can seem just *too* risky. One way to deal with the suspicion of strangeness is 'to make intimate and local the scale of human experience', even to 'make local territory morally sacred'. Community in this way becomes an extension of personality, a form of collective identification based on what is nearby, familiar, like-minded. This rehashed version of *Gemeinschaft*, argues Sennett, is in the end a 'celebration of the ghetto' (1974: 295). In such a reading, the cultural politics of community are at best conservative and nostalgic, at worst reactionary and insular. The danger is that the more 'local the imagination, the greater becomes the number of social interests and issues for which the psychological logic is: we won't get involved, we won't let this violate us. It is not indifference; it is refusal, a willed constriction of experience' (Sennett 1974: 310). In this account the idea of community is not simply an antidote to the anonymity of the city; it is a rejection of the urban as a space of strangers, a retreat to familiarity and intimacy as the safest place to be. Such a stance narrows the range of one's concern for others to those who appear familiar or who share similar problems. It stands in difficult relation to the claims of anonymity, to questions of regard between strangers, and to the kind of urban ethics that can bear difference.

Similarly, in the work of Iris Marion Young (1990a, 1990b), the turn to community is a disavowal of the city as a place of difference. The affirmation of sameness, the desire for immediacy, the premium placed on face-to-face interaction, the craving for mutuality – all appear in some sense as anti-urban. This is, to be sure, only one reading of what appeals to community might be taken to mean, but a powerful one. Such an ideal of community is troubled by difference, favours closeness and disregards moments of identity or empathy across distance and over time (Young 1990a: 227–31). It is anti-urban in the respect that cities collect differences together and spread people apart. The force of the argument here works in two ways. For Young, a politics of community fears difference close up and discounts the scope for affinity with those you don't meet or know. In this sense it both misses the proximity of difference and limits the imaginative range of identity. It is not clear, of course, that notions of community and realities of difference should be so antithetical, but it seems clear enough that the language and politics of community too often are tainted by a suspicion of otherness – whether in promoting conformity as a condition of belonging, or in marking boundaries against outsiders or incomers.

It is in a principled urbanism but also in urban realities that Young looks for an alternative ethics of being with others. The dream of the city here, and one sometimes realized in the fragile order of the street, is that of 'social differentiation without exclusion' (1990a: 238–9). It is animated by a concept of publicity in its strong sense, based on claims to urban space that are shared without being the same: 'In the city persons and groups interact within spaces and institutions they all experience themselves as belonging to, but without those interactions dissolving into unity or commonness' (1990a: 237). These shared and separate belongings have less to do with identity than with the coincidence of difference, in a field where being together in space is understood, in Young's excellent phrase, as 'side-by-side particularity' (1990a: 238). Such an idea looks to places in the city that do not reduce to blank or alienating public space, on the one hand, or to claims over territory, on the other. The everyday politics of side-by-side particularity is one cities frequently get wrong, but also routinely get right.

This argument goes beyond a notion of indifference as a bare ethical tie. If life in the city is one lived amongst strangers, it is one that requires a regard – however glancing or marginal – for the rights, the selves and the separateness of these strangers. Foreclosure of the space of encounter, via the retreat either to community or into radical privacy, is also a sealing of those imaginative properties through which one might identify with people who are unfamiliar, might recognize the other in a relation of 'mutual strangeness' (Simmel 1997b: 179). Here we come across one of the tricky and useful contradictions that run through logics of identity and difference. The power of the social imagination, that is, lies not only in making connections with others, but in allowing a latitude for disconnection, in accepting dissociation as a social relation, in valuing the very weakness of weak social ties. This negative politics of identity begins from the premise that the only way to live with difference is, first, to live with it. Most people cannot live inside community all the time, and the sociality of indifference can make it safe to venture out.

Here questions of difference in the city do not open onto a politics of recognition or claims of community, but onto an ethics of indifference and a claim to anonymity. Ideas of recognition, as Denise Riley (2002: 9) has it, are given to be 'gregarious'. They assume a certain sociality, a visible presence in social space. An ethics of indifference, in contrast, has to do with a capacity to be unseen, to be unexceptional, to be impersonal in a social field where 'differences remain unassimilated' (Young 1990a: 241) and strangeness is a matter of fact. A politics of difference in this way and at some times involves an ethics of indifference, understood as a relation between subjects, a tacit exchange of the gift of loneliness and of privacy. Cities are places in which such relations of non-identity are possible, tolerable, even normal. They can encourage an indifference to matters of difference that affords certain protections and allows certain freedoms. This is not simply to set indifference in the city against the various workings of community or identity; the solitude of the street versus the convivial politics of the street party. Rather, it is to suggest that part of a politics of difference – important because mundane – is when differences go unremarked because unremarkable, where otherness is ordinary, where a logic of anonymity displaces one of visibility. Indifference is in this sense one way in which differences are *lived* in everyday social spaces. An ethics of indifference may be (and perhaps usually is) inadvertent or unthinking; and the licence of anonymity, 'the right to be lonely' (Riley 2002) granted by the unconcern of others may be a temporary, uneven and unreliable freedom. But this negative freedom is one for which it can seem important to make positive claims.

Conclusion

The choice is not, then, between community and identity, anonymity and indifference, taken as exclusive categories. To understand oneself as alone, to mark out and protect some 'psychological private property' (Simmel 1997a: 163) in relation to others is as much the work of imagination as is the embrace of community. As Riley (2002) puts it, one is neither 'inside' nor 'outside' anything simply as a matter of fact. Rather, solitude and community are entwined in ways of thinking about and being in the city. Urban ideals, like others, are usually flawed. The impulse for community falls away on one side into pious vacuity or squeamish euphemism, elsewhere is engineered as an object of government, marked out as territory or used to police sameness. Cities' special capacity for privacy also allows for unconcern, neglect, disrespect. In Steve Pile's (1999: 18) words, 'Urban spaces make some people into strangers while others are not noticed at all.' The balance between difference and indifference is a precarious one. While the politics of difference frequently rests on a language of recognition, there is a prosaic but crucial urban freedom in having people look straight past you. Such anonymity is, surely, a partial and often a privileged right. For those whose relation to the possibility of indifference is insecure – in urban contexts where racial hatred, sexual harassment, homophobic violence are never 'indifferent' to the presence of others – the ethics of indifference is deeply ambivalent. And it may be true, as Riley suggests, 'that the concept of ambivalence cannot readily be translated into a good' (2002: 5). Anonymity and indifference sit uneasily in the margin Simmel traces between reserve and repulsion, but it is sometimes in the margins that people find room to move.

If the 'intricate order of the city' remains, as it was for Jane Jacobs (1964: 403), 'a manifestation of the freedom of countless numbers of people', this includes a critical negative freedom, the freedom that follows in part from the indifference of others – the right to be left alone. There are very different degrees of security and insecurity here, for different people, at different times, in different spaces. Cities may be the 'place where the other is and where we ourselves are other . . . as the place where we play the other' (Barthes 1997: 171), but this logic of otherness often is played out in violent modes of exclusion, or in isolating forms of disconnection and strangeness. My argument, though, is that an everyday politics of difference in the city at times works through an ethics of indifference, that there are positive claims to be made for what can appear as a negative relation. The solitude of urban life has a contrary quality. It marks a trade-off between freedom and connectedness. It has to do with the way unassimilated differences can produce *indifference* as a kind of tolerance. It is Young's 'side-by-side particularity' that, if it is not always especially companionable, is not necessarily hostile. Anonymity and indifference might be felt sometimes as loss, but they also hold out the potential to 'receive again the gift of privacy, the jewel of loneliness' (White 1999: 37). One of the things people might want from cities, after all, is to get away from the crowd.

2 Spaces of Difference and Division

According to Georg Simmel, perhaps the first sociologist of space, 'the human being is the connecting creature who must always separate and cannot connect without separating', and is 'likewise the bordering creature who has no border' (1997c: 171). People make sense of their world by connecting and separating things, by drawing distinctions and ordering relations, and these processes leave their mark in space. This chapter is concerned with the lines of social division and difference that give shape and sense to the city. How does the making of borders, both physical and conceptual, work to separate out both material spaces and social groups?

The chapter begins with Simmel's treatment of social and spatial borders. In his account the marking of boundaries translates social practice into spatial facts. The divisions that people draw between things and places harden into objective facts which in their turn organize social meanings and social action. Such lines of division have helped form an urban sociological imagination. In the accounts of the Chicago School sociologists, urban areas could be mapped around physical contours and economic functions, but also enclosed cultural groups. Spatial divisions in the city in this way reflected and reproduced social differences. The discussion sets out Ernest Burgess's mapping of urban areas, and goes on to focus on the discussion of the Jewish ghetto as a model for studying the formation of spatial enclaves and cultural communities in the city. This account points to some of the problematic assumptions which underlie early approaches to urban cultures, but also raises issues concerning the links between spatial segregation and social exclusion which remain critical to the analysis of difference and division in the city.

These early accounts within urban sociology link urban spaces to social groups. Such a connection between spatial locations and social identities has also been very clear in the development of urban policy. The identification of social problems in the city has gone hand in hand with the depiction of problem spaces and problem groups. The latter half of the discussion examines the construction of urban problems within social geographies of deprivation and disorganization. Certain urban spaces – inner cities, urban 'ghettoes' or deprived neighbourhoods – have at various times been set up as containers for urban problems. In this way questions of poverty, joblessness, urban blight or crime in the city have been explicitly spatialized and often covertly racialized. Such a social and spatial fix remains evident in recent approaches to urban neighbourhoods, notably in accounts which link pathologies of local urban areas to deficits in social capital. Here, issues of urban poverty and inequality are tied to impacted social spaces that are cut off from mainstream institutions and fractured by mistrust, and whose physical boundaries also function as lines of social exclusion.

Making boundaries

How are boundaries made in space? Divisions of space are not simply physical facts but social products. In 'The sociology of space', Simmel (1997a: 143) argues that the 'boundary is not a spatial fact with sociological consequences, but a sociological fact that forms itself spatially'. Spatial boundaries are formed and reproduced by social action, and also impress themselves on ways of thinking. Modes of both separating and connecting spaces (borders, boundaries, paths, bridges) give objective form to a subjective understanding of space, and then serve to conduct the subject in space. Simmel puts it this way in his 1909 essay on 'Bridge and door':

> The people who first built a path between two places performed one of the greatest human achievements. No matter how often they might have gone back and forth between the two and thus connected them subjectively, so to speak, it was only in visibly impressing the path into the surface of the earth that the places were objectively connected. The will to connection had become a shaping of things, a shaping that was available to the will at every repetition, without still being dependent on its frequency or rarity. Path-building, one could say, is a specifically human achievement. (Simmel 1997c: 172)

Simmel asks us to reflect on 'the miracle of the road', a social and physical fact which is born out of people's movement and then comes to command that movement. It is a very fine example of how the products of social action (at its limits, society itself) confront social actors as objective conditions. You may have made the road, but now the road directs you.

For Simmel, the work of separating and connecting are part of the same process. To draw lines of separation in space makes no sense without the idea of connection. As he has it (1997c: 171), in designating two things as ' "separate", we have already related them to one another in our consciousness, we have emphasized these two things together against whatever lies between them'. As of the banks of a river, 'if we did not first connect them in our practical thoughts, in our needs and in our fantasy, then the concept of separation would have no meaning' (ibid.). Simmel is alert to the way that conceptual connections become solid, the way in which notional borders are made real. From this early sociology of space and spatial connection comes a doubled approach to the problem of boundaries: the separation of objects, people or places is always shadowed by the idea – the 'fantasy' or the danger – of their connection.

Lines of division cut through modern cities. These are not simply questions of marks on maps, nor – after Simmel – can we think of features such as roads or bridges merely as useful objects. Apparently neutral divisions in space, the mundane geography of walls, edges and outskirts, can have effects beyond their basic function. Jane Jacobs (1964: 271) stresses the *active* character of borders in the city. Physical borders do not simply indicate divisions in space but help constitute them. She points, moreover, to the propensity of borders (railway tracks and expressways, the edges of parks or the margins between public and private spaces) to create vacuums. Such boundaries divide up space and also create new space: in-between zones whose uses and meanings often remain uncertain. More recently David Goldberg (1993) has described the way that 'buffer zones' segregate and defuse urban space, as in the division of Harlem from south-west Manhattan by Central Park and Morningside Park, as well as by the dual-lane, two-way streets that mark the area's northern and southern edges.

The differentiation of urban spaces serves practical ends, but is also crucial in producing urban meanings. Two neighbourhoods might lie next to each other on the map (think of the stark divisions that score some US cities), but 'from the moment when they receive two different significations, they are radically separated in the image of the city' (Barthes 1997: 168). The functional organization of space interacts in complex ways with its *semantic* organization. A city's 'rhythm', as Barthes puts it, is given by a tension between different kinds of signification. The question of how physical places relate to spatial meanings is one which appears often in urban analysis. The depiction of different urban zones, local areas or neighbourhoods is rarely a matter of drawing lines on a page: it also creates social categories, sets apart social groups, and demarcates social problems.

The Chicago School: spatial divisions and social ecologies

These logics of division and difference have been crucial in the formation of urban sociology. In the work of the Chicago School, lines of social difference could be mapped around functional divisions in space. Modern cities were distinguished not only by the size and concentration of their populations, but by their patterns of differentiation. Cities, that is, produce and reproduce difference in ways which are marked in space. Indeed, it is this part of the urban equation that is most interesting: not that cities contain a lot of people and pack them in tightly (of themselves, not especially interesting sociological observations), but that cities intensify and organize the differences between them.

For Louis Wirth, social diversity was both a defining characteristic of the modern city and a critical element in its reproduction. The city has

> historically been the melting-pot of races, people and cultures, and a most favorable breeding ground of new biological and cultural hybrids. It has not

only tolerated but rewarded individual differences. It has brought together people from the ends of the earth *because* they are different and thus useful to one another, rather than because they are homogeneous and like-minded. (1995: 66)

The clunking race thinking that lies behind Wirth's notion of 'biological hybrids' can put one off noticing his gesture to the kinds of cultural hybridity that are so central to contemporary approaches to the city. If Wirth's statement anticipates more recent conceptions of urban life, however, it also looks back to the founding themes of sociological thought. In highlighting the issue of difference, this approach to the city follows the classical sociological concern with the division of labour in modern societies. The differentiation of functions in a modern economy created a complex system of social interdependence between individuals, and this effect was most pronounced in the modern city (see Burgess 1967). Setting the issue of differentiation in the context of cities, though – and especially in the context of modern US cities – was unavoidably to direct critical attention to questions of social and cultural difference. In these urban settings, the economic division of labour overlapped in intricate ways with divisions of social class, with cultural and ethnic differences, and with patterns of spatial segregation. In highlighting such links the early tradition of the Chicago School offers a clear line back from urban studies' recent concern with the production and organization of difference in the city, to sociology's foundational interest in modern processes of social differentiation and integration.

This central interest in urban diversity, however – if it chimes with more current concerns – was developed in ways that betray the scientism of early twentieth-century US sociology. Famously, various members of the Chicago School used organic or biological metaphors to describe the expansion and differentiation of modern cities. For Ernest Burgess, the growth and organization of the city were analogous to the workings of metabolism in the human body (see Burgess 1967: 53). Roderick McKenzie (1967) also took the study of plant ecology as a model for 'human ecology' in order to analyze people's relationships to each other and to their environments, and the workings of competition, selection and accommodation in social and spatial life. The scientific pretensions of early sociology are standard, and can be more a matter of language than anything else, but the influence of organic metaphors is worth noting here in terms of two substantive ways that they inflected Chicago School approaches to urban life. Cities, first, were seen as complex systems based on processes that went beyond the designs of social actors. Urban processes of expansion, differentiation, organization and disorganization, that is, had a degree of autonomy in themselves and were not always subject to rational calculation or control. Robert Park (1928: viii) writes that 'the city is not merely an artefact, but an organism. Its growth is fundamentally and as a whole, natural, i.e., uncontrolled and undesigned.

The forms it tends to assume are those which represent and correspond to the functions that it is called upon to perform.'

The second effect, also evident in Park's statement, is the haze of naturalism that sometimes surrounds the Chicago School analysis. This is especially pronounced and especially interesting in the way that questions of social and spatial difference come to be naturalized. McKenzie (1967: 77) refers to the formation of distinct neighbourhoods or communities as 'natural areas', based on 'peculiar selective and cultural characteristics', whether ethnicity or language, economic interest or criminality. Wirth (1928) meanwhile undertakes to write a 'natural history' of the Jewish ghetto, and Park (1928) also writes of the ghetto as a 'natural area' in the city. This naturalistic impulse sits at odds with the wider aim of providing sociological explanations of urban processes and forms, and is particularly jarring in its tendency to confuse issues of culture with those of nature. Wirth (1928: 10), for example, intends his work on the ghetto to shed light both on 'human nature and on culture', and suggests that cultural and social arrangements can partly be read as expressions of aspects of human nature (1928: 8). The common slippage between the cultural and the natural in the works of the Chicago School produces accounts that veer between the risible and the invidious, as in Burgess's observation that occupational segregation among different ethnic groups is 'explainable more by racial temperament or circumstances than by old-world economic background, as Irish policemen, Greek ice-cream parlors, Chinese laundries, Negro porters, Belgian janitors, etc.' will attest (Burgess 1967: 57). The difficulty here is in the running together of actually quite different categories. A sociologist now might well agree that social factors ('circumstances') will influence employment opportunities and choices, that immigrants often have to work in lower-status and lower-paid jobs than those they held previously, and that labour markets can cluster members of specific ethnic groups in certain sectors. However, a contemporary sociologist would be less likely to see any of this as a question of 'racial temperament'.

This confusion of culture with 'natural' factors (including those of race) is especially clear in urban sociology's early treatment of the social geography of the city. The Chicago School model for analysing the spatial development and social organization of modern cities is exemplified in Ernest Burgess's (1925) essay, 'The growth of the city'. Here, Burgess pictures the expansion of the ideal-typical city in terms of a series of concentric rings, or 'zones', of economic activity and social distribution (Burgess 1967: 50–1; see figure 1).

The tendency of modern cities, he suggests, is to expand outward from the central business district (or downtown) via dynamic processes of 'invasion' and 'succession'. Just adjacent to the downtown area lies a 'zone in transition' where factory production gradually is being displaced by business activity or light manufacturing or, at worst, by nothing much at all. This in turn gives

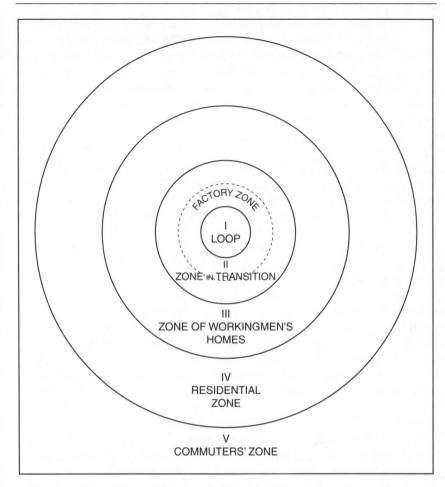

Figure 2.1 The growth of the city (from Burgess 1967)

onto a working-class residential zone, occupied mainly by those who work in the inner area. Beyond the zone of 'workingmen's homes' is a residential area of higher-grade apartment buildings and single-family homes. Further out lies the 'commuter zone' of suburbs and dormitory towns, with its primarily residential and service functions. Burgess's argument is that urban growth takes place by the expansion of each of these zones outward, by the 'invasion' of the outlying zone by residential populations and economic functions. He notes that in the case of Chicago, the downtown area or Loop would once have accommodated all the residential and economic functions which by the mid-1920s were distributed across the outer zones.

Such a model is developed as an ideal-type: it doesn't, for example, take in Chicago's extensive lake-front, the looping Chicago River, the spatial history

of local industry, or the stubborn staying-put of certain residential populations. Moreover, the visual order of regular radial zones can obscure one of
the key processes of urban development that Burgess identified. The growth
of modern cities, he suggests, does not work simply through outward expansion, but via a dual logic of decentralization and concentration. As the city
expands, new economic centres develop in outer urban areas with their own
local downtowns based around bank branches, chain stores, and so on. At the
same time, however, economic, political and cultural power is consolidated
in the centre of the city. In the Chicago of the 1920s, Burgess (1967: 52) writes,
'an agglomeration of country towns and immigrant colonies [is] undergoing
a process of reorganization into sub-business areas visibly or invisibly
dominated by the central business district'. What Burgess sets out, then, is
not a model of regular (if at times antagonistic) growth outward from the
urban core, but a distribution of economic activities around certain growth
nodes, in tandem with the concentration of activities in the centre.

Burgess's model would later be subject to intense criticism within urban
geography and sociology, not least for its ecological bent and its taint of
pseudo-science – cities, simply, are not organisms nor even much like
them. Neo-Marxist critics in the 1970s and after were particularly critical of
the way the urban ecologies naturalized the effects of market processes on
urban space (see Castells 1977; Logan and Molotch 1987; see also Saunders
2001). Nevertheless, the early Chicago models retain a real measure of
explanatory power. As Soja (2000: 88) avers, '[they] succeeded in describing,
with some accuracy, many characteristic features of the macrospatial
organization of cityspace. There was (and probably still is) some degree to
which almost every cityspace is organized around a dominant centre in a
series of concentric zones, radial sectors and specialized enclaves.' While
spatial uses and distributions may vary, Soja argues that these kinds of
patterns show up in numerous cities, ancient and modern. They also
support more critical analyzes of how urban space is organized (see Pile
1999; Bridge 2005). Mike Davis (1998), for example, uses the concentric
zones model to map what he terms the 'ecology of fear' in contemporary
Los Angeles – a spatial economy of no-go areas, highly administered and
policed spaces, edge cities and the fortified zones of gated neighbourhoods
and ex-urban 'gulags' (see figure 2).

Davis's model takes the Chicago ecology as a template for mapping lines of
segregation, division and control in a fearful late modern city. In doing so he
turns the earlier diagram of urban order into a means of representing the
spatial distribution of urban crisis in 'the thickened carceral landscape of Los
Angeles' (Soja 2000: 304). The urban zones model remains very useful in
analysing other contemporary urban processes. The twin logics of concentration and decentralization, for instance, can be seen in patterns of urban
sprawl, in the extension of strip malls, shopping centres, ribbon developments along arterial roads, and the growth of satellite suburbs and cities.

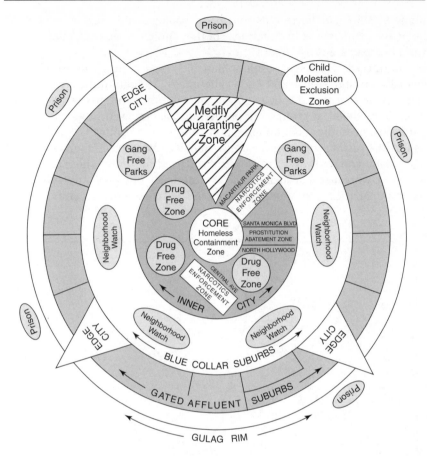

Figure 2 The ecology of fear (from Davis 1998)

Burgess's concept of 'centralized decentralization', what is more, looks like a good model of a globalized urban system, where dispersed economic sites are co-ordinated via the 'command and control' functions of key global cities (see Sassen 2001). As an ideal-type, what is more, the urban zones model of city growth provides a critical basis against which to compare contradictory processes, such as the death of certain downtowns, or the movement back into inner cities by gentrifying middle-class residents (see the discussion in chapter 4).

The original urban zones map, however, looks oddly depopulated, even if it involves a fairly clear social geography of class. The mix of people and place in the modern city becomes clearer in Burgess's charting of distinct 'urban areas'. Here the division of city space reads as a map of social difference. The language of invasion and succession by different urban populations is one

Burgess (1967: 50) borrowed from plant ecology, and there is an almost botanical exoticism in his treatment of the ethnic and cultural character of various urban areas (see figure 3).

This model depicts a cosmopolitan city organized economically and spatially around ethnic and class differences. Mobility outward from the centre is an indicator of both economic and cultural status. In the inner zones of the city, different groups are pushed up against each other in a dense patterning of ethnic and immigrant populations. As one moves away from the centre, the social geography becomes more clearly marked in terms of class, and – at least on Burgess's map – less marked in ethnic terms. Those categories of people who are most socially and economically marginal – the homeless, the criminal, the recent immigrant – are located closest to the centre. Sites of

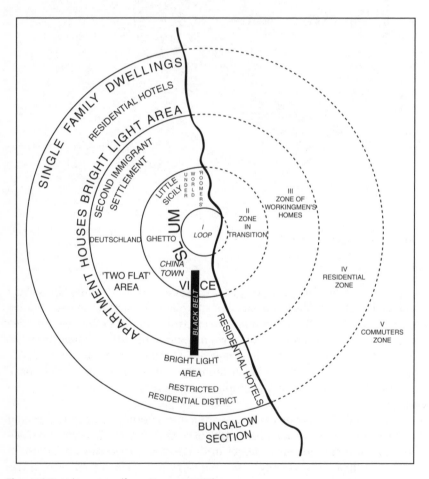

Figure 2.3 Urban areas (from Burgess 1967)

exclusion, that is, lie right alongside the centre of social and economic power. We can also note a shift in how Burgess describes this social scene – the more narrative description of urban areas abandons a scientific tenor for an almost pulp journalistic tone. Downtown, he writes, you will find 'Hobohemia', with its unstable population of homeless and itinerant people living right in the central business district, or close nearby. The inner urban area that radiates out from the centre, the deteriorating 'zone in transition', takes in

> the so-called 'slums' and 'bad lands,' with their submerged regions of poverty, degradation, and disease, and their underworlds of crime and vice. Within a deteriorating area are rooming-house districts, the purgatory of 'lost souls.' Near by is the Latin Quarter, where creative and rebellious spirits resort. The slums are also crowded to overflowing with immigrant colonies – the Ghetto, Little Sicily, Greektown, Chinatown – fascinatingly combining old world heritages and American adaptations. Wedging out from here is the Black Belt, with its free and disorderly life. (Burgess 1967: 54–6)

As one moves away from the centre, the population becomes more stable, more affluent – and is gradually de-racialized. The third zone remains predominantly working class, but the working population here tends to be more skilled and housing is of a better quality. This is the site of 'second immigrant settlement', by new residents who have prospered or by second-generation migrants. In this sense, 'it is the region of escape from the slum, the *Deutschland* of the aspiring Ghetto family' (1967: 56 – Burgess is referring here to an idea of the assimilated German Jew in their higher-status enclave). Beyond this lies the residential zone, with its gradations of housing from residential hotels and apartment houses to single family dwellings. And further out again lies the commuter zone. These outer residential zones are distinguished not only by the largely residential pattern of use but by the fact that they have apparently lost any distinct ethnic character. Such areas are implicitly coded as white (the 'Black Belt' extends only slightly into the residential zone) and are, in offering a 'Promised Land' to aspirant immigrant populations, organized by a social logic of assimilation.

This social geography of class, race and ethnicity is seen to be subject only to 'interesting minor modifications' in respect of different US cities (ibid.: 54). In general, the growth of the city works to 'sort' different economic and ethnic groups in spatially quite reliable ways. Nevertheless, Burgess's account is strongly inflected by the particular development of Chicago and by a specific concern with questions of race. Burgess and his Chicago School colleagues were writing at a period when black Americans were migrating to Northern US cities in increasing numbers: the 'Black Belt' he delineates on the map of urban areas is quite condensed, but already emergent are the outlines of a race problematic that was to become very familiar in urban discourse. Burgess's characterization of the Black Belt as 'free and disorderly' contains a couple of standard themes, and Park's (1967b) essay on juvenile delinquency develops these further. To Park, the situation of black urban communities in the United States in the first decades of the twentieth century exemplified the disorganizing effects of population mobility. While migration offered economic and cultural opportunities to migrants themselves, he argues that it destabilizes both the communities they leave behind and the ones they move into. The notion of 'disorganization' is in itself fairly innocuous – it is meant, in principle neutrally, to indicate changes in a local social and economic order. But Park suggests that such changes are also 'demoralizing', corrosive of the social and cultural values that underpin a stable urban order (see also Burgess 1967: 59). For Park, 'The enormous amount of delinquency, juvenile and adult, that exists today in the Negro communities in northern cities is due in part, though not entirely, to the fact that migrants are not able to accommodate themselves at once to a new and relatively strange environment' (1967b: 108). The same can be said, he adds, of recent European immigrants, and of the 'younger generation' of women at that time beginning to access new economic and social freedoms in the city. Processes that disrupt established social and economic arrangements in cities are also seen as subversive of conventional cultural values. This tying of social problems to mobile or unstable communities is an issue to which I return later in the chapter, particularly in respect of the more or less overt ways in which this becomes linked to race. What I wish to focus on here is how social arrangements in space are seen to be expressive of the cultural character of different groups.

Cultural difference and spatial divisions: the ghetto

The linkage of social and economic organization with cultural factors is very marked in the Chicago School's treatment of another key ethnic grouping in their map of the modern city: Jews. The analysis of Jewish immigrant settlement in the modern city works as a model of how cultural difference is organized in space. Burgess's description of mobility across urban areas encodes an exemplary story about the Jewish immigrant's path from 'Ghetto' to 'Deutschland'; from cultural and spatial isolation to integration or assimilation. It is a narrative that is realized most fully in Louis Wirth's (1928) study of the ghetto, which transposes the topography of Jewish segregation in European cities onto the map of immigrant settlement in modern Chicago. Wirth (1928: 9) notes that the European ghetto is one of the 'primary physical expressions of the social distance' between Jewish and non-Jewish populations in these old cities, regulated in many cases by law and maintained by prejudice and by more or less overt forms of violence. The ghetto offers a model of a contained social and economic order, and – as we saw in the previous chapter – something like a laboratory for urban sociology's interest in community organization. For Wirth, the 'story of the Jews' in the past thousand years 'is the story of the ghetto' (1928: 1), and the American ghetto reproduces the forms and traditions of its European origins. The Jewish quarters of New York or Chicago are, Wirth writes with horrible prescience, 'a last scene of the final act' in the long history of the European ghetto (1928: 203). While he is concerned to trace the particular spatial story of Jewish minorities, Wirth also is interested in how this account of social and spatial isolation might speak to the urban experience of black Americans, of Chinese and other immigrant groups in the modern American city (1928: 10, 20). The story of the ghetto, that is, has wider implications for the spatial organization of social difference.

In simple terms, the ghetto encloses a local urban economy, one typically situated adjacent to major commercial centres. Chicago's ghetto is close to the Loop, New York's much larger Jewish population at the same time is concentrated on the Lower East Side of Manhattan. This spatial proximity, though, belies the stark contrast between the wealth of the commercial centre and the relative poverty of the ghetto. These low-rent areas are densely populated – a consequence, Wirth contends, not only of poverty, but of the 'traditions of close community life of crowded ghetto quarters' that Jewish immigrants bring with them from Europe. Given these circumstances, Wirth remarks on the comparatively low mortality rates of Jews in the city. Whether as a result of 'acquired immunity', customary forms of diet and sanitation, or the organization of the Jewish family, it seems that 'the Jews have made some sort of accommodation to urban conditions as presented by the typical slum district' (1928: 202). The notion of the Jew as an exemplary urban type is a familiar theme – while it carries positive connotations here, it is also a basic tenet of modern anti-Semitism – but we can note that Wirth is undecided as to whether such an 'accommodation' is an effect of biology ('acquired immunity' to slum conditions), religious culture ('ritualistically prescribed diet and hygiene') or social organization ('the nature of Jewish family life').

Such an account highlights the equation of cultural and spatial forms with 'natural' tendencies which runs through the urban ecology approach. In looking at the complex of factors that shape urban areas, the tendency of different Chicago School theorists is to bring together economic and social arguments with certain assumptions about ethnic type or personality. The location and clustering of immigrant and other minority communities in the modern city are, first, explained in terms of economic factors – by access to labour and housing markets, land values, rent levels, and so on. These emergent urban areas, second, are anchored by social ties and institutions – kinship networks, churches, temples or synagogues, public baths, schools, clubs and political associations – that consolidate the community and act as a magnet for newcomers. Such a spatial effect, however, also turns on questions of habit, custom, culture and 'temperament' which are – if not always exactly *essentialized* – then certainly highly ascriptive. In outlining the ecological approach to human community, McKenzie (it must be said, one of the most dedicated 'scientizers' of the Chicago School) writes that the 'continuous process of invasions and accommodations' between different populations in the city produces distinct areas defined by 'peculiar selective and cultural characteristics'. He maintains that each such 'ecological organization within a community serves as a selective or magnetic force attracting to itself appropriate population elements and repelling incongruous units, thus making for biological and cultural subdivisions of a city's population' (McKenzie 1967: 77–8). McKenzie's work is easily the most problematic of his contemporaries. His apparently dispassionate tone and his liking for ecological jargon lead him into constructions that now read as straightforwardly racist, as in his noting the 'common observation that foreign races and other undesirable invaders, with few exceptions, take up residence near the business centre of the community or at other points of high mobility and low resistance. Once established they gradually push their way out along business or transportation thoroughfares to the periphery of the community' (McKenzie 1967: 76). The first statement makes urban populations look like rather basic life-forms, attracted to or repelled by certain areas in the city seemingly outside of their own volition. The second statement treats 'foreign races' as some especially tenacious species of pest, invading the centre of the city and then spreading outward along the lines of least resistance from existing population groups. It is not simply that the biological metaphors are awkward or inapt, here: they are ugly.

The Chicago School analyses tend to be less scientific than some of their authors might have hoped or claimed, and McKenzie's suspect conflations point to the wider difficulty of separating biological from cultural assumptions within this body of work. This has everything to do with the way a notion of 'race', treated as a social category of the same order as 'nation' or 'culture', at times slides into notion of acquired characteristics, temperament or biology. Wirth (1928: 226), for example, notes 'a constant sifting process in the course of which each racial, national, and cultural group tends to find its habitat in the various natural areas that the city affords'. This sifting and sorting of population are determined by economic considerations and social opportunities but also come to be linked to issues of 'sentiment', understood in terms of cultural ties between members of a community, but also in terms of cultural distance or alienation between distinct groups. Here, forms of accommodation or resistance organize relations between different populations along tolerant or hostile lines. Wirth (1928: 226–9) traces the various relations between Jewish immigrants in Chicago and their neighbours on the West Side of the city. Mutual tolerance between Jewish and non-Jewish Bohemian immigrants, he claims, reproduces the nature of their relations in the Old World, while ill-tempered proximity and a familiar hostility surround the close economic relations between Jews and Polish Catholics. Different kinds of accommodation take place with successive waves of Irish, Italian, Lithuanian, Greek and Turkish immigrants, who stand to the Jewish population in a range of relations shaped by history, culture, language and class. Wirth also remarks the degree of tolerance shown by Jewish shopkeepers and landlords to the recent in-migration of black residents on the near West Side, due in large part to their own experience of segregation, race prejudice and economic exclusion (see Wirth 1928: 230–1; cf. Osofsky 1971, for a contrasting account of discrimination against black residents by certain Jewish businesses in New York's Harlem).

These discussions of urban culture frequently turn on an understanding of 'personality' as a collective quality. Interestingly, Wirth does not impute the collective personality of a Jewish 'type' to any innate character, but to the impact of history and *place* on social groups. His outlining of Jewish 'personality types' is in fact a description of different social and spatial locations (Wirth 1928: 249–51), given not only by people's economic activities, their national backgrounds or their class positions, but also by their local cultural milieux. Such an idea is captured in Wirth's notion of the 'culture area', a social space in the city that is organized around particular interactions, conventions and values. Individuals' conduct is shaped in the context of a given 'culture area' – a concept which Wirth takes from anthropology. His fine distinctions among the *Deitchuks* (assimilated Jews who 'affect German ways'), *Allrightnicks* (businessmen who have jettisoned 'most of the cultural baggage' of Jewishness), the *realestatenick* (self-explanatory), the *Shacherjude* (a peddler or small-scale trader, and the typical ghetto Jew), and various other characters (including an interesting token female – the '*Radikalke*, or the emancipated woman'), are not meant merely to sketch assorted cartoon-ish types, but to describe processes of social and spatial mobility in terms of their effects on individuals' demeanour, disposition, what we might now call their 'habitus'. Wirth's argument is not simply that a pre-given cultural personality gets played out in the spaces of modern cities (as the clumsy idiom of 'natural habitats' might suggest), but that spatial conditions and social arrangements both shape cultures and in turn are shaped by cultural practices and preferences. In addressing certain common assumptions about the 'clannish' nature of the Jew, for instance, Wirth (1928: 288) writes – in what sounds like a strikingly contemporary comment – 'the Jews became exclusive because at a certain period of their history they were excluded'.

The movement away from the ghetto, in this account, is a process of deracination: spatial mobility is closely tied to social mobility and to the weakening of cultural ties, convention and practice (see pp. 245–7). The disintegration of cultural communities, driven by social mobility and spatial dispersal, is countered by the community organization that takes place in the face of external hostility, resistance and intolerance. Such a mode of community is based more clearly on social institutions and assertive expressions of identity than on either economic necessity or matters of custom, sentiment or habit. Wirth (1928: 271–2) describes how the formal organization of a Jewish community in Chicago was given impetus by increasing anti-Semitism (in the United States as well as internationally) during the early twentieth century, by changes in US immigration arrangements, and by the intensifying persecution and impoverishment of Jewish populations in Eastern Europe. This kind of organization, around formal institutions and a definite social consciousness, is distinct from the more 'natural' processes through which ethnic groups come to locate in particular areas and to associate on the basis of historic, cultural or linguistic ties. An assertive social model of community, in this sense, comes close to the synthetic and political conception of community familiar from more current debates (see also chapter 1).

For the Chicago School theorists, the relationship between spatial locations and social types is a mutually determining one. Wirth's study of the ghetto aimed to capture 'the extent to which a local culture is a matter of geographical location' (1928: 286). Culture leaves a kind of 'stain' on the urban landscape, marking out different neighbourhoods in ways which go beyond their economic functions or physical conditions. Robert Park (1967a: 6) puts it this way:

> In the course of time every section and quarter of the city takes on something of the character and qualities of its inhabitants. Each separate part of the city is inevitably stained with the peculiar sentiments of its population. The effect of this is to convert what was at first a mere geographical expression into a neighbourhood, that is to say, a locality with sentiments, traditions, and a history of its own.

The construction of ethnic enclaves, of ghettoes and other racialized spaces is in this way an effect not only of economic and social 'sorting', but of affective distance between different groups in the city:

> Physical and sentimental distances reinforce each other, and the influences of local distributions of the population participate with the influence of class and race in the evolution of the social organization. Every city has its racial colonies, like the Chinatowns of San Francisco and New York, the Little Sicily of Chicago, and various other less pronounced types. (Park 1967a: 10)

The kinds of boundaries that these thinkers describe are not simply physical (and they certainly are not fixed), but are oriented around perceptions of cultural difference, enclosing forms of identity and excluding unfamiliar others. They recall Simmel's arguments on the way subjective divisions are made real in objective forms. 'The modern invisible ghetto wall', Wirth (1928: 280) suggests, 'is no less real than the old', as these imagined boundaries give shape to the subjective reflexes which 'govern our approach to the familiar and our withdrawal from the strange' (Wirth 1928: 280).

The ghetto, whether as found in the old cities of Europe or in the immigrant quarters of American cities, gives social and psychological relations a spatial expression. In the American case, however, where the ghetto is not simply 'compulsory', the state of segregation 'is not so much a physical fact as it is a state of mind' Wirth (1928: 287). This may be overstating the point somewhat – it is not clear how far one can speak, as Wirth does, of 'voluntary' ghettoization – but it does draw out the links between the physical and mental processes of separation and connection that Simmel had theorized. Spatial segregation may be defensive, a response to intolerance, strangeness or privation, but it also may be based on the positive attractions of familiarity, shared cultural norms and practices, social and economic ties. In this sense, 'Jews drift into the ghetto,' Wirth (1928: 283) contends, 'for the same reasons that the Italians live in Little Sicily, the Negros in the black belt, and the Chinese in Chinatowns.' The sifting and sorting of different populations in the city are 'responsible for the abrupt transition in local atmosphere as we sometimes pass from one street to another in the patchwork of little ghettos that constitutes the great immigrant quarters of our large cities' (1928: 283). There is a contradiction at work, however, between Wirth's emphasis on the diversity of different cultural enclaves in the city, and the notion that all ghettoes are in some more basic sense founded on similar structures of division and inclusion. In his later work on Chicago, for instance, Allan Spear (1967: 26) argues that black ghettoes on the South and West Sides were more a result of white hostility than of economic deprivation in itself. The crucial difference that marked out the black ghetto from other ethnic enclaves 'was not the existence of slum conditions, but the difficulty of escaping the slum. European immigrants needed only to prosper to be able to move to a more desirable neighborhood. Negroes, on the other hand, suffered from both economic deprivation and systematic racial discrimination.' Racism, that is, redoubled the effects of poverty in holding certain social groups in place.

These founding approaches within urban sociology to issues of social and spatial difference leave a complicated legacy. On one hand, the Chicago School accounts emphasize the links between spatial divisions and social differences, and insist on how crucial this relation is to the organization and experience of urban space. They also stress the cultural and affective dimensions of the social and economic 'sorting' of populations in the city. Patterns on the ground which might appear as 'a mere geographical expression' of land and property values, labour markets and economic locations, take shape as social localities with their own histories, identities and cultural meanings. The problems, on the other hand, lie in the way that certain 'types' of people are pinned down in space. Ethnic identity works as both a cultural and a spatial label, such that 'the Italians . . . the Negros . . . and the Chinese' can be lumped together and assigned to their place on the map. Ethnicity in this sense becomes a kind of spatial destiny, even if only a temporary one. These minority identities are defined in their difference from an unexamined and apparently 'non-ethnic' majority – residing in those colourless zones that constitute the social field and the spatial locale of assimilation. Thinkers such as Park, Burgess and Wirth wanted to highlight the changing nature of social space in modern cities, and the mutually determining effects of culture and space, but their accounts could not always avoid lapsing into gestures of spatial and cultural fixity. The hangover from these kinds of thinking is felt in the way that different parts of the city come to be identified with particular cultural, ethnic or racial 'types'. Bounded spaces, that is, are defined, under-stood and often pathologized in terms of distinct groups. In the lines of discussion which follow, I trace the after-effects of these conceptions of spatial division and social difference in terms of two enduring themes within urban sociology: (1) the ways in which urban problems are mapped in space; and (2) the anatomy of neighbourhoods. In each case, the construction of problem spaces goes together with the identification of problem groups.

The spatiality of 'urban problems'

> The more subtle changes in our social life, which in their cruder manifes-tations are termed 'social problems,' problems that alarm and bewilder us, as divorce, delinquency, and social unrest, are to be found in their most acute forms in our large American cities. The profound and 'subver-sive' forces which have wrought these changes are measured in the phys-ical growth and expansion of cities.
>
> E. W. Burgess, 'The growth of the city'

How is it that cities, or parts of the city, come to be understood as a 'problem'? To follow Burgess, certain social problems (divorce, delinquency and social unrest remain common themes) are aggravated in urban contexts. These are, to use an old distinction, problems which are more visible *in* the city; they are not, in themselves, problems born *of* the city. One doesn't have to live in a city to get divorced, although it might help. There are other problems, however, which may be seen as the product of urban processes: that is, problems *of* the city. Most notable here are the ways in which cycles of economic and spatial change make certain spaces and certain people redundant. Cities, Robert Park (1967c: 109) asserts baldly, 'are full of junk, much of it human'. Just as the growth of cities junks the material culture of urban life as it becomes obsolete, so these processes 'scrap' those individuals who are useless or resistant to the demands of progress (see also Burgess 1967: 57–8). And as with other forms of waste, cities' human junk is clustered in specific sites. The 'Hobohemia' zone in inner Chicago, just outside the downtown, represents one such 'human junk heap'. In general, Park (1967c : 109) goes on, 'the slum areas that invari-ably grow up just on the edge of the business areas of great cities, areas of dete-riorated houses, of poverty, vice, and crime, are areas of social junk'. This is a forceful metaphor for the way in which individuals are trashed by an economic system to which they become useless, and draws a connection between marginal social lives and the marginal spaces of the city (see also Sibley 1995). Edges or border zones have a particular grip on the urban imag-ination, whether – as in the case of Hobohemia – they are situated close to the centre, or – as in the case of the outer suburbs of a city such as Paris or Glasgow – they mark the periphery of an urban order (see Mooney 1999; Wacquant 1993, 1996; see also Back 2004). If cities can be seen as primary locations for the entrenchment of social problems, and for the invention of new ones, this is not a general urban effect. There exist uneven geographies of social problems, such that certain sites in the city could be seen to incubate the 'social diseases' of 'poverty, disease and delinquency' (Park 1967d: 118).

This spatialization of social problems is typical of the Chicago School approach, and would also be central to the forms of urban policy which developed in the second half of the twentieth century. As Soja (2000: 95) writes, the 'urban crisis that exploded all over the world in the 1960s was one of several signals that the long postwar economic boom in the advanced industrial countries was coming to an end'. As well as concentrating the effects of economic crisis, however, cities also fostered their own social problems. During the 1960s a number of liberal capitalist governments – notably in the United States and Britain – set about programmes of policy intervention in response to what was seen as a growing 'urban problem' (see Atkinson and Moon 1994; Blackman 1995; Fainstein and Fainstein 1982; Halpern 1995; Kleinberg 1995; Wolman and Agius 1996). The precise nature of this problem was defined in various ways in different contexts, although it frequently circled around two key elements: poverty and race. A focus on the social and economic problems of cities was spurred by a growing poverty debate within political and public discourse during the 1960s, informed by social research and government studies into the persistence of poverty in advanced capitalist and welfare societies (see, for example, Abel-Smith and Townsend 1965, in the British context, and Moynihan 1969, in the USA; see also O'Connor 2001; Patterson 2000). This 'rediscovery of poverty' as a chronic problem – in spite of increasing economic affluence, on the one hand, and basic welfare provision, on the other – directed attention to those sites, including many inner city areas, where poverty appeared most concentrated. The development of urban policy in the United States took place against the backdrop of President Johnson's 1964 declaration of a 'war on poverty', and the unrolling of new welfare measures in the late 1960s and early 1970s (see Moynihan 1970). In Britain the introduction of the Urban Programme in 1968 signalled the formation of the first distinctly *urban* policy strategy, combining a range of social and economic initiatives on education, crime, environmental renewal and labour markets in urban areas. The spatial boundaries for these urban policies were defined by census and other research data which converged on concentrated sites of poverty, unemployment, low educational attainment, substandard housing, high crime and social tension in the city. In this way the government of social and economic problems became tied to the management of urban spaces, and questions of poverty and inequality were linked to issues of spatial order.

If poverty was the primary rationale for the development of urban policy, issues of race and ethnicity also formed part of the equation – although usually in less overt ways. Those urban areas identified as sites of acute deprivation regularly coincided with the distribution of minority ethnic

48   *Spaces of Differences and Division*

populations in the city. In Britain and in the United States, the diagnosis of an 'urban' or 'inner city problem' has in this sense been racialized from the outset. Indeed, it can be argued that from the 1960s the term 'inner city' functioned as a code for speaking about race (see Keith and Rogers 1991). As Logan and Molotch (1987: 114) argue in the US case, 'postwar urban renewal programs (lasting into the late 1960s) were truly, in James Baldwin's phrase, "Negro removal", so frequently was residential clearance to afflict poor, black people's communities'. Social and government research in the 1960s and afterwards found significant minority populations in urban areas characterized by poverty, low educational standards, poor housing stock and other indices of 'urban deprivation'. The construction of an urban problem therefore has been built in part along racial or ethnic lines. Urban processes tend to concentrate minority or immigrant groups in particular areas, based on local housing and labour markets and reinforced by patterns of both community formation and racist exclusion (see Goldberg 1993; Robinson 1999; Smith 1987). In large British and US cities, such locations typically have been inner urban areas offering manual work and relatively low-rent housing. It was these working-class areas that were hit especially hard by urban deindustrialization from the 1950s: it follows that black and minority ethnic populations would be over-represented in the geography of urban decline. Urban policy in this way became an important instrument for a politics of race in the city. Based on standard indices of social and economic deprivation, urban policy programmes allowed local and central governments to direct resources to particular sections of the urban population without appearing to give 'special treatment' to any group, especially along ethnic or racial lines. Urban interventions could be passed off as purely *spatial* rather than racial matters. Given white suspicion of special treatment for minority groups – especially in the toxic race politics of Britain in the late 1960s and 1970s – targeted urban policy based on standard indicators aimed to catch within its net disadvantaged populations, both white and non-white, without appearing to do anyone any deliberate favours.

This cuts in different ways. On one hand, the development of urban policy was supposed to be colour-blind or 'race-neutral', directing resources purely on the basis of social and economic need. On the other hand, this meant that arguments concerning race could not explicitly inform the analysis of urban problems. In using ostensibly neutral devices of social statistics to identify sites of multiple deprivation, urban policy strategies did little to explain how geographies of social inequality and racial injustice were produced and reproduced. Moreover, given that mainstream debates failed to recognize racism as a serious social factor, it became hard to explain the economic disadvantage of minority populations without ascribing some kind of deficiency to these groups themselves (see Katz, 1989; Ryan 1971; see also Jencks 1993; Murray 1995). As John Solomos has written in the British context, urban programmes targeting economic and social disadvantage in specific sites served to 'focus attention on the supposed characteristics of inner city areas and their residents without looking at the history of how such areas developed and the role of political and economic forces in the creation of "ghetto" areas' (1988: 187; see also Sugrue 1996, on the US case). The impact of discrimination in employment and housing, institutional racism and over-policing rarely entered political and public discourse. When social problems become identified with certain places, they are invariably tied to certain groups of people. As specific sites in the inner city were coded as problem spaces, particular urban subjects – young men, and especially young black and minority men – were set up as 'problems' for social and public order (see Antonopoulos 2003; Bowling 1999; Chambliss 1994; Keith 1993, 2005; see also Fiske 1998). Law and order strategies in this context have constituted the enforcement arm of urban policy, translating the war on poverty into a kind of 'war on the poor' (Gans 1996). The government of urban problems can be viewed – at the same time and without contradiction – in terms of a welfare politics of urban redistribution, and in terms of the management of urban populations.

The politics of neighbourhood

The running together of social problems and problem spaces is especially tenacious in the politics of neighbourhood. An interest in the pathologies of neighbourhood has been an enduring feature of social analysis, particularly in urban sociology and criminology, and has a clear pedigree in the ecological approaches to crime and deviance developed by Chicago School sociologists in the 1920s and after. Considered as human ecologies, certain urban areas displayed a range of characteristics that made them unusually prone to juvenile delinquency, crime and social fragmentation. The key frame at work here was that of 'social disorganization' – a general diagnosis that took in factors such as a highly mobile population, ethnic unease or conflict, sparse neighbourhood networks, lack of local organizations, social anonymity, and the formation of youth subcultures at odds with (or out of control by) 'mainstream' or adult cultures (see Park 1967a, 1967c; Shaw and McKay 1942). Burgess (1967: 59) stressed the confusing and demoralizing effects of heightened mobility in the city, arguing that in those areas where population turns over rapidly, 'and where in consequence primary controls break down completely, as in the zone of deterioration in the modern city, there develop areas of demoralization, of promiscuity, and of vice'. Ecological approaches in this way highlighted social rather than strictly 'environmental' factors in producing higher rates of crime, juvenile delinquency and disorganization in some urban locales. In line with a functionalist approach – and with the sociological imperative to explain social problems by way of social facts – neighbourhoods were seen as complex systems of social organization, and urban order or disorder was the effect of a mesh of social factors. This founding approach to studying the rules of urban order and problems of urban disorder went on to inform later approaches to social area analysis and urban ecology (see Berry and Kasarda 1977; Hawley 1950; Shevsky and Bell 1955).

Such explanations have proved very durable in studies of crime and deviance – even if they largely have discarded the biological jargon of city neighbourhoods as local 'ecologies'. While poverty was the primary spur for the development of urban policy in the 1960s, a number of later arguments suggest that 'disorganized' urban communities on the lines described above put their residents at greater risk of violence and crime, even when poverty is taken out of the equation (Burskik 1988; Burskik and Grasmick 1993; McGarrell et al. 1997; Skogan 1990). A poor neighbourhood where people don't stay around for long is, in this analysis, less safe than a poor neighbourhood where the population is more stable. Arguments of these kinds have some rather contradictory effects. On one hand, they begin with a clear understanding of the interplay of social and spatial factors in the city. Second, they aim to provide a detailed analysis of specific urban areas as social systems, rather than making generalizations about problem spaces. And they potentially shift attention away from the individual pathologies of violent, criminal or deviant actors to an account of the social environments that are likely to be most conducive to violence, crime or disorder. On the other hand, accounts of social disorganization can be given to reductive links between social factors and spatial containers. In particular, they are subject to the 'ecological fallacy' which typifies urban areas in terms of their worst features, overlooking the finer grain of interaction and organization which underlies them. It is unlikely, after all, that everyone who lives in a poor area will be poor (or jobless or violent or delinquent or fearful or hopeless or whatever). This fallacy is one that labels individuals or communities as much as places. The problem of blaming the victim continues to be as pernicious as ever in public arguments on crime, violence and urban safety: in this context, the fact of living in an unsafe or 'disorganized' neighbourhood can itself be read, by those who care to, as a symptom of individual pathology. It is always easy to run together structure and agency – 'neighbourhood effects' and individual acts – to come up with crude social explanations.

Urban ecology, like other kinds of functionalism, gets a bad press (or no press at all) these days. However, one of the strengths of ecological approaches is the focus on a complex of elements in organizing urban spaces and shaping urban processes. It is also one of their weaknesses, making it difficult to pinpoint the most immediate causal factors in respect of crime or violence. At its limits the concept of 'disorganization', rather than indicating an interplay of often complicated social features, can appear as a causal factor in itself. It follows that arguments about 'neighbourhood effects' are given to tautology: reduced to the observation that social disorganization causes more social disorganization. In unsafe or unstable neighbourhoods, the spiral is only likely to be downward.

Ideas of social disorganization, however, remain highly topical within urban sociology. In his work on *The Truly Disadvantaged* (1987), William Julius Wilson – one of the most noted later inheritors of Chicago School sociology – traces the domino of economic, institutional and cultural effects which constituted the 'crisis' of US inner cities in the second half of the twentieth century. Basing his study in Chicago, Wilson considers the long aftershock of white flight from inner urban neighbourhoods after the 1950s. The inner city problems of this period hit urban black populations especially hard; however, Wilson stresses that economic factors of deindustrialization, economic restructuring and job losses should take precedence over 'racial' factors in analysing these urban problems. The flight of jobs, investment capital and middle-class residents – both white and black – from many inner cities are crucial in this context: Wilson's analysis suggests that inner city problems can be understood to be as much a class issue as a question of race (see also Wilson 1978). While his work is sensitive to the effects of long histories of racism and discrimination, Wilson argues that the situation of poor black populations in US cities in fact worsened after the enacting of civil rights legislation, and in spite of later commitments to antidiscrimination policies such as affirmative action. The reason for this is primarily economic: urban minorities have been particularly vulnerable to the effects of economic restructuring, increasing labour market polarization, the relocation of industry out of central cities, and the deskilling and downgrading of manual work. Indeed, it can be argued that antidiscrimination policies (affirmative action measures in education and employment, the combating of residential segregation, and so on) have unintentionally compounded the problems facing inner city areas, as more socially mobile black populations move into the middle classes and out to the suburbs.

These economic processes are also linked to cultural processes. The most controversial aspects of Wilson's work concern his analysis of the social environment occupied by a 'black urban underclass' in the United States. The term 'underclass' is a very loaded one (see Devine and Wright 1993; Katz 1993; Mingeone 1996; Wacquant 1994, 2002), but Wilson is critical of analysts who – wishing to avoid the taint of racism – sidestep issues of race when looking at forms of behaviour that could be seen to stigmatize certain groups. His own account examines the connection between wider economic and demographic changes, and local problems of social organization. Economic restructuring in the 1960s and 1970s coincided with the falling age profile of urban black populations, as the slow-down of migration to northern cities from rural areas (especially in the south) meant that increases in black populations in US cities were largely due to birth-rates. It followed that inner city black populations contained higher numbers of young people, in contexts where fewer jobs were available. As Wilson points out, the lower the median age of any social group, the lower its income and the greater its rates of unemployment and crime will tend to be. At the same time the economic exodus of better-off residents weakened the basic institutions of neighbourhood life, including shops, schools, churches and community facilities. What followed was the erosion of 'social organization' in inner cities, understood by Wilson in terms of broad cultural values: 'a sense of community, positive neighbor-hood identification, and explicit norms and sanctions against aberrant behavior' (1987: 3). It was not, then, simply that an economic evacuation degraded inner urban areas, but that it weakened the social capacity of neighbourhoods to sustain local institutions and networks, and to 'police' itself in cultural terms. It is a further instance of the urban paradox under which those 'neighborhoods with the most serious need for community organizations' end up being 'those with the least capacity to create and sustain them' (Logan and Molotch 1987: 136). In such a context, fewer economic opportunities went together with fewer cultural choices as well as fewer social sanctions in fostering what Wilson calls a 'ghetto culture' in US inner cities, particularly for young black men.

In many ways this kind of argument remains tied to the problem that dogged the Chicago School's early studies in urban sociology: the vexed rela-tion between spatial arrangements and cultural processes. Between spatial determinism and cultural blame, there is a fraught field of debate over the ways in which inequality and discrimination are produced and reproduced through spatial divisions. The ghetto has been the key ground for these debates in the US context (see Keith 2005). 'The urban ghetto', Massey and Denton (1993: 18) contend, 'constructed during the first half of the twentieth century and successively reinforced thereafter, represents the key institu-tional arrangement ensuring the continued subordination of blacks in the United States.' In part, the ghetto is institutionally constructed by the system-atic effects of racism in housing, employment and spatial policing, but it is also reproduced in terms of its own institutional structures (see also Clark 1989). For sociologists, what is more, 'institutional' structures are never simply formal, they are also made and remade through informal codes of interaction and organization. This is the point where structure and culture are hard to separate: in his classic work on Harlem, Gilbert Osofsky (1971) takes the concept of the ghetto to refer to not only the social and economic, but the *psychological* conditions of black populations in the city.

These arguments over the links between economic inequality and social organization in this way are shadowed by older debates as to whether a 'culture of poverty' exists in contemporary cities. This notion is one which urban analysis has borrowed from anthropology, specifically from Oscar Lewis's work in case studies of Mexican and Puerto Rican families, includ-ing Puerto Rican immigrants in New York (Lewis 1959, 1966, 1996). Lewis explored the ways that economic inequality and cultural exclusion helped to shape subcultural values and patterns of behaviour amongst severely impoverished groups in capitalist societies. An emergent culture of poverty, he claims (1996: 220), 'is both an adaptation and a reaction of the poor to their marginal position in a class-stratified, highly individuated, capitalistic society'. In the settings he studied, these subcultural norms included: highly gendered social roles and unstable domestic arrangements; the devaluing of childhood; an orientation to the present in the absence of future chances; a focus on the immediate locality rather than on wider social contexts; a sense of fatalism or resignation with respect to life chances or events; hostility towards mainstream forms of authority (such as police, government and churches); and low levels of integration into social institutions outside the family. Lewis argued that cultures of poverty were specific to different social settings, and were relatively rare. Moreover his studies suggested that the behaviour of slum-dwellers in societies like Mexico, Puerto Rico or indeed the United States was not so much irrational, aberrant or self-fulfilling but an effect of discrimination, segregation and simple poverty. Shared cultural orientations could be seen as 'attempts to meet needs not served in the case of the poor by the institutions and agencies of the larger society because the poor are not eligible for such services, cannot afford it or are ignorant and suspicious'. In spite of these qualifications, and Lewis's sympathies for the subjects of his studies, the notion of a culture of poverty would prove easy to align with a growing assumption that deprivation in wealthy societies was on some level due to a deficit on the part of the poor themselves. The culture of poverty thesis fed into an increasingly prevalent notion that disadvantaged populations were locked into a 'cycle' of deprivation, passed on like some kind of malign cultural inheritance from generation to generation. In the 1980s and 1990s, a number of commentators argued that welfare transfers only served to entrench a culture of dependency and apathy amongst an 'underclass' that was becoming more alienated from mainstream institutions and values (see Jencks 1993; Murray 1994; cf. Katz 1993). Wilson's work occupies a critical position in these debates: on the one hand, concerned with the cultural anatomy of a disaffected and isolated 'underclass'; on the other, stressing the primacy of economic and social factors, including historical forms of discrimination, in producing 'ghetto' conditions and cultures (see also Wilson 1996). His response, moreover, was to argue not for policies targeted at specific populations, whether spatial or racial (although he insists that the struggle against race discrimination remains crucial in its own terms), but for programmes addressing the economic inequalities and injustices that affect poorer groups across the US population.

A similar concern with the local effects of larger-scale social and economic change is evident in Elijah Anderson's work in Philadelphia (Anderson 1990, 1999). Anderson, too, is interested as much in the effects of social mobility within black urban populations as in the spectre of 'white flight'. His account is built on several years of ethnographic research in specific neighbourhoods, tracing both demographic and cultural changes as well as economic shifts. He outlines two key changes in the economic and social organization of these low-income areas. First, the movement of the black middle class out of poorer neighbourhoods not only empties out sources of local capital – in terms of the consumption of both private goods (housing, shopping, leisure) and collective goods (schools, community facilities) – but also removes important sources of social leadership. Second, those 'social leaders' who do remain, whom Anderson calls the 'old heads' of the neighbourhood, are both fewer in number and weaker in moral authority. Their loss of status works in different ways. The status of older men as role models for boys is undermined by the decline of local employment, the increasing appeal of illegal economic activity, and the diminishing influence of social institutions such as churches, schools and clubs. The status of older women as family and community caretakers is weakened, meanwhile, as they become outnumbered by the ranks of unsupervised children left with the run of the street. Once given tacit and collective permission to supervise neighbourhood children – and in this sense an 'important source of social control and organization for the community' (Anderson 1990: 73) – these 'old heads' increasingly lack the numbers and the social mandate to watch out for and intervene in the activities of other people's children. Like Wilson, Anderson is concerned with the linkages between economic decline, class mobility and the social disorganization of urban areas. It is not simply the case that middle-class flight degenerates low-income areas, but rather that it forms part of a complex in which social institutions and collective norms are also reduced.

Wilson and Anderson each are quite clear about the racialized nature of the accounts that they develop in US urban settings. They are also, however, stories of class. Middle-class mobility has been an important feature of urban change at least since the Chicago School sociologists tracked the movement of economic and cultural capital through the modern city early in the twentieth century. But it is not necessarily the *physical movement* of middle-class urbanites – out to the suburbs mid-way through the twentieth century, back into the gentrifying inner cities by the beginning of the next – that is decisive for the marking of urban divisions and differences. Rather, patterns of class consumption within the city can draw quite stark lines of difference inside otherwise 'shared' urban spaces. Both Wilson and Anderson note the weakening of social institutions such as schools, community and recreational facilities following the movement out of middle-class residents, making it more difficult for remaining residents to sustain local networks and social organizations. It doesn't require the departure of the middle classes to produce this effect, however. In the 1920s Robert Park wrote of the way that the middle classes (or 'competent people', as he put it) are, 'either physically or in imagination, abroad most of the time. They live in the city – in their offices and in their clubs. They go home to sleep. Most of our residential suburbs tend to assume, as far as the professional classes are concerned, the character of dormitories' (Park

1967c: 113–14). More recently Anthony Giddens (2000: 116) has spoken of this kind of withdrawal as an effective 'social exclusion at the top'. Where middle-class residents opt out of forms of collective consumption in urban neighbourhoods – choosing private schools over local state schools, private health and support over local services, private leisure over municipal clubs and facilities – the collective and public infrastructure of urban areas tends to decrease: schools 'fail', services cut back or close, amenities degrade or disappear.

We can use categories of class and cultural capital to think about such processes, but the old bones of urban ecology have been given a shake in recent approaches to social capital. In urban contexts, 'social capital' offers a new language for talking about older themes of social organization or disorganization. The metaphor at work, however, is no longer taken from biology but from economics. While concepts of social capital gained increasing currency within social and political debates from the 1990s, the term has an older history in urban studies. In *The Death and Life of Great American Cities* Jane Jacobs (1964: 138) stressed the importance of social networks as 'a city's irreplaceable social capital. Whenever the capital is lost, from whatever cause, the income from it disappears, never to return until and unless new capital is slowly and chancily accumulated.' Jacobs was thinking about the loose networks of everyday urban life – the frequent, informal and mundane encounters with neighbours and shopkeepers that happen as part of a local routine. Such interaction can be quite fleeting or perfunctory and still help to promote a 'feeling for the public identity of people, a web of public respect and trust, and a resource in time of personal and neighbourhood need'. This sounds heavily value-laden, but Jacobs was not so interested in any sentimental attachment to one's grocer as in the idea of neighbourhood as a shared social space, in relations based on public identity rather than personal intimacy. Her version of trust had less to do with subjective qualities than with shared claims to public space. It is this type of low-level trust that makes everyday social action and interaction possible – that allows us to get on the subway every day or to walk down the street after dark. Trust in this sense is both generalized and highly situational; one draws on resources of trust routinely and often unconsciously, but always in the context of specific settings and social encounters.

'Social capital' has proved a highly mobile metaphor since Jacobs borrowed it, but it still has particular resonance in urban contexts. Its sense, however, has shifted somewhat. Jacobs was primarily concerned with the role of urban planning and design in promoting social interaction, stability and order in city spaces. In a strong sense, 'neighbourhood effects' including crime and conflict, mistrust and unsafety, could be traced to alienating urban environments which precluded informal contact, routine encounters and 'public identity' between urban residents. More recent accounts of social capital, in contrast, have centred on the role of social (rather than architectural or planning) factors in underpinning urban order. In this sense we can see a family resemblance with older urban ecologies. As in these earlier approaches, questions concerning the causal basis for neighbourhood effects remain vexed. In considering patterns of economic inequality in US cities, for instance, Fukuyama proposes a 'causal linkage between inability to cohere socially and poverty' (1995: 303). This kind of explanation – about cultures of poverty – is not at all new, even if it might carry the relatively novel label of 'social capital'. Such a culturalist argument, it is worth noting, is offered in this case as an explanation for the economic disadvantage of some African-American populations. In a watered-down version, Robert Putnam (2000: 312) cites research findings in Chicago that show 'young black men who live in neighborhoods with lots of white-collar professionals are more than three times as likely to graduate from high school than are comparable young men who lived in neighborhoods with less educated residents'.

In looking at these accounts, it is worth recalling Logan and Molotch's (1987: 132) argument that black neighbourhoods in US cities often involve 'a network of interpersonal support, and a density of internal organization that can be higher than in white areas . . . But rich interpersonal relationships within the neighbourhood may be relatively inconsequential for community defense if there are no effective extralocal ties.' This is an important rejoinder to the large body of work which tends to associate poor urban populations – especially non-white populations – with problems of 'social disorganization'. It is not only what happens inside a neighbourhood that counts, but the access its members have to connections 'outside'. We have seen a similar argument in Jane Jacobs's (1964: 126) assertion that 'economic and social self-containment' is bad for city neighbourhoods, cutting them off from wider urban flows, and minimizing the diversity of both residents and uses. Logan and Molotch also anticipate Robert Putnam's (2000) distinction between 'bonding' social capital that knits groups together, and 'bridging' social capital that creates links between and across groups. Local social networks, however rich in other respects, do not necessarily open up access to other resources or opportunities. Social capital does not simply translate into economic capital: personal networks do not of themselves create jobs; not all families can act as lenders of first or last resort. Moreover, we can describe the way that certain social networks help secure wider economic benefits as the work of 'social capital', but we also can see it as the effects of nepotism, discrimination or simply class (see Blokland and Savage 2001). Exploiting social capital can be a means of accessing opportunities but also of closing them off – in the manner that social networks, including trade unions, have worked to keep black workers out of certain jobs, or neighbourhood associations have reinforced lines of racial segregation (see Davis 1990; Forrest and Kearns 2001; Portes and Landolt 1996). It is important to note the sanitizing effects of the language of social capital, where this works as a proxy for talking about issues of racism, exclusion and inequality.

Theories of social capital, like urban ecology, have a concern with the compensating or corrosive effects of subcultures. In the older approaches the formation of subcultures at odds with a mainstream, particularly by young people, was a key symptom of social disorganization. Similar arguments have been made in the context of neighbourhoods with weak social capital – poorly integrated into wider social networks, untrusting, anonymous. 'It is in such settings', Putnam (2000: 312) suggests, 'that youths are most prone to create their own social capital in the form of gangs or neighborhood "crews".' The linking of delinquency or gang formation to disorganized areas has a long history in social analysis (see Lane and Meeker 2000; Park 1967b; Shaw and McKay 1942; Thrasher 1963). Such subcultural social forms give shape to the 'defended neighbourhood' – a local social group sealed in by clear bound-aries, the markings of gang turf, security or even just by reputation (see Suttles 1968). The defended neighbourhood, however, is not simply the preserve of the disaffected or excluded. Such markings or defences of terri-tory, Suttles suggests, matter as much to middle-class neighbourhoods as to gang turfs. Their logic is reproduced in secure or gated developments which not only set apart the rich but also enclose middle- and lower-income resi-dents in what Blakeley and Snyder (1997) call 'enclaves of fear' in contempo-rary cities (see also Caldeira 1996, 2000, on the 'city of walls'; Low 2001, 2003; Marcuse and van Kempen 2002). Susan Christopherson (1994: 410) refers to the 'emergence of "gated" housing developments as the fastest growing mode of community living'. The American city, she claims, has always been deeply privatized, and its complex of zoning laws, restrictions and covenants has been geared to the segregation of different classes, racial and ethnic groups. Even so, 'the fortress character of urban development and the inten-sive administration of urban space' (1994: 410) are distinctive and recent features of the urban scene. These defended neighbourhoods give physical form to the stark divisions which are scored across urban spaces. The discus-sion in the next chapter takes up these issues of privatization and regulation in conflicts over the use of urban public space.

Conclusion

As diverse social spaces and divided economic spaces, cities raise issues of difference and division in acute and often highly visible ways. Cities repro-duce patterns of economic and racial inequality in what David Harvey (1973) refers to as the systematic 'urbanisation of injustice'. The material organiza-tion of exclusion and inequality, what is more, exposes the limits of thinking about the city as an imagined space: how 'mutable', after all, can a housing estate or an arterial road be? These material divisions, however, feed into the way that urban spaces are perceived and practised – they are part of what Davis (1990) has called the 'archisemiotics of class war' and racial division in the late modern city.

If the modern city can be seen as 'a machine for *producing* differences amongst people' (Pile 1999: 10), this can be understood in terms both of social and cultural diversity and of division. Indeed, the two processes work together. The early work of the Chicago School showed how cultural identities were protected and promoted by spatial segregation. And as Simmel had it, it is impossible to 'connect without separating', in social as in spatial relations. The making of borders is a 'shaping of things', creating sites of encounter and zones of inclusion at the same time as it draws lines of social division and exclusion.

3 The Politics of Space: Social Movements and Public Space

> Any struggle to reconstitute power relations is a struggle to reorganize their spatial bases.
>
> D. Harvey, *The Condition of Postmodernity*

Politics, like other social relations, unfolds in space. To think about politics and power is nearly always to invoke a set of spatial relations: from the surface of the body to the distribution of property, the spatial order of the senate chamber or the 'theatre' of war. These are real spaces which are also diagrams of social power. Moreover, they point to the fact that different spaces are not merely locations in which politics takes place, but frequently constitute objects of struggle in their own right. The aim of this chapter is to consider some of the ways in which power works in the city, using this doubled sense of a politics both *in* and *over* space. Urban spaces, that is, provide sites for political action and are themselves politicized in contests over access, control and representation. Power and political organization are critical and complex themes within urban sociology, geography and political economy (see Dahl 1961; Dunleavy 1980; Judge et al. 1995; Katznelson 1981; Keating 1993; Logan and Molotch 1987; Mollenkopf 1983; Smith and Feagin 1987). The discussion in this chapter, however, has a quite specific focus. It is concerned less with an official or privileged order of power in the city – the geography of political regimes or economic elites – than with more oppositional, informal or everyday spatial politics (see also Amin and Thrift 2002; Watson 1999). Landscapes of power in the city in this sense go beyond the dominant architecture of state and capital to mark out more temporary, embattled or mundane sites of conflict and control.

The discussion sets out two key frames for thinking about such a politics of urban space. First, I consider urban social movements as agents of a distinctly spatial politics in the city, both in targeting urban space as the *point* of struggle and in using urban space as a *resource* for political mobilization. The second, and more extended, frame for discussion is the politics of public space in the city. The everyday spaces of the street, the subway or the square are sites for a micro-politics of urban life in which individuals exercise their spatial rights while negotiating the spatial claims of others. This is a politics of space as much lived in the body as it is written in law. The ways in which bodies are policed in public space, moreover, show up the partial character of different people's rights to the city. My argument suggests that conflicts at different scales over the meaning and use of public space in the city trace a line from the 'ordinary' experience of urban individuals to wider conceptions of social inclusion and urban order.

Politics and resistance: urban social movements

Power can be a difficult phenomenon to observe but it gives itself away in space. One of the most visible ways of exercising power, after all, is to occupy or to control space; architecture, meanwhile, makes power legible in material forms. In each of these senses cities are pre-eminent sites of official power. Modes of political, legal, constitutional, economic, police and military authority are materialized in space and concretized in institutions. Political power can be mapped around the spaces it occupies – as captured, very simply, in the notion of 'corridors of power'. While such a spatiality hardly exhausts the reach of the state or grasps its complexity, the architecture of authority gives physical form to official sites and concentrations of power, whether we think of this instrumentally in terms of social elites or structurally in terms of the sheer weight of institutions. The geography of political and economic privilege, however, gives us only a partial map of the organization of power in urban space. It is one version of Zukin's (1993) argument that urban architecture is readable as a 'landscape of power', a built environment of dominance and subordination that is also legible in the spatial assertions of a corporate skyline, the decaying hulks of redundant urban industries, or in the blank spaces of deteriorated zones that capital has rejected.

The architecture of authority offers a compelling but incomplete profile of power relations in urban space. For one thing, the citadels of official power – the government building, the central bank, the presidential palace, the ministry of defence, the security or intelligence headquarters – also can become targets of protest and opposition. David Harvey (1989: 237) has written that one of 'the principal tasks of the capitalist state is to locate power in those spaces which the bourgeoisie controls, and disempower those spaces which oppositional movements have the greatest potentiality to command'. One effect of this spatial strategy, however, is that sites of power are at the same time constituted as points of resistance. Such a logic is visible in the militarized lock-down around government buildings, the fortification of banks and brand outlets that has become standard preparation for meetings of the IMF, the G8 or the World Trade Organization. The geography of protest and demonstration is the spatial expression of an extended sphere of politics. Spaces of protest, even if temporary and unstable, give shape to a conception of power as something that is contested at diverse sites between different social actors. The politics of resistance – using tactics of demonstration, picket, direct action and occupation – frequently makes its point in space (see Pile and Keith 1997).

Urban spaces provide a stage for wider political conflicts, or points of symbolic contest where buildings or monuments *stand for* more anonymous structures of power. But they may also constitute political objects in themselves. As Henri Lefebvre (1991: 386) puts it, the city constitutes not only the 'setting' but the 'stakes' of political contestation. Power is made visible in the city through struggles both in and over space. One critical framework for analysing this politicization of space is that of urban social movements. Theories of new social movements, which gained increasing currency within social and political analysis from the early 1980s, have sought new ways of conceiving the agents, the objectives and the techniques of politics outside both established political institutions and conventional forms of opposition. Such accounts centred on the shift, particularly within advanced capitalist economies, away from a politics of class and economic distribution to a politics of identity, non-material interests and styles of life (Giddens 1991: 214; see also Larana et al. 1994; Melucci 1989, 1996; Nash 2000; Touraine 1981). Class identities and inequalities did not always trump forms of identity and lines of inequality based on gender, race, culture or sexuality; nor did questions of economic justice take precedence over the politics of nuclear proliferation, environmental degradation, civil liberties or human rights. Within urban theory such arguments took a specific form, focusing on the emergence of specifically *urban* social movements. The concept of urban social movements referred to a politics of protest and of activism concerned with the character, freedoms and control of urban space.

Manuel Castells's work has been important for the wider analysis of social movements, and was central in thinking about the particular character of urban social movements (see Castells 1977, 1983; see also Lowe 1986). In his work in the 1970s and 1980s the broad elements of new social movement theory were applied to specific features of urban politics. The forms of political agency to be found in squatters' groups or community development movements, for instance, were typical of a new politics that involved struggles going beyond the sphere of work and production, and formed outside political parties or trade unions. While urban social movements often were concerned with a politics of equality and distributive justice, this centred less on relations of production than on questions of consumption, especially issues of *collective* consumption in the city (Castells 1977; see also Harvey 1973). The politics of collective consumption focused on the provision of and access to public goods – addressing such issues as environmental quality and access to public space, policing, transport and public services, social and affordable housing. These represented struggles over the spaces and the politics of everyday urban life, the equity of different people's rights to the city. Such a politics is distinguished both in terms of content – questions of collective consumption in the city – and in terms of form – its membership, modes of organization and practice.

Urban social movements politicized the city as a context for distinctive problems of social and economic justice. Cities might capture and concentrate wider struggles over exploitation and inequality, but they also posed specific questions of justice on the ownership and distribution of public space and collective goods. In organizational terms, however, urban social movements shared key features of new social movements more generally. These included an emphasis on autonomy and self-management, and a suspicion of representation or mediation by official leaders, delegates or spokespeople. A focus on direct action and participation went with a will to work outside the formal structures of political power, even if the new politics frequently targeted the central and local state as sites of lobbying and protest. Finally, Castells suggests that while the politics of urban social movements was directed to specific issues and localities, it also tended to raise wider questions of cultural identity and lifestyle, especially as these were linked to the uses of space or to forms of spatial practice. As well as sharing these characteristics with a broader social movement politics (the same elements might be seen in environmental or anti-nuclear movements, for example), urban struggles had certain basic features which distinguished them as a group. While urban social movements ran from counter-cultural squatters in Western Europe to middle-class neighbourhood associations in the United States to shanty town defence groups in Third World cities, these diverse mobilizations centred on some common themes. First, such movements understood themselves as distinctly urban, addressed to the special conditions and problems of the city. Second, these movements were orientated around place; they were at the core 'place-based and territorially-defined', even if they might make links with other struggles across space. Third, they mobilized around three key issues in the urban context: those of collective consumption, cultural identity, and political self-management (see Castells 1983: 328). In bringing together these three goals, such movements were set against an urban system dominated by private capital, by an advancing technology of 'informationalism' which undermined the meaning of local contexts, and by an increasingly remote statist politics.

Castells developed his work in the 1970s in the wake of the radical politics of the late 1960s, and at this stage he viewed urban social movements as potential agents of broader social transformation through alliances with worker and other left movements (see Castells 1977). Castells's early work in this sense saw the growth of new social movements as consistent with a Marxian analysis of social crisis and change; in other contexts, an interest in new social movements formed part of a critique of Marxist politics, especially in terms of the primacy given to capitalist economic relations and to class struggle (see Touraine 1981). Castells was later to refine his work considerably, and to place greater importance on struggles that were not primarily rooted in material inequalities or in class relations. In *The City and the Grassroots* (1983) Castells analysed, for example, the politics of gay liberation in San Francisco, as well as the struggles of squatters in Latin American cities, and the Citizen Movement in Madrid in the 1970s. The effect was to extend the concept of urban social movements beyond issues of economic inequality and exclusion, and to open up certain cultural and 'symbolic' dimensions of urban politics. As his work developed, Castells reinterpreted urban movements as foregrounding conflicts over urban identities and meanings, as well as over urban resources (see Castells 1983, 1989, 2004). One could argue of course that the contest of meanings is always implicit in struggles over access to, and distribution of, urban resources. However, we can see here a shift to a more serious engagement with the politics of urban meaning, in ways which do not treat this as always secondary to, or merely reflective of, the more primary conflict over who gets what in the city. People, to put it simply, want different things from a city, and competing visions of the 'good' city can be a basis for political action. Castells's work is valuable, in this context, in that it does not reduce on either side to the prior claims of economic conflict, or to the vagaries of a politics of image. Who and what a city is *for* is a matter of diverse social, economic and cultural claims. These competing claims open onto conflicts over space and power, cut lines of division and difference in the city, and are fought out in disputes over meaning and representation.

These arguments about the politics of urban social movements remain highly relevant to struggles over urban space (see Mayer 1999; although see also Pickvance 1995). Questions relating to how the city gets carved up, and the functions for which its spaces are used, are always tied to questions of who exactly gets to use it. Social movements politicize urban spaces in terms of ownership, access, uses and meanings. Where squatters or urban travellers occupy empty buildings or land, for instance, the claims of private property in the city are at least momentarily subordinated to claims to housing as a social right. Of course, property rights have a legal force which social rights mostly do not, but squatting challenges the order of private property as the 'natural' order of the city. It is, to use Michel de Certeau's usage (1984: 37), a tactical move 'within the enemy's field of vision'. This is the tactic as 'an art of the weak' or the excluded – the homeless, the jobless or the dropout – in the order of the strong. A similar effect is visible in movements such as Reclaim the Streets or Critical Mass, which contest the privatization and regulation of public spaces, the concretization of the urban environment, or the ubiquity of the motor car. These political forms challenge the order of a city given over to capital and to a logic of development. While this works through a quite particular politics of location – targeted at this landfill, that road project, those developers – it is also a politics that has been mobilized in different and distant cities in terms of common movements, campaigns, language, images and tactics (see Mayer 2000). Movements such as these politicize urban space as an object of contestation between private and public property, development and environmental quality, the interests of the motorist against those of the rest. They also politicize spaces in the city through tactics of occupation, protest, sabotage and play (see Cohen 1993; McKay 1998). Urban space is both the object of political agency and its medium.

This picks up on the double sense of an urban 'politics of space'. Social movements target the uses and meanings of urban space as the point of contest, and also transform these uses and meanings through practice. Such modes of spatial practice dispute established uses and rights of ownership, and make embodied claims to the freedoms of the city. The politer kind of demonstration, of course, operates within very clear rules, occupying public streets and squares at times and in ways allowed by the municipal authorities and usually agreed with the police. Acts of spatial opposition can take place through staged encounters, explicit manoeuvres and sometimes through pitched battles, but also via little incursions in official territory, small acts of resistance. We might think about this spatial politics as the production, even if temporarily, of what Lefebvre called 'counter-spaces' in the city. These are sites that question the dominant organization of space and which refuse a predatory logic of capital; they are places valorized in terms of use value rather than exchange value. For Lefebvre (1991: 381–2) this is quite a simple point:

> What runs counter to a society founded on exchange is a primacy of *use*. What counters quantity is quality. We know what counter-projects consist or what counter-space consists in – because practice demonstrates it. When a community fights the construction of urban motorways or housing developments, when it demands 'amenities' or empty spaces for play and encounter, we can see how a counter-space can insert itself into spatial reality.

Counter-spaces are the work both of political imagination and of practice. They are implied in the criticism of normal spatial arrangements, and realized when existing spaces are remade in contrary ways. They run from the everyday to the experimental. Lefebvre offers the case of Les Halles as an example of the inventive 'diversion' of a space from one use to another. Having outlasted its function as the central market in Paris, for a time between 1969 and 1971 the site 'was transformed into a gathering-place and a scene of permanent festival – in short, into a centre of play rather than of work – for the youth of Paris' (1991: 167). Les Halles, of course, was later reappropriated as a space of commerce and alienated leisure in one of the uglier projects of urban renewal in Paris. Counter-spaces in the city can be enduring or very provisional, entrenched or highly vulnerable, mundane or risky. But they open up cracks in the totalizing logic of the capitalist city, liberated zones in the fields of regulation and order.

New social movements reject the party as the primary model of political agency on the assumption that individuals may engage with a range of politics and enlist in various alliances at different points. There is not necessarily any high (or straight) road to politics. The politics of urban preservation often has brought together motley coalitions of conservatives and radicals, self-interested residents and itinerant greens, in shared opposition to particular developments (see Lefebvre 1991: 380–1). Airport noise, road-building projects or the spectre of a new McDonald's franchise can spur very contrary actors to make common cause. Recent urban social movements, too, take in aspects of anti-capitalist, anarchist and environmental politics without reducing to any of these fronts. Quite different interests may be mobilized around specific issues or spaces, which makes it hard for political parties (with their urge to control manifestoes and membership) to co-opt them (see Lefebvre 1991: 381). Such creative or unlikely alliances are especially possible in the complex social space of the city. As well as social movements which politicize urban spaces as the point of contest, cities are important contexts for the development of social movements more broadly. In providing a site for alternative forms of political organization and action, cities offer a number of spatial and social resources. First and most obviously, the city provides public space in itself – streets, squares, parks, bridges – and therefore provides an informal spatial infrastructure for political action and association. Second, cities offer information and mobilization networks, from dense transport networks and a concentration of press and broadcast media, to the informal communications technology of bill-sticking and graffiti. Third, cities bring together the social networks that support pressure groups, campaigning organizations and community movements. While such groups have developed capacities to exchange information and mobilize across space, cities still provide crucial sites for a politics of assembly, collectivity, spontaneity, and for spatial expressions of solidarity. Fourth, cities are conducive to the formation of communities of interest – whether based on identities, ideologies or 'lifestyles' – which provide the critical mass to locate politics in space.

Wider social and political movements, while they might not always focus on urban or spatial politics, can include these as part of a broad agenda or draw on the spatial and political resources cities have to offer. In a stronger sense, as in the arguments of Lefebvre or Harvey, all politics implies an effort to remake space. As Lefebvre (1991: 386) has it, 'How could one aim for power without reaching for the places where power resides?' Movements of anti-global or anti-capitalist resistance, for instance, have been made possible in part by a new information infrastructure that stretches across space, but still have been actualized in urban protests in Seattle, in Washington, in Prague, Genoa and so on. These actions – like the IMF riots of the late 1970s and 1980s in cities such as São Paulo and Kingston (see Walton 1987) – put in place a local politics of global resistance. This politics of space has a highly symbolic form, instantiating globalization in the form of its political vanguard and bureaucratic functionaries (as well as its preferred blend of coffee or signature burger). But urban protests also represent situated moments in a much larger politics of space. These spatial practices have sought to connect privileged and very visible sites of political and economic authority, usually in the North, with less visible spaces of exploitation dispersed across innumerable sweatshops, factory floors, plantations or forests, mostly in the South. The sites of urban protest in this way are politicized in terms of a much larger spatial system of global relations and inequities (see Smith 2001).

By the late 1980s, Castells's work was concerned less with the politics of place than with the growing economics of placelessness: with 'the historical emergence of the space of flows, superseding the meaning of the space of places' (1989: 348). Such an effect was the result of a mode of 'informational-ism' which disconnected production, consumption and exchange from distinct cultures of place. Anti-global movements, among other things, resist this emptying out of meaning from place. As David Harvey (1989: 238) writes:

> Movements of opposition to the disruptions of home, community, territory and nation by the restless flow of capital are legion. But then so too are move-ments against the tight constraints of a purely monetary expression of value and the systematized organization of space and time . . . And from time to time these individual resistances can coalesce into social movements with the aim of liberating space.

Such acts of opposition rely, of course, on making links across space, but also on localizing this politics in particular sites at particular times. The 'space of flows' – if it offers an analysis of changing socio-economic conditions – is also an alibi for the movements of power, which nevertheless continues to stick quite reliably in certain locations and with specific agents. A politics of protest rejects the fiction (or the ideology) of boundless flow, and tries to target power in place. One measure of its success in localizing these struggles might be the way in which urban police forces, otherwise the keepers of local order, at times appear in these encounters as the enforcement wing of global capital. Furthermore, the exclusion zones that are thrown around the sites of trade negotiations, presidential visits and finance talks – and the forms of policing to which anti-capitalist or anti-imperialist protests have been subject – clearly mark the limits to public space and to rights of protest in the city. It is the question of public space to which the discussion now turns.

The uses of public space

Forms of urban protest – whether taking the city as the object of contest, or using it as a resource for mobilization – have a critical relation to public space. The distinction between public and private has been a key device used by social theorists to analyse the organization of modern societies, and is a scheme which maps very clearly onto spatial divisions in the city (see Lofland 1998). It is a primary instance of the way that categories of thought can be seen to extend across and become 'real' in space. The conceptual and spatial senses of a public sphere are given to run together, but it is not always clear how – if at all – public spaces relate to notions of a public sphere (Amin and Thrift 2002: 136). It may be helpful to start by thinking about public space in a quite schematic fashion. For this purpose we can sketch three ideal-types of public space, which in turn capture three different senses of being with others in public. These three types are: (1) the square – representing collective belonging; (2) the café – representing social exchange; and (3) the street – representing informal encounter. In the first sense, as a site of collective belonging, public space refers to those places provided or protected by the state, affording equal and in principle free access to all users as citizens. Such public spaces range from the monumental or symbolic – the square or piazza – to the local and everyday – public parks and green spaces, for example. This most literal version of public space is also its deepest ideal, premised on a notion of the public as a political community and a claim to certain spaces as a simple expression of citizenship. In this way, common spatial rights are an everyday aspect of social and political belonging.

The second type of public space refers to sites of sociality, exchange and encounter with others. These may be privately owned and regulated, but still involve a sense of being out in public. 'The fact remains,' Lefebvre (1991: 57) noted – and in spite of the best efforts of capital – 'communal or shared spaces, the possession or consumption of which cannot be entirely privatized, continue to exist. Cafés, squares and monuments are cases in point.' Here, the 'publicity' of a place is not a question of who owns it, exactly, but of the sense of public life it engenders. Jürgen Habermas (1974) famously wrote of the salons, theatres and coffee-houses of eighteenth-century London as formative spaces for a bourgeois public sphere in which opinions could be traded and connections made outside the formal exchanges of economic life, the prescribed codes of political debate or the strictures of status hierarchies. This 'architecture of sociability' was the spatial counterpart to new mediated forms of social exchange, represented by the spread of newspapers, the growth of popular literary forms, and the expansion of postal services. Habermas takes these historical spaces as precedents for a more abstract concept of the modern public sphere, understood as a field of communication and debate in which versions of public opinion are formed and contested (see also Habermas 1989). Contemporary perspectives tend to focus on this discursive sense of the public sphere, particularly the role of communications media in public exchange, rather than on its forms of spatialization. Even so, ideas of place continue to hang around the concept of the public sphere. Some of those eighteenth-century coffee-houses still exist in London after all – and if they didn't, the notion that the liberal chattering classes broker opinion over café latte has been a standby of the conservative right in recent years.

The easy dismissal of liberal opinion in fact points to a primary criticism of the public sphere as both an ideal and an actuality: one which is mirrored almost exactly by its critics on the left. The idea of the public sphere, in these accounts, remains irredeemably *bourgeois* both in the structure and sensibilities of debate (codes of legitimacy and politeness which determine what is sayable in the public field), and in respect of who gets to takes part in the public conversation. In practice, it can be argued, participation in a modern public sphere has not extended much beyond the privileged class of men who met on equal terms in Habermas's coffee-house (see Robbins 1993). This is an important criticism of the public sphere ideal, but the 'architecture of sociability' has a wider relevance to the texture of social life. Certain spaces of social interaction (whether bars, pubs, clubs, community centres or churches) are basic to everyday modes of being together in public (see Fleischacker 1998) – and affluent white men don't get in everywhere. Moreover, the overt and the tacit exclusions that operate around the informal spaces of public life are fractures in the corpus of a liberal public which open up the possibility of 'counter-publics' and other spaces. Different senses of a public might be traced around the neglected or 'hidden public spaces' that make room for those whose opinions are marginal or antagonistic to a main-stream, or whose spatial freedoms are limited by law, hostility or harassment (Gilroy 2003: 387; see also Fraser 1991; Negt and Kluge 1993; Warner 2002). Gilroy is thinking of the spaces in which black music cultures were repro-duced in British cities in the later part of the twentieth century, and the importance of those sounds from these spaces for particular claims of iden-tity and belonging. One might also think of the private apartments or houses used for dissident meetings; the shared or squatted spaces of grassroots and community movements; the improvised sites where young people get together; the importance of women-only spaces in feminist politics; the formation of queer publics around sites of sociality, seclusion or activism. Dominant conceptions of the public sphere may be abstract or exclusive but the possibilities of public space – the intricate architecture of social life – offer more local and critical ways of thinking about places of social connection and exchange. Even if the public sphere is now largely imagined in terms of mediated connections (via print and electronic media, and especially via the internet), being together in place remains an important aspect of how people engage with various 'publics'.

Public space, third, can refer to more mundane spaces of communal use: places that we share as a matter of fact, rather than as a gesture of belonging or as a ground for social exchange. The street – as the basic unit of public life in the city – is the best and most obvious example of a shared public space in which individuals are brought to interact, however minimally, with others. This is to think about public space less as an architecture of sociability than as a 'landscape of marginal encounters' (Gornick 1996: 2). In these pedes-trian spaces we are obliged to accommodate others whose claims to be there are, at least in principle, equal to our own. On the streets and sidewalks of the city, on benches and at meeting places, on public transport and in the bus queue, social difference is resolved in terms of identical rights to ordinary and crucial public spaces. That at least is the theory: the ways, in fact, in which different individuals' simple rights to the street are constrained make visible certain logics of regulation and exclusion in contemporary cities.

I return to this issue in the later part of the chapter; first, we might look at the rules of social engagement in this minimal public space.

The micro-politics of public space

The street, as the simplest form of public space in the city, is more complex than it looks. These everyday public spaces are subject to different uses and meanings: they are means and media of getting about, meeting places or places to hang around in, forums of visibility and display, sites of protest. Carrying off these different uses of space is an art or skill that is carried in the body. Jane Jacobs (1964) spoke about the 'ballet of the streets', that dance without a choreographer through which people negotiate each other's presence in proximate space. Erving Goffman wrote in a similar manner of the unspoken codes that govern people's conduct in public places, the tacit rules which give order to informal behaviour in public and which imply a momentary and minimal relation. 'City streets,' he proposes, 'provide a setting where mutual trust is routinely displayed among strangers' (Goffman 1973: 17; see also Goffman 1963). This is a benign version of Lefebvre's (1991: 57) blunter observation that 'In the street, each individual is supposed not to attack those he meets.' Each person has some sense of how these encounters (or non-encounters) should be managed, and assumes the same informal knowledge on the part of others. When someone invades your space in public (heads lolling on strange shoulders on the bus, a stranger making contact with bare flesh or with a fixed stare), the discomfort is not only physical but social. *Everyone knows*, after all, but without knowing how they know, the basic protocol of the street and the subway. Defying this code is to make a tiny, stinging cut in the social contract.

A critical perspective on these forms of public behaviour is found in Elijah Anderson's ethnographic studies in the city of Philadelphia (Anderson 1990, 1999). Anderson's work is shaped by a more explicit conception of urban tension – especially in relation to issues of race and class – and a more fraught model of urban space than is found in the work of Jacobs or of Goffman. The edge is given by a shift from thinking generally about strangers in public space, to thinking about specific kinds of strangers in specific places (see also Lee 2002). *Streetwise* (1990) is based on fieldwork in two adjacent neighbourhoods which Anderson calls Northton and the Village (see also the discussion in chapter 2). Both are formerly white working-class areas which had become sites of transition; each had seen a substantial growth in the local black population in the middle decades of the twentieth century, and deindustrialization after 1960. More recently, the two areas had been subject to different patterns of middle-class mobility. In the case of Northton, black middle-class residents had moved away in the years prior to Anderson's study. The Village, meanwhile, had been subject since the 1950s to successive waves of inmigration by sections of the white middle class, particularly those associated with liberal, bohemian or alternative cultural identities. As Northton became more black and increasingly impoverished, the Village became increasingly affluent and more white. These adjacent neighbourhoods, then, told two different stories of class in the city – one of movement away and growing deprivation, one of incoming and gentrification – inflected in crucial ways by race. Neighbourhood relations appear in this setting as a complex mix of spatial proximity, deepening economic division and fragile social encounter.

The two neighbourhoods, as noted in chapter 2, had undergone the kinds of 'disorganization' detailed in the early urban sociology of the Chicago School – population shifts, economic restructuring, social fragmentation. From Anderson's ethnographic account we get a sense of how these processes play out in local spaces. For one thing, the 'disorganization' of social space can make the street much harder to read. To Anderson, encounters across and within the local boundaries of neighbourhood are not simply questions of abstract strangers behaving properly in public space. Rather, these border skirmishes involve quite definite relations and tensions between familiar strangers who are marked and read in terms of difference. To illustrate how this works, Anderson draws a distinction between two modes of behaviour in public: street etiquette and street wisdom. Street etiquette, first, refers to the knowledge and deployment of minimal codes on the street (in the manner described by Goffman), accommodating the presence of others and – if not exactly expressing relations of trust – at least communicating a lack of positive *mistrust*. This system involves a formal code of behaviour that might be applied in various spatial contexts. The details that Anderson provides are familiar: conventions of 'passing behavior' (how you cross someone's path or overtake them on the sidewalk); 'eye work' (meeting someone's gaze for a moment to indicate your awareness of their presence, then averting your eyes); 'civil inattention' (appearing to ignore offensive, embarrassing or distressing scenes on the street); scowling and other kinds of pre-emptive face work; dealing with money (how much to carry, how to use it safely in public), and so on (see Anderson 1990: 213–21). All of this can be hard work to keep up, but it creates a 'protective shell' against contact with strangers in public. The effect, Anderson argues (1990: 230), is to give individuals a kind of 'tunnel vision with regard to all strangers except those who appear superficially most like themselves in skin color and dress'. Street etiquette, that is, works to ward off all-comers without discriminating in any very informed way between them. The basic line of discrimination, rather, is racialized: for whites, especially, who tend to manage encounters with any black stranger through these bare strategies of blanking and evasion.

Street wisdom, in contrast, refers to a more subtle, more savvy, more resourceful alertness to events and individuals in the street, based on a kind of informal 'field research' which allows individuals to negotiate the streets with a greater degree of confidence. Being streetwise is an agile and knowing strategy for dealing with diverse situations and different kinds of stranger in the street. It is a practical form of spatial knowledge which translates into social practice: simply, you don't play everyone in the same way. This sort of nous is based on familiarity with a place – the streetwise are 'veterans' of public space (1990: 232) – and the development of a social sense that can read the minor signs in the street, the way someone dresses or walks, the meaning of a look or a 'vibe'. Street wisdom and street etiquette, Anderson writes (1990: 231), 'are comparable to a scalpel and a hatchet. One is capable of cutting extremely fine lines . . . the other can only make broader, more brutal strokes.' The 'streetdumb' can never really be at ease in public space, handling it via a series of avoidance tactics. The streetwise, though, take on rather than warding off the street. This involves not only a sense of how to read 'incomplete strangers' (1990: 212), but also a certain presentation of the self in public, an acting-out of personality in the space of the street. The trick here is one of communicating that you are unconcerned by the presence of the other, that you are no victim, but nor are you dangerous. Such a form of self-presentation to strangers can be less about investing trust in them than in communicating confidence in yourself. It might include a preparedness to talk back (or talk first) to strangers or half-strangers, a readiness to make eye contact, a posture of ease in the body. The more fraught, contested or threatening the urban scene, the more crucial street wisdom becomes as a spatial strategy. Writing later, in *Code of the Street*, about an inner city area in Philadelphia scarred by crime and thin on trust, Anderson observes that 'it is important, as people here say, to "know what time it is" – not by the clock, but by reading people, places and situations' (1999: 23).

The street, in this account, is not an abstract space of social encounter, but a thicket of social codes and potentially risky contacts. Mutual suspicion can be in much greater supply than mutual trust. Behaviour in public, then, is not merely about accommodating faceless others (who, in this sense, look a bit like you), but it is being attuned to what kinds of others you might come across. In Anderson's account, the ballet of the streets is highly nuanced in race and class terms, even as individuals might try to efface such distinctions. For the liberal whites of the Village, for instance, there is the embodied labour of carrying off a certain ease about 'being middle class in an environment that must be shared with the working class and the poor' (Anderson 1990: 216). And street wisdom is a basic spatial strategy for a black man in the everyday politics of street and neighbourhood that routinely reads 'male gender and black skin' as dangerous (1990: 230; see also Chiricos et al. 1997; Keith 2000; Lane and Meeker 2000; St. John and Heald-Moore 1995, 1996; Parker 2001). This is especially acute in encounters or near-encounters with the police, where a long history of bad experiences (their own or those of others) means that a young black man can rarely feel secure. It also underpins the 'hatchet' code of the street which can only distinguish between unknown others on the crudest basis and which works to deflect any encounter, however minor, that might go outside the range of the familiar. Anderson's work traces a micro-politics of public space as this is negotiated by incomplete strangers, one shaped by the signifiers of class (a man in a tie or carrying a newspaper is not a threat) or else by a reflex mode of race thinking premised, as so often, on not having to think. In localizing the rules of the street, giving shape and skin to the actors that encounter each other there, Anderson traces the lines of social distance that can typify being 'together' in shared public space.

Privatization, exclusion, and the order of public space

Anderson's analysis suggests that the street works differently depending on who is standing in it. The way difference operates in public space questions the idea that rights to shared space are a basic expression of political and social membership. This is a simple and a crucial idea. The civil rights movement and the women's movement, for instance, both understood that equal claims to mundane public space – on the bus, in the diner, on the street – were the everyday correlate of larger claims to equality. And it follows that the official, the private, the informal and the covert means by which rights to public space are policed, restricted or denied continue to point up the practical limits of equality (see Mitchell 2003). Unequal rights to public space are just one of the ways in which – in the city, as elsewhere – some people remain more equal than others.

The primary ideal of public space, I have noted, is based on equality of access. The real life of public spaces, though, suggests that these are not constituted purely in terms of access but also are organized through forms of control and exclusion. One site of especially intense regulation in contemporary cities is the always unsteady boundary between public and private spaces. The division of public from private space is complicated by the various ways in which urban environments become 'privatized', not only in terms of the private development or redevelopment of property, but also in the use of public spaces or services for private profit, or the role of private interest in urban government. Where public transport is privately owned, or planning decisions are geared to private gain, or access to public space depends on consuming while you're there, the line that distinguishes public from private becomes hazy. Managing the boundary is a complex matter of demarcating spaces, ordering behaviour and sorting out bodies. There are different degrees of formality at work along this front, governed by explicit and more tacit logics of inclusion and prohibition. Public policing, private security, social aversion, hostility or harassment, codes of consumption and conduct interact in various ways to determine both the rules of access to public space and the exclusion zones of the private.

To some critics, the erosion of both the extent and the worth of urban public space marks a general devaluing of public life, and a failure of inclusive notions of who the 'public' might be. The privatization of the city is in this sense both economic and cultural, altering not only the ownership of urban space but also the dimensions of urban experience. In *The Fall of Public Man*, Richard Sennett (1974) takes the city as a stage both for the play of public life and for a contemporary turn to the private. The modern tension which Simmel traced between the claims of individuality and those of collectivity has been, in Sennett's account, resolved decisively in favour of the individual. Like Simmel, Sennett draws out the connections between the mental life of the urban subject, their modes of social interaction, and the spatial order of the city. He sketches the lines of a late modern retreat into privacy – in its various forms of social insularity, self-regarding psychologies and narcissistic consumerism – which can also be read on the surfaces of the city. At the level of subjectivity the cult of privacy has 'raised claustrophobia into an ethical principle' as the work of the self and the drama of intimacy assume the centre of moral life (1974: 295). Privacy also becomes a spatial principle: if strangers are of little interest and less concern to me, why would I want or need to share space with them? This subjective turn is therefore reflected on a larger scale in the creeping privatization of urban space. The meaning and the contours of public space are redrawn, Sennett contends, as more and more of the contemporary city is given over to private consumption and private concerns. Sennett's text is taken from the experience of New York, but his arguments are hardly limited to that context. Rather, they speak to a much more common urban trade-off between private development and public use, one which has only intensified in the period since he wrote of *The Fall of Public Man*. In numerous advanced or developing capitalist cities what passes as public space increasingly is an addendum to private development – the atrium, piazza or *porte cochère* of international corporate style which stand as vacant temples to an urban cult of privacy. Offered as empty civic gestures by developers (a small price to pay for planning permission, a sop for getting around height or street-front restrictions, or simply a matter of standardized postmodern vogue), these bits of 'dead public space' too often are perceived as blank, forbidding or alienating by potential public users (1974: 12; see also Sorkin 1992).

The distortion or disappearance of public space can be seen as an index of the weakening of public life and also a causal factor in its decay. Public spaces are downgraded by the same processes that reduce any coherent notion of a public sphere in itself. Rights to communal space are an obvious, routine and basic expression of public belonging. Where public spaces are rendered inaccessible or unaccommodating or expensive, or simply are killed off by privatization, this compounds the dwindling of a public sense that makes such developments expedient in the first place. Such a process is reinforced by the fact that claims to public space are often a matter of potentiality (anyone could in principle use the harbour-side park), while the claims of private space are meant to be directly calculable (three hundred seats in the harbour-side restaurant or the rental yields of harbour-side apartments). As consumption becomes the 'primary urban function' (Christopherson 1994: 410), it follows that spaces of private consumption are paramount in the design of the contemporary city. Logan and Molotch (1987) argue that the conflict between use and exchange values is crucial to the shaping of cities, and it is particularly visible in transfers from public to private space. It can be hard, simply, to argue for the use value of a public space – a city garden, say, or a sports field – over its potential exchange value on the property market. If different types of public space stand for different ways of being together in public (collectivity, social exchange, informal encounter), the privatization of public spaces valorizes relationships based on private interest. In an unhappy spiral, the shrinking of public space is both a symptom of the reduced status of publicity as a social value and a key agent in its erosion.

Mike Davis (1990: 226) suggests that one need only think of the repugnance that now attaches to the figure of the 'street person' to get some sense of how far public space has been downgraded in contemporary urban life. The street and those associated with it are seen as suspect, smacking of the marginal, the criminal or the dysfunctional. They are out of place in the social and spatial order. In this representation of the street person, moreover, problems of homelessness are posed as a question of the visible presence of some homeless people on the street; a wider social condition is reduced to what are seen as intolerable public spectacles, such as begging, drinking or rough sleeping. One response is to further restrict or disfigure public spaces, by locking people out or moving them on, or in the design of 'sadistic street environments' whose narrow seats or corrugated shopfronts prevent people from lying down or even sitting comfortably in common spaces (1990: 232; see also Lippard 2000; Mitchell 1997). Such tactics of exclusion form part of what Davis terms the 'social relations of the built environment', the way that urban spaces inscribe and reproduce social and economic divisions. The political economy of the city is not confined, after all, to questions of who owns what, but with how this spatial economy is regulated in terms of access, exclusion and control. Writing about Los Angeles in the latter part of the twentieth century, Davis offers a radical analysis of the markings of power in space. The privatizing logic that has colonized this city, he argues, means that really accessible public spaces have been steadily degraded and destroyed, while 'pseudo-public spaces – sumptuary malls, office centers, cultural acropolises and so on – are full of invisible signs warning off the underclass "Other"' (Davis 1990: 226). Such spaces signify in a language of design and discrimination that serves as well as any door policy. These rules of access may work via tacit codes of social distinction, but 'pariah groups – whether poor Latino families, young black men, or elderly homeless white females – read the meaning immediately' (ibid.). The semiotics of exclusion (which even if invisible to many architectural critics, he argues, are often 'about as subtle as a swaggering white cop') act as a first line of defence against those whose presence is seen as disruptive, undesirable or simply unprofitable.

Signs of social distinction may delimit access to privatized or pseudo-public space, but lines of urban partition are also backed by explicit shows of force. The semiotics of exclusion are not always enough to ensure people leave quietly or stay outside. For Davis, Los Angeles is not only a deeply divided city but one whose spatial and social divisions have been virtually 'militarized'. The metaphor of militarization describes the increasing use of security and surveillance (including more and more privatized security and surveillance) to protect pockets of wealth against the incursions of the poor (see also Fiske 1998). To Davis, an effective kind of 'urban apartheid' has come to separate spaces and social groups in a city which is 'brutally divided between "fortified cells" of affluent society and "places of terror" where the police battle the criminalized poor' (Davis 1990: 224; see also Massey and Denton 1993). Private security, in this account, is used to fortify and defend the property of the rich, while public security in the form of increasingly aggressive policing is used to maintain order among the poor. Davis's work offers a critical engagement with the history and the present of Los Angeles, but also the outline of a more general urban future whose implications go beyond that particular city. In writing of the 'apartheid' tactics of urban security in Los Angeles, or the 'Ulsterization' of ethnic difference in its highly segregated urban areas, Davis takes the brutal partitions that have disfigured cities in South Africa and Northern Ireland as templates for the future of other cities striated by race or culture and riven by inequality. The modes of violence, militarization and segregation which have marked the limit cases of divided cities, he suggests, now function as normalized strategies of urban order.

Davis makes a powerful case around the security tactics which work to divide and to police the contemporary city. His harrowing analysis of Los Angeles suggests that the future of the city is already with us – or at least with some of us, caught up in the logics of fortification or crackdown. But Davis's concern with the social relations of the built environment, with the semiotics of exclusion and the control of public space, can also be traced in less violent methods of maintaining urban order. Aggressive tactics of control point to a breakdown in spatial consent, in the normal order which governs relations in urban space. These moments of crisis question the wider terms of the 'spatial consensus' that ordinarily regulates the use of communal spaces in the city. In Lefebvre's account, such a spatial consensus operates via codes of access which define proper spatial conduct and acceptable kinds of use. It 'valorizes certain relationships between people in particular places (shops, cafés, cinemas, etc.)' and carries with it a set of conventions about how people should behave in these sites:

> such and such a place is supposed to be trouble-free, a quiet area where
> people go to have a good time . . . there is to be no fighting over who should
> occupy a particular spot; spaces are to be left free, and wherever possible

allowance is to be made for 'proxemics' – for the maintenance of respectful distances. (Lefebvre 1991: 56)

Such spatial protocols are basic to the urban social contract, and are as much a part of the civilizing process as are 'prohibitions against acts considered vulgar or offensive to children, women, old people or the public in general' (1991: 57). At the level of everyday practice, then, the problem of urban order is that of inculcating and maintaining consensus, securing the consent of those who might resist, and excluding those who refuse to consent. Lefebvre may see this spatial consensus as essentially conservative, but it is hard to argue with anyone's wish to have a good (or a quiet) time, avoid trouble, and be treated with spatial respect. The more critical question, as Susan Christopherson (1994: 413) puts it, is 'what rules and interventions they are willing to accept in order to ensure that security'.

The rules for upholding spatial order in the city range from the tacit codes of bodily demeanour to the strong arm of the law. At a primary level, urban spaces are governed by the work of the eye, by strategies of visibility and surveillance. Visual order and public order are closely linked in the regulation of space. Jacobs (1964: 45) wrote of the value of the informal policing that put 'eyes upon the street', the regular presence of different people in common space which served to monitor and to manage behaviour in public. In her account, the safety of the street was secured by the informal action of people out and about in a familiar space, watching what went on, keeping the peace. Ordinary social actors in this way enforced the spatial consensus by ensuring that what happened in public space was *seen*. The widespread deployment of CCTV has realized this visual logic in a cautionary fashion, used as it is not only to watch over property but also to keep a blurry eye on people in public spaces (see Crang 2000; Fyfe and Bannister 1996). While Jacobs meant for her watchful residents and shopkeepers to have a deterrent effect, though, the camera can act only as an onlooker to events. As a passive spectator, it mimics the common stance of actors in public space. At times the appearance of spatial order is maintained precisely by *not* seeing, by rendering people and incidents invisible – overlooking people in distress, discounting odd or aggressive behaviour, ignoring someone who asks you for money or time. This is the 'civil inattention' that Anderson (1990) described, the blanking of others' presence or actions in order to preserve the veneer of spatial order and personal security. If visibility is an important element in the regulation and order of the city, selective vision and non-contact are common defensive strategies for individuals in everyday urban space.

Where spatial consensus breaks down, policing becomes a formal matter. The policing of public space involves some very fraught boundary problems. These sit on the lines between offensive behaviour and criminal behaviour, private and public property, policing and security, individual freedoms and public standards. Such dilemmas are particularly sharp in spatial strategies of policing, including forms of community or neighbourhood policing, 'zero tolerance' and 'quality of life' programmes, surveillance and the use of stop-and-search tactics in public spaces (see Body-Gendrot 2000; Burskik and Grasmick 1993; Chambliss 1994; Cunneen 1999; Davis 1990; Evans 1995; Greene 1999; Herbert 1997; McArdle and Erzen 2001; McLaughlin and Muncie 1999; Skogan 1990; Smith 2001; Walklate and Evans 1999; Wilson and Kelling 1982). These modes of policing public space define problems of order in particular ways, as well as the proper means of securing it. Zero tolerance, the strategy for urban policing minted in New York in the 1990s, is particularly significant here – not because it was especially radical or even really distinctive but because it seemed to concentrate a broader set of arguments about the spatial order of cities. Its conception of public space therefore goes beyond the zero tolerance 'brand' to exemplify wider rationalities of urban control. At the level of the street it underlined the assumptions that lie behind tactics of stop and search in different cities, and the visibility of police patrols and surveillance in urban areas. A key concern within this policing framework was with everyday 'quality of life' in the city, and with managing forms of behaviour which degraded the ambience and safety of urban environments. In such an approach to the regulation of city space, nothing should go unnoticed or unpoliced; anti-social or simply annoying behaviour being taken not only as a quality of life issue but also as a lead into disorderly or criminal conduct. The range of behaviours subject to zero tolerance could extend from the irritating to the illicit: riding bikes on sidewalks, loitering, littering, graffiti, turnstile jumping, vandalism, sleeping rough, begging, illegal street enterprise, petty street crime, and so on – any of these might provide occasions for being stopped, searched, cautioned, fined or more. Such modes of policing assume that there is a continuity between minor infractions of the spatial consensus and criminal behaviour; that stamping out the small transgressions might help to prevent more serious offences. There may be something in this, but one effect of such an approach is to run together quite different categories of behaviour which offend against the order of public space – from the criminal to the unfortunate. What is deemed unacceptable to an official version of spatial consensus becomes susceptible to a policing solution. Public order and urban quality of life in this way provide a framework for understanding and addressing not only anti-social annoyances or minor crimes, but also symptoms of poverty or social crisis. A marked example of this kind of thinking has been the popular representation and official treatment of homeless people, beggars or panhandlers as blots on the urban landscape, an obtrusive presence in public space (see Mitchell 1997; Smith 1996a, 1996b). The 'quality of life' that is at issue here is not that of the homeless individual, but of the offended passer-by.

In her version of city living Jane Jacobs (1964) made much of the 'uses of sidewalks' – as spaces of encounter, passage, commerce and visibility.

Among the primary uses of sidewalks were those of safety, contact, of assimilating children into the urban scene. The safety and the freedoms of urban life, she held, depended on this kind of life on the street. What does it mean now, though, for a city to have a 'street life'? Such a term becomes deeply euphemistic in urban contexts where so many people make their lives on the street, or where poverty or hostility is too visible on the pavements of the city. The problem for city authorities that want *al fresco* dining but not rough sleeping is one of managing the competing uses of sidewalks. It is evident in the social cleansing of the streets for Sunday mornings, state visits and major sporting events. These represent forms of 'purification' that connect spatial order with social order, which separate out proper from improper behaviours, bodies and uses (see Sibley 1995). The order of the street, for instance, includes distinctions under which you may be able to drink alcohol on the pavement outside a restaurant but not on the pavement outside a supermarket. In this way the legal and economic regulation of space is underpinned by social distinctions that proscribe individuals as well as activities. They serve to mark out differential 'rights' to public space, in part by drawing fine legal or social differences between private and public behaviour, between property rights and spatial freedoms. Witold Rybczynski (1995: 210) contends that people are attracted to malls because these 'are perceived as public spaces where rules of personal conduct are enforced'. They offer, he goes on, 'a reasonable (in most eyes) level of public order; the right not to be subjected to outlandish conduct, not to be assaulted and intimidated by boorish adolescents, noisy drunks, and aggressive panhandlers'. Nobody wants to be assaulted, to be sure, but here 'outlandish conduct' in public space becomes an offence against others' *rights*. Open public spaces – spaces without private security or clear rules of exclusion – in this sort of social cringe are left to the 'outlandish' and the intimidating. Certain spaces become problems together with certain forms of behaviour (begging, some kinds of public drinking, loitering or just hanging around), and certain categories of person (the rough sleeper, the unsupervised juvenile). As Dick Hebdige (1988: 17) has argued, in the representation of public spaces, 'youth is only present when its presence is a problem, or is regarded as a problem'.

Urban theory is given to celebrating the freedoms of the city, the space it permits for expressive and non-conforming styles of life. As Robert Park (1967a: 41) put it, 'The small community often tolerates eccentricity. The city, on the contrary, rewards it.' There are limits, however, to how much difference contemporary cities can take and these limits tend to be marked in public space. Here, as Neil Smith (1996b: 230) has argued, 'white middle-class assumptions about civil society retrench as a narrow set of social norms against which everyone else is found dangerously wanting'. If various forms of eccentricity are all just part of the urban spectacle, visible displays of social crisis, mental distress or simply of poverty seem to take unconventionality too far. Different people's access to and use of public space are policed, both formally and informally, by rules decreeing what is tolerable behaviour in public and which kinds of individual have a legitimate claim to communal space. In London in the late 1990s a public information campaign advised people against giving money to beggars, its message promoted on billboards and posters and announced via recorded messages over public address systems in railway and underground stations. As such, it slotted in with already familiar campaigns that asked people not to litter these public spaces, or advised what to do if they saw a suspect package. Other people, that is, became one of the nuisances or threats that had to be handled in public space. There was, moreover, no individual ethical decision to be made if someone asked you for money: there was a policy to follow. This officialized means of coping with others compounds the way in which physical closeness can sit with moral estrangement in the up-close alienation of urban life (see Bauman 1990).

Conclusion

As places where social questions are posed in spatial forms, cities are critical contexts for thinking about issues of power. Urban spaces provide a stage for an official geography of authority as well as for the mobilization of alternative politics. They also are sites for enacting certain everyday rights of belonging. The discussion in this chapter has drawn on a notion of public space that is both idealized and very ordinary. It describes those sites of commonality, of exchange and encounter to which different people's access is, in principle, equal. From the square or park to the street or subway, these are places which cannot, as Lefebvre put it, be entirely privatized: whether legally – in terms of ownership or access – or subjectively – given that they are based on shared use. In fact, urban public spaces involve numerous strategies for securing order and regulating public access. This is all part of the work of maintaining spatial consensus, of ensuring that people observe the accepted codes of social conduct and spatial use. Such a spatial consensus, though, is split by urban divisions. Patterns of inequality and lines of exclusion are scored across the common spaces of cities. The degrading, disappearance and policing of public spaces do not simply question what such spaces are for, but also what the public itself might mean and who it might include. In this sense the prohibitions that operate in public space mark the limits of everyday spatial citizenship. The order and disorder of the street point to the way public space is governed through forms of pacification and exclusion, and underline the fragile nature of spatial consensus in contemporary cities. While concepts of public space are meant to capture certain principles of equality and inclusion, the real life of public spaces shows how social distinctions work through spatial exclusions.

4 Capital and Culture: Gentrifying the City

A photograph in a real estate agent's window in Sydney's inner west shows what you used to get for your money around here. The picture is less than thirty years old, but it has an almost antique quality: black and white, faded, distinctly amateur. The period aspect, though, is really given by the price, typewritten and stuck across the top. As an adjacent note exclaims, you couldn't buy a decent car for that today. It's a neat visual relic, with all the usual kitsch value of 1970s style, but there is a larger story behind this image of an ordinary house in a less than desirable area. The photograph is from another time but is also, it might be said, of another place. It sits next to colour snaps of current market offerings, several of which lead on their enviable 'inner city' location. Set alongside these domestic glamour shots of original features and courtyard gardens, the older picture captures a shift not only in what it costs but in what it *means* to live in the inner city.

Changes in the social and physical fabric of cities are reflected, and sometimes presaged, in changes at the level of representation and meaning. This chapter is concerned with the connection between material and symbolic processes in the city. In tracing such a connection, the discussion focuses on the social and symbolic restructuring of the inner city through processes of gentrification. The inner city is never simply a spatial fact: the various associations that cling to it mark how cultural values, as well as economic processes, are composed around urban forms. There are narratives of both economic and social change in the transformation of urban spaces. The remaking of contemporary inner cities operates in terms of their physical form, their economic function, their social make-up, but also in terms of how we think about living in the city. Recent shifts at the level of class and capital – the accelerated gentrification of certain parts of the late capitalist city – produce new patterns of spatial stratification and also reshape urban identities.

The inner city has always been as much a social as a spatial category. While it has been a familiar theme for urban sociologists since the Chicago School thinkers charted the modern city in the inter-war period, its haze of meaning goes back to those urban explorers – novelists, journalists, reformers, artists, agitators – who plotted their maps of the nineteenth-century city around the wretched quarters that bordered its centre. Such explorations did not merely chart spatial locales but sought to describe social worlds. This doubled meaning was central to the concept of 'the inner city' that developed within urban theory and policy in the latter half of the twentieth century. The twin senses of the inner city – as both a social and a spatial label – came together most powerfully in the 1960s and after, in a range of political strategies for the renewal of urban areas afflicted by social or environmental blight. The inner city came to be understood as a dense space of government, where impacted sites of multiple deprivation stood in close proximity to centres of growth, areas of decline smudged an expansionary urban landscape. Census data, government studies and planning surveys all plotted the contours of poverty, entrenched male unemployment, low educational attainment, substandard building and various other ills in certain inner urban areas. The identification of urban problems in this way was bound up with the construction of urban places. Within the frame of the inner city, complex social and economic conditions could be spatialized in quite specific ways.

The statistical snapshot, however – while it acts as a powerful representation – never quite captures its object. Nor have policy instruments been the only means of transforming urban spaces. Policy-makers have constantly been shadowed by other actors in the inner city, state strategies have been trailed by market processes. If the inner city has been a site, at once figurative and very real, of urban decline and acute social deprivation, it also and increasingly has become a site for development. In recent years, new patterns of residential development have redistributed urban spaces and altered the meaning of inner city living.

The discussion which follows traces these changes in terms of processes of urban gentrification – the market renewal of low-rent areas, especially inner city areas, by middle-class or higher-income populations. Forms of gentrification have been visible in cities across North America, Europe and Australasia since the 1960s: while they vary in different urban contexts, certain common themes are also evident. The early period of gentrification is associated with particular segments of the middle class, who were attracted to inner urban neighbourhoods both for their affordable housing and for their social mix (see Smith and Williams 1986). These middle-class incomers to the city tended to reject suburbanism as a way of life. They also rejected (and in any case couldn't afford) the more established urban lifestyle of the affluent middle classes who have long occupied the better parts of the central city – as Benjamin wrote of Berlin's West End in the 1930s – 'in a posture compounded of self-satisfaction and resentment that turned it into something like a ghetto held on lease' (1986f: 10). If the early gentrifiers were drawn, however, by cheap housing, their renewal of run-down property helped to inflate prices in these inner urban neighbourhoods. Once the 'gentrification frontier' had been opened up, moreover, the attractions of the inner city came to be less those of social and economic diversity than the effects of gentrification itself: renovated housing, new spaces of consumption and middle-class residents. By the 1990s processes of gentrification had become the spatial expression of a new urban middle class which had largely displaced not only working-class populations but lower-income middle-class residents from the centre of the city. In the advanced stage of gentrification, I suggest, higher-rent housing has become the norm rather than the exception in many central cities.

There are clear social and economic factors underlying these processes of urban change: the deindustrialization of inner urban areas from the 1950s onwards; changes in household forms; the growth of urban service and cultural economies; the workings of urban land and property markets. Approaches to gentrification have often split between those which emphasize the role of class, capital and changes in the material production of economic space in the city, as against those which stress culture, lifestyle and patterns of consumption. This opposition between production-side and consumption-side arguments, however, can obscure the extent to which the production of consumption goods, services and spaces has become central to economic accumulation in many contemporary cities (see Smith 1996b). Gentrifying fractions do not simply represent a consumption class based on their ownership of private housing and their patterns of activity in urban consumer markets, but they are also constituted through changing strategies of accumulation as urban economies are restructured around the production of services, culture and information (see also Castells 1989). This points to the material as well as the symbolic dimensions of consumption in the city. Within processes of gentrification, the material and the symbolic production of space come together, as shifts in cultural meaning help to secure the ground for social and spatial restructuring. Urban meanings, that is, form part of the fabric from which buildings, spaces and images of the city are made and remade.

Inner city living

The inner city has a special hold on the modern urban imagination. Those spaces that lie in the shadow of downtown promise to tell the real secrets of the city. The local knowledge of the *demi-monde*, the romance of the margins, is the stuff of pulp fiction, of *film noir* and true crime. But it has also been subject to more rational readings. Mapping the ecology of the modern city between the wars, Chicago School sociologists marked the inner areas as a 'zone in transition': between populations, between functions, between use and disuse, between growth and decline. Even so, the language they used – of the 'underworld', 'Hobohemia' and the 'bad lands' – suggests that the urban ecologists were not wholly unmoved by those other ways of writing about the city (see Burgess 1967; McKenzie 1967; Park 1967a, 1967c). It is easy to overwork the clichés, and the charts of urban areas can appear to fix things too rigidly in space. But the maps were meant to capture something of the dynamic admixture of people and place in the modern city, the changing nature of urban forms and urban life. Between the economic order of downtown and the social order of the suburbs, what is more, lay a less orderly zone that told different stories.

These were often stories of other places. Although the garbage and the dilapidation unnerved him at first, Herbert Gans wrote that being in Boston's West End in the 1950s 'left me with the impression that I was in Europe. Its high buildings set on narrow, irregularly curving streets, its Italian and Jewish restaurants and food stores, and the variety of people who crowded the streets when the weather was good – all gave the area a foreign and exotic flavour' (1982: 11). It is the mix of associations that draws out the 'flavour' of the scene, which places it, hazily, somewhere 'in Europe'. With its Jewish restaurants, after all, there are plenty of places in Europe this couldn't be, and irregularly curving streets are not unusual in Boston. Just as contemporary cities are to a great degree constituted through networks of exchange – of ideas, images, information and people – so ways of thinking about the inner city are heavily shaded by meanings borrowed from other places. Gans shows us on the street what the urban ecologies tried to map from above: the mix of people, the farrago of meanings, and the flux of urban change. He catches the West End at a particular moment, before slum clearance remakes quarters such as these on another plan, one designed with even higher buildings and much straighter streets.

To Gans, the post-war inner city told a spatial story of 'group and class' which linked social and economic identities. Boston's West End was an ethnic enclave in the city with a sizeable population of first- or second-generation immigrants, mainly from Italy. It was also a lower-class area, with more than its share of poor housing and economic hardship. Later accounts have re-worked these themes in different ways: group and class, ethnicity and economy, race and poverty, culture and capital. The conjunction of social and economic factors has been critical to how inner city areas have been identified and understood. It was these factors, above all, which would define the inner city as a problem for government. By the end of the 1960s, the term designated the worn-out zones of northern US cities, abandoned by capital and evacuated by 'white flight'. The economic migration of capital and the social migration represented by white flight left behind spaces populated by the subjects of 'deprivation': the old and the very young, the unemployed, the poorly educated and badly housed, the criminal and the victimized, and – more or less explicitly – the non-white (see the discussion in chapter 2). This conception of the inner city, whatever the specifics of the US case, travelled. Informed by the language of debates in the United States, from the late 1960s the inner city in Britain was set up as a distinct site of government, mapped along lines of socio-economic deprivation and heightened racial divisions (see Blackman 1995: 43; see also Keith and Rogers 1991).

At the various meeting-points of public policy, social science and moral panic, social and economic pathologies seemed to converge on parts of the inner city. Mapped along lines that were physical, social and – in notions of a 'culture of poverty' or 'cycle of deprivation' – even psychological, the inner city was laid out as a suitable case for treatment. It stood at the centre of a contemporary urban problem: marking the ways in which forms of privation seemed to cluster together in space, in which social inequalities were reinforced by the physical organization of cities. As a distinct body of urban policy developed in different national contexts from the 1960s onwards, a range of government initiatives were addressed to the stubborn spatial concentration of unemployment, substandard housing, poverty, educational failure, victimization, ill health and environmental blight that seemed to characterize certain urban areas, and for which the term 'inner city' came to provide a convenient shorthand (see Halpern 1995; MacGregor and Pimlott 1990). Within urban policy programmes the inner city was set up as a space that must be pacified, whose commerce must be cleaned up and spurred on, and whose social and physical environment must be regenerated.

Gentrification and the inner city

Such policy strategies have not disappeared from the field of urban government. However, more recently, a different set of meanings has become attached to living in the inner city. These meanings emerge from the market processes that have run alongside public regeneration programmes from the start, and which have become increasingly important in reshaping contemporary cities. Since the 1960s numerous cities, from London to Melbourne or Toronto, have seen a movement into their centres of new groups of middle-class residents (see Smith and Williams 1986; Ley 1996). To be sure, this represents only a partial correction of the large-scale move to the suburbs of the post-war period, and in advanced capitalist cities such as these suburbanization remains the typical middle-class residential experience. Gentrification began as a vanguard practice and remains something of a minority taste. The early period of gentrification in the 1960s and 1970s was associated with particular class fractions; it went with a self-consciously alternative taste culture or progressive urban politics, and often with a more marginal economic position (see Smith and Williams 1986). In this context, inner city housing combined the cultural virtues of urban authenticity or social diversity with the economic realities of austerity. The draw of such factors for particular sections of the middle class is not, in itself, exactly new. Although the concept of gentrification usually refers to processes of urban change dating from the 1960s and after, the gentrifiers of this period were hardly the first wave of pioneers in the inner city. Indeed in the 1920s Ernest Burgess argued that the inner zone of deterioration in Chicago, 'while essentially one of decay, of stationary or declining population, is also one of regeneration, as witness the mission, the settlement, the artists' colony, radical centers – all obsessed with the vision of a new and better world' (1967: 56). What marks the period after the 1960s, however, are the social and economic conditions which opened up parts of the city for gentrification, the social and economic impact of the inward migration, the new cultural significance of inner urban living, and the gradual displacement of existing populations by higher-income groups. The 'vision of a new and better world', too, would shift in focus somewhat. While the Chicago School sociologists had understood urban change in terms of outward migration from the centre of the city – a model borne out by post-war suburbanization – here was a case of relatively advantaged groups wanting to get back into the city.

In pointing to the social, artistic and political interests of his various agents of regeneration, Burgess signals something which will be critical to later accounts of gentrification. This is the interaction of culture and politics in the remaking of urban spaces. Sharon Zukin (1982), to take a prime example, plots the inter-relation of culture and economy in the gentrification of parts of lower Manhattan from the 1960s onwards. Patterns of economic restructuring in the 1950s and after, particularly the loss of light industry and manufacturing from downtown districts, left behind a stock of empty commercial and industrial spaces (lofts, workshops, warehouses, and so on) at low rents and often in poor condition. Such sites proved attractive to artists and other creative workers, drawn by the availability of large, cheap spaces in or close to areas such as Greenwich Village with already established bohemian credentials. The origins of loft living in lower Manhattan mark a shift in patterns of spatial use – from manufacturing or craft production to aesthetic production, from industrial spaces to residential and creative spaces. Although such changes in use violated existing zoning laws and lease arrangements, by the 1970s many artists had secured their right to live and work in disused industrial spaces. It is this legal adjustment which really serves to open up the 'gentrification frontier' for large-scale urban recycling and for the entry of wealthier residents (Smith 1986, 1991, 1992, 1996b). A process that begins with artists looking for cheaper working and living space ends with developers capitalizing on added value in downtown locations where building stock has been revived and cultural stock greatly enhanced.

In other cities – and in other parts of New York – the narratives were somewhat different (see Carpenter and Lees 1995; Smith and Williams 1986). Processes of gentrification more typically referred to the renewal of run-down housing (rather than industrial) stock in working-class areas by incomers who were attracted not only by cheaper rents but by these areas' social mix and proximity to the centre. The economics of gentrification in this sense went together with an informal urban politics which rejected the cultural homogeneity and social conformity of the suburbs (see Caulfield 1994; Ley 1994; cf. Smith 1987). As Lefebvre wrote in the 1970s of the 'influx of an élite element' into the Marais in Paris: 'this is an élite made of intellectuals and of members of the (old and new) liberal professions, which does not look down its nose at the common people. In this respect, it differs from the old-style bourgeoisie, still solidly ensconced in the city's "residential" *arrondissements* and suburbs' (1991: 385). Lefebvre's notion that this class politics might allow for the continued existence in the Marais of 'a proletarian or even sub-proletarian population' would prove, however, wide of the mark. What was common to different cities was the way that capital followed the early gentrifiers, as the pushing back of the gentrification boundary over time opened up new markets for property developers, consumer services and higher-income residents. Cultural and economic values, that is, were closely linked, and together were subject to intense valorization. If an 'artisan' or 'craft' model could be broadly associated with the early period of 'sweat equity' gentrification (whether undertaken by artists or by do-it-yourself householders), this later would give way to the mass production of gentrified spaces along increasingly standard lines. By the end of the 1990s, gentrification had translated into a tide of urban developments based less on a segmented class politics or alternative urban culture than on a more aspirational kind of lifestyle in the city. Neil Smith's original work in this field drew a distinction between gentrification, as the renewal of existing housing stock, and new-build urban development. This works, he thinks, for the early period of gentrification – from the 1960s to the early 1980s, say. Such a distinction, however, becomes harder to draw when urban development is so extensively styled in terms of gentrifying gestures and homogenizing class effects. As Smith (1996b: 39) himself puts it: 'Gentrification is no longer about a narrow and quixotic oddity in the housing market but has become the leading residential edge of a much larger endeavour; the class remake of the central urban landscape.'

Class distinction and urban design

There are definite social factors underlying these spatial shifts, so that the new urban middle class goes beyond the parameters of the original gentrifiers (see Butler 1997; Ley 1996). Most marked here is the impact of changing domestic arrangements in the later decades of the twentieth century. These changes have been especially pronounced in the social make-up of cities: the increase in urban centres of dual-income, childless, same-sex and single-person households, in their various combinations. The typical suburban model based on a male commuter, female homemaker and at least a couple of dependent children breaks down along several lines, here. Of particular significance is the presence of a certain type of woman within these new urban households – more highly educated, more fully employed, better paid, less inclined (or later inclined) to have children. Inner city living, for the new urban class, offers a number of advantages. It allows for proximity between home and workplace (also allowing, it might be noted, for an extended working-hours culture). It provides access to centres of urban consumption. It localizes particular social milieux. Gentrification in this way helps to constitute a particular class culture in the city. This class narrative, it should be noted, is also racialized – particularly in the US context. The inner city had been defined as a problem partly in terms of the effects of 'white flight'. The trend of gentrification, however, is to reverse that effect, with the movement of mainly white middle-class residents into ethnically mixed urban areas. This gives quite a different tone to accounts of urban population shifts. As Logan and Molotch (1987: 115) note, while 'a "good neighbourhood" into which poor people move (especially black poor) is usually considered a tragic example of urban decline, the invasion of affluent whites is considered – among the press, the public bureaucracies, and the entrepreneurs – grounds for celebration'. Movements in property values index movements of class and racial populations. Although the tame language of urban 'renewal' or 'regeneration' may work to 'blunt the class and also racial connotations' of these processes, the gentrification of many US inner cities nevertheless can be seen as a form of 'urban cleansing by the white middle classes' (Smith 1996b: 32; see also Smith 2001). If gentrification speaks a language of class, it is one that is cut through by issues of race, gender, sexuality, culture and consumption (see Anderson 1990; Bondi 1991, 1999; Bondi and Christie 2000; Bouthillette 1994; Butler and Robson 2001; Castells and Murphy 1982; Lauria and Knopp 1985; Quilley 1997; Rothenberg 1995; Smith 1987, 1996a, 1996b; Warde 1991).

These urban changes are also legible at the level of built form, in the varied architecture of renewal, conversion and invention. Different modes of gentrification might be plotted, that is, around the regeneration of run-down housing; the conversion of industrial buildings for residential use; and new-build apartment projects in and around city centres. In each case the tenor of inner urban living alters somewhat. Renovated housing, in the first instance, establishes degrees of distinction among common building types: the terrace or brownstone with the restored sash windows makes a different cultural claim from its neighbour with the concreted front yard. Disused industrial or commercial buildings, in the second case, offer new conceptions of domestic space, based on open internal plans behind unhomely façades. New-build developments, meanwhile – the architecture of invention – finesse an urban lifestyle out of the most unpromising bits of infill or car park. In each of these modes gentrification is a means of restoring the 'waste products' of a city – degraded housing, obsolete buildings, under-utilized land – to the circuits of visual and economic order (see de Certeau 1984: 94). The narratives that might be read in these transformations of urban space have symbolic as well as material content. They get at what Zukin (1996: 45) calls the 'synergy of capital investment and cultural meanings' through which urban spaces are produced, the link between the political and visual economies of the modern city. In the architecture of conversion, the import of the 'post-industrial' has to do not only with economics but with style. The idea of post-industrial spaces refers not just to a pattern of use but to a certain kind of *look*. Although such a style makes strong claims to the contemporary, it also deals in bits of 'architectural anti-quarianism' which seek to preserve or retrieve some version of the past (Jacobs 1964: 150). This is the logic of the postmodern pillar that doesn't hold anything up, the original but redundant feature (the crane attached to the warehouse apartment building), the aesthetics of Factoriana, the neo-Deco façade. And if the shift from industrial to residential usage of redundant buildings marks a set of changes in urban economies, the fact that some new housing developments are designed to look as if they might once have been warehouses brings us surely into the realm of simulation.

Such an architecture of invention combines post-industrial aesthetics with postmodern quotation. Years after Manhattan's original loft-livers have moved off the island, a derivative loft style ripples through any number of late capitalist cities (see Smith 2002). You don't have to be in New York, simply, to live in a 'New York loft'. Exchanges of meaning between different urban places proliferate. One exemplary advertisement in the mid-1990s promised 'Manhattan luxury in a Miami landscape . . . and it's called Alaska!' – all in the less fabulous ambience of Bermondsey in inner London. As ever, changes in the city's social and built forms are tracked at the level of representations. Back in inner western Sydney, an array of billboards on adjacent building-sites hold out an image of the lifestyle to come, where it seems martinis and evening dress will constitute an ordinary night in. Across the road, mean-while, more subtle images make a gleaming fetish of doorknobs, tap fittings and other minor fixtures – distinction, here, being in the detail.

The placards give us a picture of the projected residents of these new devel-opments: effortlessly moving between work and play, they move from laptop to running machine to cocktail bar with consummate ease. These displays of conspicuous, if clichéd, consumption recall Jane Jacobs's older comments about 'luxury housing projects that mitigate their inanity, or try to, with a vapid vulgarity' (1964: 14). Of course, real people generally do not turn up in the form proposed by advertising hoardings, just as not everyone who lives on outer suburban developments necessarily plays golf. There is (usually) something very knowing, consciously artful – sometimes ironized – about these images. Advertisers after all, like real estate agents, politicians and other urban fabulists, are in the business of boosterism. The point is that the images aim to shape perceptions in something like the manner that archi-tects and designers shape space. The making of buildings goes together with the making of meanings.

It is notable that even in different cities ways of talking up such urban developments draw on a very limited set of references. The design references are also standard. The loft, the warehouse, the penthouse, are less building types (or even bits of buildings) than gestural 'styles' which translate into numerous design contexts. There are only so many actual warehouses avail-able for conversion, but a galleried sleeping area, exposed brickwork and double-height ceiling offer a fair imitation. Given the common language of design and distinction, these are buildings that do not necessarily remind you which city you are living in. On one level this points to a new international style in urban domestic architecture – the SoHo effect, as it were, in its various translations. It also stems from a certain hotel lobby aesthetic, reflective of patterns of investment in rental property markets. The idea of downtown living may still gain points from its association with the bespoke conversions of the original loft-livers, but the economics frequently has more to do with the mass production of investment units in urban centres. Charges of uniformity have customarily been levelled at the project homes of suburbs and new towns, or the systems-building of 1960s public housing estates. (Uniformity, of course, has generally not been seen as an error in the case of Regency terraces.) Yet the glut of 'architecturally-designed', 'boutique' developments which fed urban property markets from the mid-1990s – the jargon is meant to signify a distinctive style of urban living, but appears everywhere – signals another kind of uniformity.

'There is no longer an elsewhere', Michel de Certeau (1984: 40) reflected in his writing on modern cities. This sounds like a lament, but it doesn't have to be. It can do away with what Georges Perec (1999: 77) called 'the surprise and disappointment of travelling'. These urban non-places – the standard issue spaces of mass-produced gentrification – offer metropolitans a sort of tourist experience at home, with easy access to the cultural attractions of the city and all the amenities of a resort right there in their own building (see Lash and Urry 1994: 30; Urry 1995; see also Augé 1995). Such domestic tourism, however, also gives a particular slant to the ideas of 'diversity' associated with city living.

Diversity and undiversity

In certain versions of city living, diversity is taken to be not only an urban fact but a principal urban value. City life is held to thrive where there is a density of different kinds of people and a diversity of uses (see, classically, Jacobs 1964). There is, to emphasize, a basic relationship between 'functional physical diversity' and 'diversity among users' (1964: 107): a mixture of uses implies a mixture of people. In these terms social mix is not simply a cultural but a *functional* feature of urbanism as a way of life. It entails a range of occupations, of incomes, of building type, age and tenure. These are, simply, the conditions for the 'economics of generating city diversity' (1964: 224). Such an ideal is not entirely captured in strategies of urban development in which 'mixed use' refers to live/work spaces with rapid internet access, just as a shop stocking six different types of olive oil does not in itself indicate diversity. Neil Smith (1996b: 115) refers to a kind of 'gentrification kitsch' in which 'cultural difference itself becomes mass produced'. Moreover, the functional distribution of difference is lost when diversity comes to be understood primarily as an aesthetic category. Reduced to a set of cultural referents, 'difference' might connote little more than Gans' 'exotic and foreign flavour'; a sun-dried cosmopolitanism which points to certain modes of urban consumption, rather than to the forms of social diversity the latter increasingly displaces (Jacobs 1998; Zukin 1996, 1998). 'Urbanity', as Susan Christopherson (1994: 413) puts it, 'has been redefined as a consumption experience.' While notions of the cosmopolitan may work as a code for ethnic difference in the city, sometimes they are just a simulation of it.

In its early stages gentrification had clear (if not untroubled) associations with issues of urban diversity. The attraction of inner urban neighbourhoods for certain middle-class incomers was due not only to their cheaper housing stock or proximity to city centres, but to the perceived social and cultural mix of these areas – understood in class or ethnic terms or both. Gentrifying residents themselves could be seen to enhance the diversity of these neighbourhoods, adding to the local mix of occupations, income groups and housing tenure. Smith (1996b: 171) calls this 'ecumenical gentrification', a process which supports – at least temporarily – a certain class mix. New businesses also tend to follow higher-income residents, including banks and other financial institutions, shops and consumer services. This diversifying effect is reversed, however, at the point where existing populations and uses are displaced by higher rents and rates. As gentrification advances, 'social mix' can become a simpler matter of social inequality, as social and economic distance polarizes different groups of residents within urban areas. In the 1980s and 1990s, Smith suggests, gentrification was often more consistent with polarization than with diversity. This effect stems in part from the intense valorization of gentrifying markets from the late 1980s: the shift, as it were, from gentrification by schoolteachers to gentrification by stockbrokers which created sharp disparities of wealth inside very local geographies (see, for example, Foster 1997, on the case of London's Docklands). It is also a consequence of large-scale new residential developments in inner urban areas which rule out lower-rent uses and users. The mid-1990s marked the start of accelerated growth in urban property markets across Europe, North America and Australasia – with of course various dips, reversals and cold spots. David Harvey (2003: 112) has noted that 'the most important prop to the US and British economies after the onset of general recession in all other sectors from mid-2001 onwards was the continued speculative vigour in the property and housing markets and construction'. This pattern of growth was based both on strong house price inflation for existing urban properties, and a surge in new-build housing in cities – especially on the model of medium-density apartment living. Such an increase in urban housing, if largely market-driven, has also been supported by two key political objectives. One is the desire on the part of city and regional governments to curb urban sprawl, to prevent the poorly planned spill of low-density residential developments beyond the urban fringe and especially into greenbelt areas, as well as the new infrastructure demands and costs such expansion entails (see Hayden 2003). The gentrification model, in contrast, is one of 'spatial reconcentration' within the existing limits of the city (Smith 1996b: 36). The second objective is the renewal of urban areas themselves, led in this case by escalating housing markets rather than by government programmes.

Residential strategies of inner city development have become an import-ant component of local policy and planning in urban contexts, but these can work to zone out or to price out alternative uses and other populations (see Atkinson 2000). A degree of public use or a proportion of low-income hous-ing may often be a condition for developers seeking to gain planning permis-sion for large-scale projects, but the balance remains weighted towards the most profitable uses, and in particular towards investment property markets. In cities such as London, San Francisco or Sydney, moreover, these market processes tend to exclude not only low-income populations from the central city (or even anywhere very near it), but also middle-income residents, including such key public workers as nurses and teachers, police and other emergency services. The niche demographic of the gentrifier – higher-income professionals, double-salary households, few children or none – comes to describe less a distinct market segment than the conditions for entry into urban housing markets. This can have a perversely homogenizing effect on the culture of cities. If the early gentrifiers rejected the sameness of the suburbs, the mass production of gentrified spaces now creates suburbs in the city – higher-rent enclaves of visual and social sameness. In its advanced stage, then, gentrification has become a key way in which parts of the city 'undiversify' themselves (Jacobs 1964: 256).

While a functional sense of urban diversity may have weakened, however, its aesthetic sense intensifies. The aesthetic experience of urban difference is a feature of tourism at home. It draws in part on 'cosmopolitan' modes of urban consumption, but also on the older meanings which attach to the inner city. A kind of aestheticized slumming sits, sometimes uneasily, between the old and new versions of inner urban living. A sense of that other inner city adds to the atmosphere but it is present in more real terms in the security logic of the underground car park or video-entry system. State-of-the-art security will be just as important, in luxury inner city developments, as a state-of-the-art kitchen. Imaginative locations, after all, can bring with them forms of unwanted proximity. The shape and scale of many new resi-dential developments incline to a turning away from the street, as collective amenities – the municipal baths, the public park – are brought inside or on top of the building in the form of private gyms, swimming pools and roof gardens. Social life and public space come in off the street. The seam between the interior and the street here is marked and secured, between enclosed private spaces and the dead public space outside.

Elijah Anderson (1990: 216) wrote of the self-understanding of the gentri-fier as one which 'affirms the belief that "city people" are somehow special, deserving commendation for tolerating the problems of being middle class in an environment that must be shared with the working class and the poor'. In the advanced stage of gentrification, however, the social environment does not really have to be shared. Secure and gated developments, rather, are like a new kind of plague village, locked in and surveyed in the manner of a medieval town under quarantine (see Blakeley and Snyder 1997; Christopherson 1994; Foster 1997; Low 2003).

Conclusion

Social change in the city, and material change in urban forms, invariably are expressed in contests over urban culture and meanings. As we saw in the previous chapter, following the work of Manuel Castells, the 'symbolic' dimensions of urban politics are hard to separate from disputes over the distribution of urban resources. The contest for the contemporary inner city can be read all over the place – in the ethnography of the street or the iconography of the sign, in the urban graffiti imploring some kind of fight back or in the fantasies of the real estate agent's window. These are only ever partial representations of what the inner city is and means, but that doesn't make them wholly fictional. Forms of urban representation – however calculated, inept or banal – have a role in shaping urban identities and expectations, and in making legible the way economic and social power plays in the city.

The inner city remains a space full of meaning. Indeed, it works most effectively as a container for meaning: as a spatial marker, it is often imprecise. The outer fringes of cities, based on one reading, may display typically 'inner-city' characteristics if these are to be measured via standard indices of deprivation. On another reading, aspirant suburbs might affect a revamped 'inner city' air, especially if transport times into the centre can plausibly be talked down. In one version the idea of the inner city is pathologized, in the other it is aestheticized. In the kinds of urban process I have been concerned with in this chapter, the two versions come together. The spectacle of development, that is, gains an edge from the spectre of decline.

These exchanges of meaning are part of the urban alchemy through which living in the inner city comes to connote affluence rather than privation, desirable location rather than spatial disadvantage. They bring about the inversion through which 'cosmopolitanism' or 'diversity' indicates a culture of sameness. It is always an unstable fix, and it doesn't entirely disrupt the way that older meanings are given to cling to certain places. Still, the role of language and meaning in social and economic change is bluntly apparent when what was once a flat in a council tower block becomes a high-rise apartment for private sale.

Henri Lefebvre (1991: 75) wrote that there was 'no need to subject modern towns, their outskirts and new buildings, to careful scrutiny in order to reach the conclusion that everything here resembles everything else'. This has been a common criticism of modernist architecture and planning, usually levelled at public design, social housing and the less imaginative tracts of commercial and suburban development. Another kind of uniformity, however, may be seen in new styles of inner urban living which fetishize quite standard gestures of distinction, in the design logic of developments concerned to show that they are just as different as anywhere else. It is not clear that the visual uniformity which Lefebvre remarked is always a key to social uniformity. It is clear, though, that the mass production of gentrified spaces is strongly linked to patterns of urban consumption, work and lifestyle which aestheticize rather than represent urban 'diversity'. In its advanced stage, the gentrification of contemporary cities sets out an increasingly standard template for social life in the production of urban space.

5 Embodied Spaces: Gender, Sexuality and the City

What kinds of spatial difference do different bodies make? This chapter considers how issues of gender and sexuality affect the perception and the use of urban spaces. Looking at gender and sexuality in the city directs attention to the material ways in which cities conduct us as bodies, and to how urban experience shapes us as selves. It highlights the interplay between social relations, material forms and subjective positions in the city. Spatial arrangements help to reproduce structures of gender and sexual difference, but also to articulate identities. Lines of social division and dominance are reinforced by urban environments, but individuals also find spaces in the city in which to perform or express difference. To think about gender and sexuality in the city, then, is to think about the interaction of spatial practice, social difference and symbolic associations in urban contexts.

Setting gender and sexuality in the city is partly a question of putting bodies in space. But it is also to ask how embodied subjects are located within more general social structures and relationships. Gender and sexuality, after all, are not defined by the limits of the individual body: they involve social relations that extend across and are shaped by space. The difficulty here is that of making visible categories which can be seen either as obvious and highly normalized (gender), or as private, subjective, mutable (sexuality). How can we *see* gender or sexuality in space as social factors, rather than simply as subjective details? The aim of the chapter is to address gender and sexuality in terms of social and material relations which leave an imprint on urban forms and urban processes. It suggests that the problem of gender or sexuality in the city is not merely a question of what kind of body is walking down the street, but of the social and physical environments which they inhabit and reproduce. The street, that is, can be seen as 'sexed' and 'gendered', not just the person who uses it.

The discussion that follows is necessarily selective, bringing together different critical perspectives on gender and sexuality in the city. Its larger aim is to examine the spatial impact of these subjective identities and relations on three levels: on the meaning, the use, and the shape of urban spaces. The first part of the discussion considers how the *meaning* of urban spaces is composed around gendered bodies – focusing, here, on the representation of women in the modern city. The argument goes on to examine the gendered *use* of urban space – looking to recent studies of how women's spatial practice is constrained by geographies of violence and fear. The latter part of the discussion explores the impact of sexuality on the *shape* of urban space – tracing patterns of lesbian and gay residential and community formation. Taken together, the argument is concerned with the roles of cultural meaning, spatial practice and physical forms in 'sexing' the city. The discussion is also selective, it should be noted, in concentrating on women and sexual minorities: not because I assume that gender is women's problem or sexuality a queer thing, but because paying attention to these spatial subjects can unsettle 'normal' conceptions of social space. Examining how difference is organized around less dominant actors indicates the extent to which social space is tailored to conventional gender roles and sexual codes.

The opening section considers different ways of posing the problem of gender in space. It begins with the symbolic organization of gendered spaces and looks to accounts within feminist art history and cultural history of the representation of women in nineteenth- and early twentieth-century European cities, London in particular. These accounts reflect on the links between the conceptual categories used to organize urban space – particularly the separation of public from private – and the positioning of the female body in the city. Uncertain meanings attached to the figure of the woman in public, who variously signified disorder, danger and desire. By putting themselves out of place, individual women not only unsettled the dominant order of social space, but created spaces of movement for themselves. If the pace, diversity and instability of urban life disturbed established social forms, this included gender roles and codes of gendered conduct. In this sense, the modern city could be seen as a potential site of freedom for women. The metropolis offered women new social and spatial liberties, political visibility as well as the pleasures of anonymity. Cultural and historical analyses of women in the city play on the double edge of visibility and invisibility, suggesting that women are located in the urban landscape not only as a troubling visual presence but also by the trick of disappearing into the urban scene.

This relation between being seen and going unseen is critical not only to women's freedoms in the city, but also to their safety. The discussion moves on from cultural and historical accounts of the representation of women in cities, to more recent geographical and sociological analyses of women's routine spatial practice. One of the starkest forms in which gender difference and gender inequality appear in the city is in the geography of violence against women. Even in urban contexts where cultural or legal dictates do not deny women full access to public spaces, it can be argued that many women's perceptions and use of urban space are restricted by logics of sexual dominance and fear. Against that backdrop the city appears not simply as a space of freedom for women, but also as a site of danger. The gendering of space becomes especially evident in this geography of danger, as women's fear of male violence is manifested as a fear of *space*.

Given the highly charged figure of the woman in the city, and the work of feminist theorists in putting bodies in urban space, it is not surprising that issues of gender and sexuality are often run together in spatial studies, or that both tend to be associated with feminist analyses (see Domosh 1999). Moreover, it is easy to reduce these twinned concepts of gender and sexuality to certain primary themes: sexual violence against women, prostitution (generally understood in terms of women's work and men's desire) and male homosexuality. Women, in this division of intellectual labour, are gendered, while men – as clients of prostitutes or as gay subjects – get sex. Recent approaches to sexuality and space, however, have sought to decouple (although not entirely dissociate) sexuality from gender, and to set out a broader agenda for the spatial study of sexualities (see Bell 2001; Bell and Valentine 1995a; Ingram et al. 1997; Mort and Nead 1999). Part of the task of looking at sexuality as a spatial fact is to think about how questions of identity help to shape urban spaces. This goes beyond treating sexuality merely as something that happens in space, to examine sexuality in terms of social relations and practices that themselves work to produce space (see Kitchin 2002; Knopp 1992).

The latter part of the chapter, then, is concerned with how lesbian and gay subjects make space in the city through patterns of politics, residence, consumption and sociality. Such an analysis works on a certain scale and in something of a positivist manner. That is, it sets up sexuality as a social fact which can be observed in terms of household and neighbourhood formation, collective organization and assertions of identity. It has less to do with hidden or momentary spaces of sexual expression – and little, really, to do with sex. You don't have to buy a house or open a bar, after all, in order to queer space, you just have to kiss your partner in the street. In taking up accounts which map residential communities or consumer spaces, though, my aim is to get away from a notion that sexuality simply slips into the urban environment, usually in private and preferably behind closed doors. The emphasis here is rather on how a factor such as sexuality – which might otherwise be seen as private or mutable or purely a question of subjectivity – moulds the material and social environment of the city in visible and fairly permanent ways. Moreover the focus on 'other' sexualities shows up the extent to which urban spaces are organized around the representation and social reproduction of heterosexuality. Sexuality only becomes marked in space when it is non-straight. Heterosexuality, in contrast, is like white noise in the urban environment. Thinking about spaces in terms of sexual difference, then, can press the issue of just what it is these 'other' spaces are different from. Studies of queer space have the effect not only of locating dissident sexualities, but of drawing notice to the forms of exclusion, erotic spectacle and everyday practice through which dominant versions of sexuality are reproduced in urban space.

Gendered spaces

Spaces are gendered through both social practices and symbolic associations. It can be hard, of course, to separate the two: the practical ways in which people 'do' gender in space tend to be overwritten, whether consciously or unconsciously, by a tangle of meanings and images. These extend from the most abstract representations of space to the minor detail of ordinary conduct. Some very basic conceptual devices for understanding social space turn on gendered meanings, the modern exemplar being the division between private and public. Such a distinction works not only to organize space in terms of specific functions, relationships and rules, but also affects the meanings that hang upon different bodies. The ways in which bodies take on and reproduce these social codes can make the gendering of certain spaces seem – if not exactly *natural* – then at least normal and certainly tenacious. When gendered subjects walk down the street, enter the workplace or stay at home, they are dealing not only with physical and social environments but with symbolic spaces. The relation between the symbolic organization of different spaces and the comportment of different bodies within them is a critical example of the way that 'the body', as Pierre Bourdieu put it (1990: 71–2), 'takes metaphors seriously'. Conceptual divisions in space are closely aligned with the division of gendered roles and practices, the location and conduct of gendered bodies. This demarcation of spaces and practices along gender lines can be traced from the abstract geography of public and private spheres to the local geographies of everyday life – the street, the office, the kitchen, the bedroom – and the micro-divisions of space within them (being at the head of the table, say, as opposed to having one's arms in the sink). Anthropologists have been especially assiduous in mapping social space in terms of specific gender functions, and the most compelling of these accounts suggest that such spatial divisions are neither given nor obvious, but are enacted and reproduced through embodied practices (see Bourdieu 1977; see also Moore 1994). Urban spaces make excellent contexts for thinking about how gender works, following Bourdieu, as an 'embodied idea'. This goes beyond saying that certain sites (the courtroom or the football ground or the trading floor) are 'masculine' because one finds men doing their thing there, to point to the continual exchange of meanings between the social and the spatial in putting gender into place.

An important framework for exploring these continuities between the organization of space and the positioning of gendered bodies has been developed within feminist art history and cultural history, notably in studies of women in the nineteenth-century European city (see Epstein Nord 1995; Nead 1988, 1997, 2000; Nochlin 1992, 1999; Nochlin and Bolloch 1998; Walkowitz 1992, 1998; Wolff 1990). These accounts provide both an historical context and a critical frame for thinking about the persistent if sometimes shaky distinction between public and private in the modern city. Representations of women in the arts, journalism, literature, social investigation and political debate of the period reveal how norms of gender and sexuality were conceived and situated in social space. This relation between representations of gendered space and sites of gendered practice, however, was a fraught one, and no more so than in the demarcation of public from private spaces: neat in theory, more messy in practice. Judith Walkowitz (1992) argues that a tension between public and private was threaded through questions of moral and spatial order in late Victorian London, particularly in terms of the order and disorder of the street and of those gendered bodies found in it. In Walkowitz's analysis of contemporary debate, this tension was concentrated in particular ways around the figure of the 'public woman' – strictly the prostitute, but referring by extension to the ambiguous presence of *any* woman out in public (see also Nead 2000; Radner 1999; Walkowitz 1998). The term in this way carries a double meaning: it both tags the prostitute and names a larger paradox – a 'public woman' is a woman out of place. In this slide of association, public debate and moral panics over prostitution – which played out in newspapers and popular literature, social surveys and reformist tracts, parliamentary discourse, police and public health measures – touched upon wider anxieties about the position of women in the city. The arguments and images that circulated around the figure of the prostitute distilled more general concerns over women and public space. Most obviously, women's presence in public spaces interrupted a normative separation of an urban public sphere, encoded and enacted as male, from a feminized private or domestic sphere (see Pollock 1988). This ideal spatial settlement was troubled by the evidence of a range of women who were out and about in the city – including prostitutes working on the streets, working-class women and lower middle-class women who entered the labour force in increasing numbers in the late-Victorian period, bourgeois consumers, social reformers, charitable workers and political radicals. In crossing over into public space these different women suggested that there are practical limits to just how far bodies will take metaphors seriously. Indeed, Walkowitz's work tends to assert the tenacity of the public–private distinction in the moral and spatial imagination of the times, only to show how unsteady such a distinction was in practical terms.

The figure of the prostitute disturbed the separation of public and private in a further, more specific sense. Her sexualized presence confused the distinction drawn between the public sphere as a space of civility, formality and rationality, and the private as the site of intimacy (see Nead 1999). On one level, the prostitute represented the incursion of the body and sex into public space. At the same time, however, sex became an alienated object of economic exchange – no longer intimate and not even especially private, but instead instrumental and frankly workaday. Walkowitz (1992) notes the significant numbers of women who were involved in prostitution in mid-to-late nineteenth-century London, as selling sex featured as one element in a range of insecure occupations which working women might put together in order to get by (see also Walkowitz 1980; and Gilfoyle 1992, on the case of New York). Sex, however, was not only lower-class work. The cartography of prostitution in London could be read as a kind of shorthand for the class profile of the city:s

> When commentators detailed the social geography of vice, extending from the courtesans of St John's Wood, to the elegantly attired streetwalkers who perambulated around the fashionable shopping districts, to the impoverished women – the 'kneetremblers' and 'Round-the-corner-Sallie' – committing 'acts of indecency' in the ill-lit back alleys and courts of the city's slums, they brought into relief the class structure and general social distribution of London. (Walkowitz 1992: 21)

Here, the *demi-monde* of the prostitute acts as a mirror for the social map of the city. It reflects a social order, however, that is cut through by unease about gender. The class meanings that attach to the figure of the prostitute are complex. Her encounter with the higher-class man – whether as sexual client, social voyeur or moral campaigner – was one charged along class boundaries understood not only in terms of social and economic location but also in terms of moral conduct and bodily demeanour. Moreover, if she was an object of desire, shame or disquiet, she was also an object of inquiry. Walkowitz (1992: 20–2) remarks the fascination of the prostitute for a range of Victorian journalists, urban explorers and social reformers, from Mayhew to Dickens and Gladstone, and argues that this socially and often spatially peripheral character played a critical role in the way the city was conceived in terms of danger, deprivation and desire.

In the urban interplay of danger and desire, the public woman cuts a deeply ambivalent figure. The woman in the street carried various significations of sexual commerce or sexual licence, sexual danger or prohibition. Her equivocal nature is especially pronounced in the way she is positioned as both endangered and dangerous. The prostitute, for instance, was seen as vulnerable to physical and moral harm, but also as an agent of moral and physical corruption. She appeared as 'both an object of pity and a dangerous source of contagion' (Walkowitz 1992: 22), preyed upon by men but also threatening to their moral and physical health, and subversive of female propriety and convention. It followed that the prostitute was set up as an object of moral concern and public regulation both for her own good and for the public good (see also Bartle 2000; Mort 2000a). Within late-Victorian discourses of public decency, the woman's body became something like a visible symptom of the moral health of the social body. The regulation and policing of prostitution tightened the identification of the body and the city, the arrest and moving on of prostitutes acting as a social cleansing of the streets in moral as well as sanitary terms. Determined efforts to remove the problem, however, may only have made it visible in other ways. In Walkowitz's account, police crackdowns in the late nineteenth century – which frequently netted 'respectable women' in the street as well as prostitutes – served to 'keep prostitution in the "public eye" as a confusing and protean identity that invoked the larger question of women and civil society' (1992: 24). Whether 'respectable' or not, the woman in the street remained a dubious and confronting figure. The presence of any woman in public space without the protection and the legitimation of a man could be a basis for suspicion or at least uncertainty, raising as it did the issue of what right (never mind what business) she had to be there.

This focus on the public woman in the late Victorian city is premised on the idea that marginal figures can be crucial carriers of meaning (Walkowitz 1992: 21; see also Ogborn 1992; Stallybrass and White 1986). Social anxieties about the prostitute opened onto wider concerns over the place of the woman in the city. In debates over prostitution the city appeared as a danger-ous and decadent environment, corrupting of female virtue and male decency. As Walter Benjamin's treatment of the *flâneur* in the nineteenth-century city linked forms of spatial practice with a certain kind of masculine subjectivity, so representations of the prostitute (who was also one of Benjamin's key urban types) offer insights into how women were positioned in urban space. These urban types tell of different ways of being a gendered body in the city. They are quite particular stories, but they do point to some keynotes in the gendered organization of space. It is not incidental, for instance, that the *flâneur* is positioned in terms of detachment and distrac-tion, while the prostitute is depicted in terms of encounter and infection. And while each has a critical relation to desire and to consumption, their agency in these respects is counter-opposed: the *flâneur* appears as the consuming and desiring subject, the prostitute as their troubling object.

Spatial freedoms

The woman in the city, though, is not simply an object in space. Urban life also provides sites of agency for women. If the rhythms of the modern city were subversive of established social roles and spatial order, this was parti-cularly true of conventional models of gender and domestic relations. While such subversion might be threatening to certain kinds of entrenched mascu-line authority, it offered forms of freedom to women as both individual and collective subjects. Another key character in the parade of 'public women' in the Victorian city was the feminist reformer or campaigner, and she represents a determined assault on the gendered organization of social space (see Ryan 1990; Walker 1998). Such women were disruptive of the spatial and symbolic order of things in wilfully putting themselves in the wrong place. As Henrietta Moore (1994: 83) has commented, early feminists recognized the necessity of changing spatial relations, literally of *invading* space, 'in order to resist or combat and then to change the conceptual and social relations of gender'. This bore not only on the symbolic and material reconfiguration of domestic spaces but also involved claims to a presence in public space.

Claims to representation, claims to identity, claims to public and citizenship rights, claims to a public life, have also been claims to visibility in public space (see Green 1994; Staeheli 1996). In struggles for female suffrage and movements of women's liberation, in feminist pacifism and anti-nuclear politics, in campaigns for abortion rights and against sexual violence, gender politics invariably has made its case on city streets and in public spaces. Such political movements highlight and sharpen the meaning of women's more everyday spatial claims. The occupation is a standard part of the repertoire of political resistance and struggle, and for women simply being – legitimately, independently, unaccompanied and unmolested – in the street, the public building or the workplace has something of the logic of trespass and occupation about it.

The disruptive charge of women's presence in urban space derives in part from the tricky interplay between freedom and danger. Writing in the 1920s, Robert Park remarked on the 'disturbing influence' on social and moral order represented by 'the younger generation of women who are just now entering in such large numbers into the newer occupations and the freer life which the great cities offer them' (1967b: 108). This was a disturbance which combined equal parts of anxiety and pleasure: 'Apparently', Park noted, just about 'anything that makes life interesting is dangerous to the existing order' (ibid.). The dangerous freedom of the city remains a critical theme in work on women in the modern metropolis (see Ankum 1997; McDowell 1999b; Showalter 1990; Wolff 1985). It plays a central role in Elizabeth Wilson's study of the female metropolitan in a range of modern contexts, drawing on literary and cultural representations from such cities as Chicago, London, Lusaka, Moscow, New York, Paris and São Paulo (Wilson 1991; see also Wilson 1992). Wilson's arguments hinge upon the deep contradictions at work in urban space. On one hand, she suggests, modern urbanism has been defined by rationalist principles of government, regulation, design and planning. Yet modern cities offer, on the other hand, unrivalled spaces of freedom, licence and excess. These two urban currents exist in tension with one another: the freedoms of urban life are continually but always incompletely subject to modern disciplines of urban control and order. Indeed, it may be this tension between discipline and subversion that gives the freedom of the city its particular kick. For Wilson, such an opposition might be conceived in gendered terms. The tension between order and disorder, control and freedom, can be read as a conflict between masculine and feminine principles at work in the city: 'urban life', she writes (1991: 7–8), 'is actually based on this perpetual struggle between rigid, routinised order, and pleasurable anarchy, the male-female dichotomy'. Of course – regardless of how spaces of order and disorder might be coded – women's pleasures in the modern city were hardly unmitigated. The experience and consumption of urban delights have rarely been accessible to all who might want them, and women have been particularly subject to the controls of 'rigid, routinised order'. If the modern city opened up potential sites of freedom for women, it would also create new forms of 'spatial entrapment' for women in the social geography of the suburbs (see England 1993; see also Dowling 1998).

While women's visible presence in urban space could signify forms of disruption and disorder, more covert subversions followed from going unseen. Wilson (1992) argues that one of the attractions of the modern city, for women as much as anyone, is the possibility of losing oneself in the crowd. Urban spaces offer plenty of chances for disappearing acts. It is one of the pleasurable contradictions of city life that these sites of spectacle and surveillance are also exemplary spaces of privacy and seclusion. Visibility and invisibility hold out different kinds of presence and freedom in the city. While women have sought, especially via collective politics, to make themselves and their claims visible, a different claim to urban space concerns the chance to pass unnoticed. 'Visibility' – as Foucault wrote in his reflections on the Panopticon (1977: 200) – 'is a trap', and women can be too visible in the city: as symptoms of disorder and signals of danger, maybe, but more often as objects of hostile or demeaning regard (see Gardner 1995). This has to do with what Wilson calls the 'ambiguous freedoms' of city life. We have been here before, of course. Simmel saw the downside of urban freedom in the loneliness and the isolation of the anonymous individual (see the discussion in chapter 1). There was always a trade-off to be made between anonymity and connectedness. For women, though, this trade-off can appear more sharply as one between autonomy and security. While the city may be perceived as a space of freedom, it is also experienced as a site of danger.

Violence, safety and fear

Women's ambivalent relation to the city in terms of freedom and danger goes beyond the symbolic coding of space. It boils down to critical decisions about spatial practice. In this context, the geography of gender in the city involves not only margins of freedom but maps of danger. Perceptions of safety and danger in the city affect the ways gendered subjects use space. It is common criminological knowledge that women typically are more afraid of becoming victims of crime than are men (see Ferraro 1996; Stanko 1995; Warr 1984; cf. Gilchrist et al.; on males see Goodey 1997). This pattern of fear, it can be argued, has a particular basis. Women's more general fear of crime is underlined and heightened by the specific fear of rape and sexual assault (see Ferraro 1996; Pain 1991; Stanko 1995; Warr 1985). The fear of sexual violence in this way 'shadows' women's broader sense of danger in relation to other kinds of risk (Ferraro 1996). Women are not alone, of course, in feeling unsafe – especially in the city. Older people and members of ethnic minorities tend to express similar senses of vulnerability (see Pain 2001; Parker 2001; Warr 1984), but my interest here is in the distinctly gendered nature of women's sense of risk. Women's fear is gendered in that it is based on feelings of vulnerability to men, and framed by the threat of sex-related crimes. Women's fear, moreover, is spatialized. Their perceptions of danger have a specific geography and this can determine women's routine movements in urban space. The 'geography of women's fear' gives us a map of gendered spaces which are both overlaid by symbolic associations and reproduced through spatial practices (Valentine 1989; see also Valentine 1992). It is a mental and a practical geography that influences how women perceive and use space in the city. Feminist geographers have tracked a variety of defensive spatial strategies which women adopt to stay safe and avoid danger (see Bannister and Fyfe 2001; Burgess 1998; Koskela and Pain 2000; Pain 1991, 1997, 2000, 2001; Valentine 1989, 1991, 1992). Such tactics suggest that women's cognitive maps of the city – and their everyday spatial stories – are frequently organized around calculations of safety and gendered readings of danger.

Gendered perceptions of safety and danger in the city are based on an unstable geography. This works on two levels: in terms of the different groups that occupy urban space; and in terms of the ways space changes over time. A railway station or park that might seem quite safe at midday appears unsafe at midnight. In a practical sense, it is no longer the same space. Gill Valentine (1989, 1992) has argued that women's fear of danger and defensive use of space starts from the assumption that male violence is unevenly distributed across both space and time. A primary spatial strategy, then, is to avoid particular 'dangerous' places at particular 'dangerous' times. Shopping precincts that are full of women during the day can be emptied out of women after dark. The daytime population of the city includes more women, more children and more elderly people than does the night-time population. At night, the streets are more likely to be populated by couples, by groups, and by individual men (see Worpole 1992). Valentine suggests that women perceive space as dangerous when people's behaviour (especially men's behaviour) is seen as unregulated. This can be true of open spaces – parks, towpaths, wasteland – which can be difficult to get out of or to quickly get across (see also Burgess 1998). It is equally true of 'closed spaces' which are sealed off and where behaviour is relatively concealed – subways, alleys and laneways, multistorey car parks, train carriages.

In this understanding of space, issues of human behaviour intersect with questions of urban form. Women's cognitive maps of safety and danger are both traced around specific social geographies and shaped by the physical environment of the city (Koskela and Pain 2000; Pain 1997; 2000; Valentine 1991). This is an environment which can appear distinctly 'gendered', in neglecting the spatial needs and the security of women users (see Boys 1998; Durning and Wigley 2000; Hayden 2000; Little et al. 1988; MATRIX 1984; Weisman 1992). The meaning of a space, and the kinds of behaviour associated with it, will be tied to its degree of visibility or transparency, its openness and ease of access or exit. One way of making urban spaces safer (or feel safer) is to 'design out' the potential for threatening behaviour from the built environment (Newman 1972). Better street lighting is one standard measure in this respect, as is the increased use of closed circuit television cameras in public and common spaces. The logic of CCTV is interesting in this context, in that it not only aims to make certain spaces visible; it also imitates a social geography. The camera's disembodied eye carries with it the pretence that we are not alone on the empty subway platform, that we are visible to others walking down the late-night street. Such a simulation of visibility in the absence of any social life bears comparison with Jacobs's (1964: 52) comment on the usefulness of streetlamps in deserted spaces: 'Without effective eyes to see, does a light cast light? Not for practical purposes.' The camera has an ambivalent role to play in creating defensible space, sitting uneasily on the margin between safety and surveillance, deterrence and protection, doing something and doing nothing (see Ainley 1998; Parenti 2003). Alongside these technical adjustments to the built environment, women learn to make practical adjustments to their behaviour. Defensive tactics might mean avoiding particular places at certain times, using private transport or, most simply, not going out alone or at night. Such tactics also affect the conduct of the body in space. Like most children and some dogs, women are trained in how to use the street. Negotiating space becomes a question of learning how and where to walk, who to watch out for, what to do if things turn bad (see Stanko 1996). There is something troubling in the standard advice that women should not walk 'like a victim', as if ready-made victims somehow gave themselves away – set themselves up, even – through their spatial demeanour. There is more than a twinge of the blaming the victim reflex here, one which is all too familiar in the context of crimes against women. In relation to sex and hate crimes, one might just as well say: 'Don't walk like a woman, don't walk like a black or a gay.' People are victimized in these cases because their assailants are violent or misogynist or racist or homophobic – not because they themselves are victims. Still, women put their shoulders back and their heads up, walk purposefully, hold their keys or some other makeshift weapon at the ready (see Koskela 1997). The charged nature of space for many women, and the fraught nature of the female body in space, are evident in the advice commonly offered to women if they should find themselves on a deserted street after dark: the notion that you should walk in the middle of the road and not on the pavement literally puts women out of place in ordinary public spaces. It might be good advice, but it underlines the way that having a female body can be a spatial liability, and how certain spaces in the city are experienced as a kind of conflict zone.

Women's use of urban space is constrained by perceptions of danger in spite of two well-known facts about violence. That is, violence is most likely to occur to men in public places, usually from strangers or near-strangers, and to women in private space, usually in their own homes at the hands of someone they know and often know well. In this sense it is not facts about crime but perceptions of danger that condition women's spatial strategies. These strategies, moreover, are complicated by factors of age, income and lifestyle which can determine how different women negotiate space – staying in after dark, using cars or taxis, seeking the protection of men, facing the necessity of getting to work at unsocial hours or in un-salubrious places. Women's perceptions and use of space are also tied to issues of race. A number of white women in Valentine's study in Reading in southern England perceived a predominantly black area as dangerous – based, she argues, on racist assumptions about the character of black men (see also Chiricos et al. 1997; St. John and Heald-Moore 1995, 1996). Day's (1999) study in Orange County, California, examines how black and minority women's perceptions of public space are determined by their experience of racism; while Hutchinson (2000) notes the reliance of black and minority women on the Los Angeles bus and subway system in a city where, it is otherwise popularly believed, 'nobody walks'. Although there may be common patterns in how gender relations impinge on women's spatial practice, there remain different ways of being a female body in space. Negotiating urban space may be a very different proposition for an older as compared to a younger woman, a woman with and without a child, a straight woman and a lesbian, an able-bodied woman and a woman with a disability. At a general level, though, women's fear of violence or harassment can be seen to foreclose certain of the spatial freedoms and some of the independence that city life otherwise might offer. Valentine (1989) reads these constrained patterns of use as a 'spatial expression of patriarchy', a means by which gendered power relations are reproduced in the order and practice of space (see also Peake 1993). She argues that women's fear of male violence, and the limits that govern their movements in urban space, act as a further spur to women to seek protection from a man within the heterosexual couple. In this sense, the fear of violence, which functions as a fear of *space*, joins with other social forces in making conventional models of heterosexuality a compulsory 'choice' for many women.

Sexuality and urban space

> The path out of the ghetto is neither straight nor unobstructed.
>
> L. Wirth, *The Ghetto*

These different ways of locating women in the city emphasize the extent to which urban space is organized via a heterosexual matrix. Whether women represent an unsettling agent in urban space, or see themselves as vulnerable to danger, the positioning of women in urban space is commonly understood in relation to that of men. Heterosexuality is like the prevailing conditions in the urban environment: something one takes for granted, adapts to, dresses for. From workplaces or sites of consumption to shared public spaces and the billboards on the street – gender relations are reproduced and represented in urban space in terms of a normative sexuality. Yet as Bell et al. (1994: 31) point out, 'not all space is "straight".' How, then, do 'non-straight' spaces insert themselves into urban contexts that are so extensively shaped by the images, the interests and the claims of heterosexuality? Thinking about alternative sexual identities in the city has particular relevance to the issues of visibility raised earlier. The expression, articulation or concealment of sexuality are worked out in practices of seeing and going unseen in urban spaces. Cities both provide a stage for enacting sexual identity in various ways – whether through personal identities or collective sympathies, political platforms or expressions of style – and offer forms of cover for perverse, proscribed or private sexualities. And again, visibility has a double edge. While the modern city has been the most visible site for the articulation of gay identities and the formation of queer solidarities (Chauncey 1995; Fischer 1982), visibility cuts in other ways when the expression or simply the suspicion of homosexuality in public renders people vulnerable to policing, hostility, harassment and violence (see Herek and Berrill 1992; Herek et al. 2002; Jarman and Tennant 2003; Mason and Palmer 1996; Mason and Tomsen 1997; Moran 2000; Morrison and McKay 2000; Rothblum and Bond 1996).

This question of visibility also raises critical issues for the spatial study of sexualities. In order to 'see' sexuality at work in space, it becomes necessary to define it in terms of certain social facts – locations, populations, practices – that mark out a more or less stable geography. Sexuality is, one presumes, fairly portable, so pinning it down in space is a somewhat artificial exercise. One established line of research in urban sociology and geography has treated gay men and lesbians as 'subcultures' that may be studied in terms of community formation, migration and residential patterns, and associated forms of political and cultural agency (Canavan 1988; Fischer 1982; Levine 1979; Lyod and Rowntree 1978; Wolf 1979). The origins of such an approach lie in the Chicago School's interest in cultural communities, and borrow from methods developed to study ethnic neighbourhoods in the city. Lesbians and gays – where there are enough of them to show up on the map – become a kind of proxy 'ethnic group', a distinct urban minority whose members tend to locate or to socialize in certain parts of the city on the basis of common identities and cultural affinities, and in the interests of self-protection and safety (see Bell and Valentine 1995b: 4). Homosexual spaces in the city in this sense could be read as one of the 'non-Jewish ghettos' to which Louis Wirth's work referred (1928: 282; see also Levine 1979). The 'gay ghetto', like the classic ghetto of urban sociology, offered a space of sociality, identity and at least relative safety – although without quite the same air of claustrophobia or, usually, the 'narrow, dark and filthy' streets (Wirth 1928: 243).

Mapping lesbian and gay populations, however, is not an exact science. There are, after all, few official census data to go on, and researchers often have relied on the distribution of gay venues (bars, saunas, and so on) to suggest some kind of critical mass in an area, or else have drawn on the kinds of common or inside knowledge that pass as ethnographic instinct. There is a very basic contradiction in studying hidden populations at precisely those points where they are visible, and it is commonly understood that the focus on specific commercial, cultural, residential and political sites tends to settle on gay male geographies, themselves often quite particular in terms of class, lifestyle or age (see Binnie 1995; Binnie and Skeggs 2004; Castells 1983; Forest 1995; Forrest 1994; Mort 1998; cf. Lynch 1987; Phillips et al. 2000). Lesbian geographies can be harder to map in terms of established or discrete cultural and commercial venues, counter-public spaces or recognized neighbourhoods, given that women are less likely than men to own businesses or homes, generally have less disposable income or time for cultural consumption, and can feel more vulnerable to violence or harassment in public. Studies of lesbian community formation have tended, therefore, to trace networks of women through social contacts and insider ethnography, rather than via the architecture of cultural and public life (Adler and Brenner 1992; Lapovsky Kennedy and Davis 1993; Rothenberg 1995; Valentine 1995; Wolf 1979). Hemmings (2002) shows how difficult or provisional it can be, furthermore, to chart the contours of bisexual spaces which endure over time and do not simply get recoded as lesbian, gay or straight spaces.

These problems, while they can make things difficult for researchers, are also productive in pointing to the complexity of social space and of sexualities within it (see Valentine and Skelton 2003). The translation between identities and places is never a complete one. Not everyone will appear on the map, nor will want to. Sexuality is figured in space in terms of different social and economic relations, forms of cultural or political expression, sites of shared identity and agency. There is always something that gets away from attempts to fix sexualities in space, to track the moving body or map the desiring subject. While turning sexual acts into social facts may be a reductive process, however, it is one that allows us to see sexuality as involving material relations which have a legible impact on urban space.

Sexuality, community and the urban process

Urban studies of sexuality frequently have centred on the formation of gay communities in the context of cities' broader attractions of size, diversity and anonymity. Cities in this sense provide the setting for a doubled experience: the freedoms afforded by the proliferation and toleration of differences, and the solace to be found in various urban subcultures. If such geographies of gay sexuality inherit a great deal from the urban ecologists, then San Francisco has been their alternative Chicago (see Castells 1983; D'Emilio 1983; Fischer 1982; Lyod and Rowntree 1978). In his study of the formation of gay community in San Francisco, Claude Fischer (1982) takes the impeccable Chicago School line that urban contexts allow social networks and forms of identity to proliferate, since people can choose a variety of elective bases on which to build connections with others. The density and diversity of urban populations support the formation of numerous subcultures, often located in space. In the case of San Francisco, Fischer traces how selective migration to the city on the part of gay men over an extended period served to create a 'critical mass' large enough to support distinct social networks and cultural forms (see also Castells and Murphy 1982). In the wake of this 'first wave' of settlement, new populations of gay men – often moving from more conformist or repressive provincial centres, rural areas and smaller towns – were encouraged to migrate to San Francisco, reinforcing and extending the emergent subculture. The narrative, however, is not simply the happy story through which increasing numbers of gay men chose to 'dwell among friends', to borrow Fischer's title. Rather, conflicts with and crackdowns by public and private authorities – police and other public institutions, private employers and property owners – as well as the everyday violence of heterosexism's self-appointed vigilantes, served both to make visible and to strengthen gay culture in the city, as groups of gay men came to organize in terms of a politicized identity, and increasingly as an electoral force (see also D'Emilio 1983).

This political dimension is critical to Manual Castells's analysis of the development of San Francisco's Castro as a gay neighbourhood. Castells departs from older urban studies paradigms of 'community' or 'subculture' to consider gay men as an urban social movement (Castells 1983; see also the discussion in chapter 3). The politics of liberation, equal rights and representation was inseparable, his argument suggests, from the occupation and transformation of space. Castells and Murphy (1982) see spatial organization as a key resource for political identity; the neighbourhood offers a local stronghold in which cultural networks could be developed, social institutions embedded and political claims advanced (see also Bailey 1998; Forest 1995; Knopp 1998; Myslik 1996). Such an approach emphasizes the politics of urban community and the assertive spatial claims this can involve. Such claims to space, moreover, were distinctly gendered. In staking out territory, Castells (1983: 140) argues, gay men acted 'first and foremost as men'. There was no comparable 'lesbian territory' in the city; lesbian politics were 'placeless', even if – not coincidentally – 'much more radical'. Whatever the consolations of greater radicalism, such gender difference reflected men's economic advantage in relation to women, and their enhanced power in housing and labour markets. Men, simply, could afford to make claims to urban space. Apart from these broad-brush social and economic factors, however, Castells suggests that the spatial politics of gay men in the city had something to do simply with the way men are: the will to power, for men, typically involves a will to space. 'Men', he writes, 'have sought to dominate, and one expression of this domination has been spatial' (ibid.). In linking political claims to claims over space, that is, gay men were acting out a masculine tendency to colonize space, whether in the street or the subway, in the turf wars of young male gangs or the politics of militarism.

Castells's take on masculinity has garnered a fair amount of criticism, although the supposed errors of essentialism do not exactly invalidate his point, given the continuing practical evidence of men's general spatial dominance. Other accounts have taken up the social movement framework to address lesbian as well as gay male politics (such as Knopp's 1987 work on Minneapolis) or to analyse a queer politics that takes in a broader range of sexual identities (see Davis 1995 on Boston), while more than one study since Castells has managed to locate lesbians in place (Adler and Brenner 1992; Rothenberg 1995; see also Valentine 1995, 1996, 2000). The larger import of Castells's work, however, had less to do with the residential patterns or spatial assertions of gay men as opposed to lesbians, than with the relations between cultural identities and spatial politics, and with the ability of urban social movements to mobilize resources and access power. These issues of economic and social power and their impact on urban forms have been especially evident in work on the role of gay men and lesbians in the processes of gentrification in the city (Binnie 1995; Binnie and Skeggs 2004; Bouthillette 1994; Kitchin 2002; Lauria and Knopp 1985; Quilley 1997; Rothenberg 1995; see also the discussion in chapter 4). In this context sexual minorities might be seen less as either 'communities' or 'social movements' than as class fractions – specific elements of a middle-class movement into low-income, run-down or marginal economic and social spaces. The production of San Francisco's Castro as a gay neighbour-hood, for instance, could be read as a fairly straightforward account of gentrification, given the in-migration of higher-income residents, the reno-vation of housing stock and enhancement of property values, and the development of new cultural and consumer spaces. Similar narratives appear in Greenwich Village or Chelsea in New York, the Marais in Paris or Paddington in Sydney. The social and cultural associations of gentrifica-tion – new household arrangements, socially liberal politics, cosmopolitan preferences in consumption, the cultural appeal of the urban – might be seen as especially compatible with certain kinds of gay lifestyle. Indeed, gay men can appear as something of a cultural vanguard in pushing back the gentrification frontier.

Economic and childcare constraints, in contrast, are more apt to limit the residential choices of lesbian or bisexual women, making them more likely to locate further out of the centre, or in precisely those 'ethnically mixed, older, working-class areas' that become ripe for later gentrification (Wolf 1979: 98). Rothenberg's (1995) study of Brooklyn's Park Slope as a neighbourhood with a relatively high concentration of lesbian residents suggests that female households are associated more with the counter-cultural politics and 'sweat equity' investments of the early period of gentrification in the 1960s and 1970s than with the increasingly affluent urban lifestyle signalled by gentrification in the 1980s and after. As the area becomes more gentrified, Rothenberg reports that lesbians find it increasingly difficult to move into or remain in Park Slope, especially given women's generally lower rates of home ownership. Against this backdrop, the migration of lesbian households into lower-rent neighbouring areas can be seen either as a further advance along the gentrification frontier, or as simply a process of economic displacement by wealthier incomers: 'In this respect, lesbians are much like other "named" groups that have been credited, for better or worse, with initiating the gentrification of a neighbourhood – such as artists or moderate income professionals: in a crude sense, victims of their own success' (Rothenberg 1995: 178).

Sexual geographies

In this focus on neighbourhood and community formation, gays can appear as just a kind of better-dressed residents' association. Such an account may have come some distance from the older ecologies of the margins, but whether queer populations are seen as marginal subjects in the city, sequestered in their ghettoes (see Winchester and White 1988), or as a gentrification niche market, looking at patterns of settlement and sociality still tends to reduce to disembodied points on a map. Nor is the narrative of homosexual spaces in the city simply one of increasing affluence or cultural capital – even if only on the part of some groups of gay men. It should be impossible not to notice, for instance, that the body of writing produced in the early 1980s on the emergence and entrenchment of a gay community in San Francisco appeared just prior to the assault on that community of the AIDS epidemic. This gives a new dimension to the political understanding of gay men as an urban social movement. Apart from medical maps of transmission and infection, the geography of HIV/AIDS can be read in terms of what might be called 'pathways of politics', which both work on a very local scale of organization and mobilization, and also seek to make connections across international space (see Geltmaker 1992; Brown 1995).

Sexual bodies, sexual identities and sexual spaces are knitted together in complex ways in the geography of HIV/AIDS. In this sense it points to a critical problem for spatial studies of sexuality. Looking at the residential patterns of gay and lesbian populations, or the spatial politics of queer identity and organization, has rather little to do with sex itself. The cartography of sexual identity – which might be charted around claims to political and public space, community services and social institutions, places of memory and pilgrimage, sites of commerce and consumption – does not simply coincide with the geography of sexual practice – which may be harder to see, less stable or more transitory, sometimes illicit or at least unmarked, given over to privacy and intimacy rather than to publicity or identity (Humphries 1970; Bell 1995a, 1995b; Mort 1999, 2000b). This is not to say that sex is never about identity or indeed publicity, but that they are not always co-extensive in space. Sex happens, after all, in the closet.

This uncertain relation between sexual identity and sexual agency is partly reflective of the unstable balance between what are to be considered public and private spaces. The claims to public visibility of minority sexual identities – as citizens, as communities or as social movements – have been an important response to mainstream sensibilities and hetero-normative laws that can tolerate sexual dissidence so long as it remains 'private': that is, invisible. It is an even more pronounced response to those delicate constitutions – whether anxious individuals, state agencies or religious hierarchies – which cannot tolerate it at all (see Stein 2001). The public and visible spaces in which claims to sexual equality or rights of sexual difference are declared operate on a somewhat different scale from micro-geographies of the body, desire and sexual encounter. The policing and the articulation of sexualities, however, produce a series of border skirmishes along the unsteady lines that mark out public from private spaces. This works both in the direction of legislation and repression, and in that of sexual expression and autonomy. The legal regulation or prohibition of certain kinds of consensual sexual activity – in respect of specific sexual practices, differential ages of consent, and so on – makes a public issue out of private conduct. What might otherwise be viewed as a matter of privacy and personal consent becomes a matter of public discourse and official interdiction (see Mort 2000a). In a different way, sex in public places confuses conventional distinctions between publicity and privacy, intimacy and anonymity. Sexual encounters in parks, woodlands, alleyways, docksides, public toilets, motorway lay-bys, bath-houses and clubs create private spaces in public landscapes and provide sites of intimacy between strangers – often in contexts where same-sex desire cannot be expressed in the 'privacy' of the home (see Bell 1995b: 306–8).

Conclusion

This point returns us to the spatial and symbolic division of public and private which has been so central to the understanding of modern social space, and so easily troubled by questions of gender and sexuality. The discussion in this chapter has set out three different levels on which these factors impress themselves on urban spaces: the levels of meaning, of use, and of material form. Such categories, however, are harder to separate in practice. Women's defensive use of space, for instance, is based not only on material facts (the dark street, the empty car park) but on meanings and representations (narratives of sexual danger, the associations of certain 'bad' places). Gender and sexuality become visible in the city in the symbolic coding of spaces, through modes of spatial practice and interaction, in terms of material divisions and exclusions in space, and in the 'micro-geographies' of the body.

Issues of gender in the city are not identical to those of sexuality – even if they overlap at various points – but both have something to say about the dangerous freedoms of the modern city. Urban contexts have been critical sites for remaking gender relations, as well as for the expression of sexual identities. The freedoms which have been claimed by different gendered and sexual subjects, though, have always been shadowed by certain dangers. The threat and the reality of sexual or homophobic violence mean that streets and other public spaces will look and feel differently depending on the bodies that use them. Geographies of danger map out another city from the one inhabited by those who can wear their bodies more lightly, more carelessly, in urban space. These other cities, however, are not solely defined by fear or constraint; they also are composed of bold moves and ordinary gestures which alter the everyday run of space. Looking at how gender or sexuality makes a difference to the meaning, the practice or the shape of urban spaces raises the question of what 'normal' space would look like; unsettles the taken-for-granted order of the city. The everyday man in the street, after all, might actually be a woman.

6 Spatial Stories: Subjectivity in the City

Cities may be the densest of object realities but one comes to know them as a subject. These contraptions of material form and hit-or-miss human design never look quite the same on the ground as on the page. The view will depend, partly, on where you are standing and where you have come from. This chapter is concerned with the city and subjectivity, with how individuals engage with urban spaces at the levels of perception, memory and agency. Alongside a conception of the city as defined by built forms or demographic facts, might be posed an alternative version that understands it in terms of modes of consciousness or experience. People's experience of the city is not only or always determined by larger social or economic structures, but also fashioned by their individual perceptions, mental maps and spatial practices. Different social actors, it follows, will have quite different 'spatial stories' to tell about their routes through the city (de Certeau 1984; see also Keith and Pile 1993; Pile and Thrift 1995).

The discussion that follows takes three of the central stories told within urban social theory about subjectivity in the city. Each foregrounds different themes: (1) the impact of urban life on human consciousness; (2) the city's relation to memory, dream and perception; and (3) the role of people's everyday practice in making space in the city. The first section focuses on Georg Simmel's 1903 treatment of the distinctive nature of mental life in the modern city. This discussion expands on the brief account of Simmel's ideas in the first chapter to consider more closely his arguments about how cities elicit certain responses on the part of the subject, an 'adjustment of the senses' which makes it possible for individuals to withstand the sensory excess of the urban scene. The emphasis here is on the management of subjectivity, the development of a mode of self-conduct which is also a disposition towards others in urban space. Simmel is interested in the continuities between the mental life of the urban subject, their styles of interaction with others, and the larger social order of the modern city. In this way a concern with subjectivity opens onto much broader questions regarding the modern social condition and what Simmel sees as its central problematic – the uneasy relation between individuality and collective life, played out more vividly than anywhere else in the lonely and crowded spaces of cities.

The central part of the chapter draws on aspects of the work of Walter Benjamin from the 1920s and 1930s to consider how urban meanings are formed by memory and perception. Like Simmel, Benjamin is concerned with the encounter between the individual and the sensory environment of the city. His subject, though, is defined more by their imaginative engagement with the city than by an evasive detachment from it. Benjamin's memoir of his early life in Berlin offers a remarkable treatment of the city as a site of memory. The city appears here not simply as the background to events in a life, but as an agent of memory, a store of meanings that belong as much to the place itself as they do to the individual who retraces their steps through it. In seeking to decipher those meanings that are held in place, Benjamin's writings throw up numerous metaphors for the ways a subject makes sense of the city – variously likened to the work of digging, collecting, listening, botanizing, reading. In these descriptions the city is understood as a material form that embeds or encodes meaning, and which surrenders these in the form of fragments or clues, hints or echoes, symptomatic readings or the flashes of memory.

The idea that these splintered perspectives might offer insights into the city which are not available to a more rational eye is critical to Michel de Certeau's notion of spatial stories. The final part of the discussion takes up de Certeau's argument in *The Practice of Everyday Life* to consider the spatial practice of the city's ordinary users. De Certeau was concerned with how subjects make room for themselves in urban spaces which are overdetermined by maps, plans, rules, codes and schemes. At the mundane and barely visible level of everyday practice, people trace their private maps in ways which are known only to themselves – and even then only sketchily. For de Certeau, these many routes through the city constitute an unsigned gesture of refusal in the face of the official city, with its logics of planning, of surveillance and spatial order. If rationalist fantasies have held that the modern city might be laid out and governed as a total environment, a kind of social machine, the artful manoeuvres of everyday users are always slipping between the lines, vanishing out of sight.

The contrasts that both Benjamin and de Certeau draw between rational knowledge of the city and the idiomatic ways subjects imagine and practise space parallel some of Henri Lefebvre's larger arguments on the social production of space. In particular, they resemble Lefebvre's distinction between formal 'representations of space' and the kinds of 'representational space' that subjects invest with meaning. In Lefebvre's account, representations of space involve systematizations, plans and designs which are linked to formal 'knowledge, to signs, to codes' (1991: 33). This is a scientific or architectural treatment of space typical of what de Certeau calls 'the concept city', the modernist dream of a thoroughly rational urban environment.

Representational space, meanwhile, refers to 'space as directly *lived* through its associated images and symbols, and hence the space of "inhabitants" and "users" . . . This is the dominated – and hence passively experienced – space which the imagination seeks to change and appropriate.

It overlays physical space, making symbolic use of its objects' (Lefebvre 1991: 39). For Lefebvre, such a space is tied to memory and folded through intimate sites. It 'is alive: it speaks. It has an affective kernel or centre: Ego, bed, bedroom, dwelling, house; or: square, church, graveyard. It embraces the loci of passion, of action, and of lived situations, and thus immediately implies time . . . it is essentially qualitative, fluid and dynamic' (ibid.: 42). There is a lot (maybe too much) going on in this version of space, but the notion that spaces might 'speak' – like the fluid relation of space to time – is also present in Benjamin's work. For him, spaces and things in the city speak to the subject in a language which has the quality of memory or dream. The 'dumb' language of things is a medium for sensory knowledge of the city, a form of knowledge which does not lend itself easily to representation or explanation (see Benjamin 1986a: 321). As Amin and Thrift (2002: 9) suggest, the phenomenology of the city 'cannot be known through theory or cognition alone.' Elsewhere in his work Benjamin (1977: 201) contrasts 'intoxicated spoken language' with 'signifying written language'; one is sensuous and unruly, the other captures and fixes meaning. This gap between what is given to the senses and what can be formally signified also runs through de Certeau's account of the everyday subject's use of space. If the official order of the city is *written down* as so many rules, codes, maps and plans, the individual's version is a spatial story told as if out loud in the streets of the city, leaving no trace other than a movement in the air.

Consciousness in the city: Simmel

Louis Wirth (1967: 218) described Georg Simmel's 1903 essay, 'The metropolis and mental life' as 'the most important single article on the city from the sociological standpoint'. It remains one of the most brilliant turns in urban sociology, giving a vivid account of metropolitan experience at a certain historical moment even as it resonates with far more recent versions of urban subjectivity. The pleasure of the text, over one hundred years on, is in part the tremor of recognition for anyone who has ridden a subway or enacted the drama of the crowded street. Simmel's point, though, was the way these routine moments offer insights into far larger questions of social order. For him, the central problem of modern social life – the tension between individualism and collectivity – is posed nowhere more clearly than it is in the city. To examine urban 'sociation', then, is no less than to enquire 'into the soul of the cultural body' (Simmel 1997b: 175).

Simmel's account of metropolitan life moves between the levels of individual subjectivity, social conduct and collective order. The mental life of the urban subject can be understood in terms of the same conditions that shape social relations in the city and which are typical of modern social life more generally. For Simmel, as we saw in chapter 1, sociality in the city is primarily a question of dissociation. Surrounded by all those others to whom you have no direct relation, you can only disconnect. This is a means of coping with the sheer weight of numbers; it is not possible, nor is it necessary, to engage with everyone you come across. So you sit next to somebody on the bus, or wait next to someone at the traffic lights, or ride in a crowded elevator – the examples are mainly trivial and probably endless – without speaking, without looking at them, acting as if you were quite alone. Conduct of this sort remains a mode of social action, though, in that it is oriented towards others. My way of accommodating a stranger's presence in shared space is usually to ignore them. The discussion in the opening chapter suggested that the peculiar kind of solitude one finds in the city should be seen as a social relation, a condition of being with others based on detachment. Being 'alone' on a crowded train, after all, looks and feels different from being alone in an empty room. It requires you to carry yourself in a certain way, to tailor your use of space to others' movements, to communicate using the tacit social language of indifference. Acting as if you *really* were alone (talking to yourself in the street, singing on the subway, preening at the mirror in the lift) could, in contrast, be something of a false move.

The detached way in which people conduct themselves in the city is not simply a matter of social form. On another level, it has to do with the special nature of the urban psyche, with the forms of consciousness which characterize city life. The modern city produces new kinds of social relationship and with them a particular psychology – a self fashioned by the city, reactive to the flux of urban life and its intensification of nervous stimulation. Simmel writes (1997b: 175), 'Man is', essentially 'a differentiating creature': people create meaning, make sense of things, by drawing distinctions between various sensory impressions. We work out when and where to look, which sounds to tune into, what we can ignore. This ability to filter one's perceptions, however, is stretched by the sensory excess of urban environments. In the city one encounters an explosion of the sensory in a rapidly shifting scene, a mess of random spurs to the senses that exhausts the capacity to discriminate. The basic condition of mental life in the modern city is one of overload, as the individual is subject – daily, everywhere and in the most mundane ways – to a battery of visual and mental stimulation. It becomes difficult to process everything you see or hear, hard to make sense of the city as it insists at you from all angles.

Robert Park (1967a: 40–1) later will write in a similar vein of the intense 'stimulus of city life' which 'gives it, for young and fresh nerves, a peculiar attractiveness. The lure of great cities is perhaps a consequence of stimulations which act directly upon the reflexes.' The downside of such a scene, presumably for those whose nerves are less young or fresh, is that such intensity can leave you stranded somewhere between agitation and enervation. Such a sensory onslaught has the potential to drive you quite literally to a state of distraction. More commonly it produces a negative reaction, in the form of a typical urban attitude that Simmel memorably termed 'blasé'. The blasé posture is exemplary of subjectivity in the modern city. A blank reaction to over-stimulation, this reversal or 'peculiar adjustment' of the senses (Simmel 1997b: 179) inures the urban subject to the hectic ambience of the city. It works against the basic impulse to differentiate and to make sense, it becomes a way of not seeing and not listening in the city. An acquired indifference is both the side-effect of, and the best defence against, what Susan Sontag called 'too much indulgence in the nervous, metallic pleasure of cities' (1982: 373). Such an attitude involves a flattening of impression, a deadening of the sensory. It gives us the rule about not making eye contact in public places and the fiction that people who speak to you on the street cannot be heard. Simmel's Berliners in the early twentieth century had to effect this kind of social distance by themselves. Now, the mobile technologies of the personal stereo or telephone have made technical what otherwise was simply learned. These are devices which realize the logic of urban detachment perfectly. Immersed in a private soundscape, engaged in another interactive scene, you can set certain limits to the city as a shared perceptual or social space (see Bassett 2003; Bull 2000; Thibaud 2003).

The blasé attitude is a response – in the form of a lack of response – to the sensory overkill of the urban environment and the social overload of the urban crowd. Such a subjective stance, for Simmel, also reflected a more basic feature of modern social exchange. In the modern context more and more aspects of social interaction are reduced to the terms of the market. The impassive face worn by the urban subject is consistent with an overriding money logic that does not discriminate between things other than on the basis of price. If a person is in essence a 'differentiating creature', this sense-making process is greatly simplified in the modern city, whether by the subject's blanking of their surroundings or by the primacy of price as a market signal. In either case, you don't have to draw fine distinctions. The spectacle of the city is in large part the spectacle of the marketplace; Benjamin (1986f: 40) will call it a 'theater of purchases'. And the dominance of the money economy in modern cities has particular implications for personality as both urban sociation and money exchange produce 'a matter-of-fact attitude in dealing with men and things' (Simmel 1997b: 176) – hard, but mainly fair.

Relations of indifference in the city in this way can be seen as part of a general 'dulling of the senses' which serves to abridge the terms of social contact, to mark and maintain the psychological boundaries between individuals. If this represents some kind of social loss, it is a necessary one. Simmel writes that 'the indifference to that which is spatially close is simply a protective device without which one would be mentally ground down and destroyed in the metropolis' (1997a: 154). Even so, the metropolitan attitude does not simply betray an indifference to others, but 'more often than we are aware . . . a slight aversion, a mutual strangeness and repulsion' (Simmel 1997b: 179). There are always those moments (maybe Simmel felt them, too) when you want to push someone down the escalator. The point here is not simply that any one person might be too much to take, on top of everything else, but that they are potentially an object of casual or more serious hostility. Bleak as this view may seem, Simmel sees such aversion as functional for the reproduction of urban order, and the only viable way of conducting urban lives: 'A latent antipathy and the preparatory stage of practical antagonism effect the distances and aversions without which this mode of life could not at all be led. . . . What appears in the metropolitan style of life directly as dissociation is in reality only one of its elementary forms of socialization' (Simmel 1997b: 179–80). It is mutual aversion, then (if not exactly murderous impulses), that helps hold everybody together in the city.

The rules of repulsion are part of a 'spatial economy' that sorts bodies in space, obliges them to keep a proper distance, and minimizes social exchange (see Lefebvre 1991: 56). Such a social logic produces the deep anonymity of the crowd but also can encourage a perverse desire to stand out. When nobody is listening, after all, it can be hard for a person to 'remain audible, even to himself' (Simmel 1997b: 184). The dissociation typical of modern city life, the freeing of the person from traditional social ties as from each other, has its contrary effect in a loss or diminution of individuality. Being just another face in the crowd, an object of indifference to strangers, liberates the individual from a whole range of obligations to others – not least the necessity to engage. But it also can lead to feelings of insignificance and the impulse to exaggerate one's individual qualities, to emphasize the matter of personality in the realm of the impersonal. As Vivian Gornick (1996: 1) more recently has put it, 'on the street: nobody watches, everyone performs'.

The anxiety of anonymity is one sense in which the city provides a stage for the tricky mediation of individual and collective life. In this way it opens onto a larger theme in Simmel's argument concerning the modern trade-off between freedom and impersonality. Simmel identifies a tension around the figure of the individual that can be traced through dual movements in modern social thought, and which becomes visible in the dilemmas of the urban subject. On one side lies the notion that individual liberty is the expression of a common ethical substance, an idea which finds its high point in eighteenth-century thought and specifically in the rhetoric of the French Revolution. This position makes the case for individual freedom on the basis of common rights of man; the claims of the self are inseparable from the recognition of the other. The individual, then, is understood in terms of a broader solidarity. On the other side of this tension lie arguments premised on difference. These typically nineteenth-century positions have their philosophical rationale in the individualist precepts of Romanticism; they appear somewhat differently in social and economic thought in accounts of the division of labour. These dual arguments over the nature of the modern individual mark a theoretical but also a lived tension between, on one hand, solidarity or collective life, and on the other, the coinciding claims of an aesthetic quest for individuality and a functional need for difference. Such movements in modern thought – which pitch Rousseau or Paine against Goethe and Durkheim – can also be figured, at least to Simmel, as the problem of subjectivity in the modern city. The recognition of and regard for others, as an ethics of identity, stand in tension with the separateness of the self and the social actuality of difference. In this sense a central problem of modernity is manifest in the common anxieties of the metropolitan, the banal manoeuvres of urban life. Blanking people on the subway, we might console ourselves, is all just part of the unhappy struggle between the individual and the 'supra-individual' in the modern city.

This modern tension between the collective and the individual, between solidarity and difference, is felt most clearly in the crush of the city. Here the sense of detachment between oneself and others is underlined, as 'bodily proximity and narrowness of space makes the mental distance only the more visible' (Simmel 1997b: 181). Dissociation is a subjective reflex in response to the mass of people and things in the city; it is also an index of one's autonomy. Individual freedom, in the city as in modern life more generally, depends in part on the estrangement of others. And for Simmel, it 'is obviously only the obverse of this freedom if, under certain circumstances, one nowhere feels so lonely and lost as in the metropolitan crowd' (ibid.).

Landmarks and footfalls: memory in the city

To Walter Benjamin, writing some three decades after Simmel, this state of being 'lonely and lost' in the modern city could be a source of pleasure. He wrote of Baudelaire (who was, for Benjamin, an exemplary modern figure) that the poet 'loved solitude but he wanted it in a crowd' (Benjamin 1983: 50). Elsewhere he speaks of the adventure of getting lost:

> Not to find one's way in a city may well be uninteresting and banal. It requires ignorance – nothing more. But to lose oneself in a city – as one loses oneself in a forest – that calls for quite a different schooling. Then, sign-boards and street names, passers-by, roofs, kiosks, or bars must speak to the wanderer like a cracking twig under his feet in the forest. (Benjamin 1986f: 8–9)

This brief excerpt tells us quite a lot about Benjamin's ways of conceiving the city. The city is, first, a kind of labyrinth, a spatial riddle whose inner logic is hidden from those lost within it, 'entangled in the ribbon of the streets' (1986f: 28). Like the labyrinth or the forest, the city is an enchanted space. To become lost is to give oneself over to the spell of the city, to find different ways of making sense. Benjamin looks for meaning, especially, in the trace of minor details. The mute language of things – here it is rooftops, bars, street-signs – speaks to the urban subject like the cracking of twigs underfoot. Benjamin, who was short-sighted but finely tuned to sound, was given to play with the order of the senses, such that the modern city, like the silent cinema, was a space in which one might learn to 'listen with his eyes' (the term is Abel Gance's – see Conrad 2000: 159). Urban planners would later borrow from psychology the term 'cognitive mapping' to describe how people make their peculiar ways around the city (Lynch 1960), but Benjamin has the rudiments of the theory already. Odd things in the city help you to find your place. This attentiveness to what is stray, hidden or dilapidated is a keynote of Benjamin's approach to the city. After all, as he writes, 'to live means to leave traces' (Benjamin 1986g: 155). Such a regard for details and dregs recalls the method of certain other modern figures who paid attention to small things. Benjamin's reading of the city in terms of its fragments sits alongside the Freudian reading of the symptom or slip of the tongue, the detective's reading of the clue (see Ginzburg 1990). All deduce bigger stories from the hints or trails that are left behind.

For Benjamin, the city was a complex site of perception and memory. This is especially clear in his account in 'A Berlin chronicle' of 1932, and also runs through the Arcades Project which occupied Benjamin during his last decade and remained unfinished when he died in 1940 (see Benjamin 1999). Throughout his work the meaning of urban spaces is bound up in individual and cultural memory. Though Benjamin was intensely interested in *things* – he wrote about glass buildings, arcades, apartments, and so on – he did not see urban meanings as simply contained in the physical forms of the city. Rather, these forms gave themselves to the subject at different moments; the sense of material space was filtered through experience. Nor was this merely a matter of individual perception but of an engagement with the stores of meaning gathered into place. In Benjamin's writing, places and objects have effects which cannot be fully explained by their official uses or representations, nor wholly reduced to the responses of the subject. There remained something intrinsic to the place itself. Things speak, if you have the eyes to listen. It is a commonplace to wish that walls 'could talk' – to imagine the stories they might remember and retell – but for Benjamin, in a way they do. The stones, quays and kiosks of Paris, he claims, speak in a language which has the texture of dream. It is as if the city had a memory. Buildings, spaces and objects hold onto meanings as pasts that are no longer visible press on the experience of the present. These past lives of a place represent layers of memory, what Michel de Certeau will later call 'the invisible identities of the visible' (1984: 108). Benjamin was not concerned with the obvious architectural gestures of memory, with the monuments and buildings that are meant to preserve official histories. Indeed, he decried the fact that there were so few public spaces left in Europe 'whose secret structure was not profaned and destroyed by the monument in the nineteenth century' (Benjamin 1986b: 125). Rather, the relationship of memory to space operates somewhere between the landmarks of the official city and the footfalls of the solitary subject.

Urban meaning in this way can be seen as a property of spaces, buildings and objects; one deciphers these meanings in something like the way archaeologists make sense of ruins. In 'A Berlin chronicle' – a chronicle of his earlier life which is at the same time a chronicle of the city – Benjamin writes that one 'who seeks to approach his own buried past must conduct himself like a man digging' (1986f: 26). This is good advice, too, for how to read Benjamin: digging in odd places, turning over the words to reveal glimmers of memory, the scintilla of meaning. You can gut his work for suggestive phrases. It is this kind of 'reading' that Benjamin practises in the city as a store of things, of clues, of ruins. Cities, like selves, do not give themselves up easily to either rational knowledge or transparent biography. The sense of a place, rather, is opened up in imagination, reverie, in what Benjamin calls 'waking dreams'. Such forms of knowing are mirrored in the fragmentary and sometimes poetic quality of Benjamin's writing on cities – especially in the pieces contained in *One Way Street* (1925–6). Here, hidden or occluded meanings are glimpsed via crabwise moves, sidelong glances, agile conceits and unlikely juxtapositions. These may provide only fragmentary perspectives, but ones which also can disclose unexpected lines of sight.

The intricate relation between individual and collective meanings in the city, personal and cultural memory, is woven through Benjamin's writing in 'A Berlin chronicle'. The partial map of Berlin that he draws in this piece is also an incomplete map of a life. The writer remembers the 'dreamy recalcitrance' with which his childhood self accompanied its mother on walks in the city (1986f: 4), and this dreaminess inflects his whole way of recalling both places in the city and events in his own life. The 'fan of memory' folds and unfolds as places and moments are given up to 'dreamlike representation' (1986f: 13). While Benjamin writes of the spaces of memory, therefore, there is little sense of a flow of time – the Berlin chronicle is a memoir or souvenir, but not a biography. It is clear that this is not a straight transcription of events from an earlier life but an act of imagination in the present, just as memory is not a means to access the past but the medium for its experience. One's past does not sit complete, waiting to be remembered, but is put together in the creative process of memory. This is what Benjamin calls the 'mysterious work of remembrance – which is really the capacity for endless interpolations into what has been' (1986f: 16).

In this work of memory the city is more vivid – because stiller and more enduring – than its inhabitants. You remember people in terms of the places you went with them, the spaces they filled. One's relationships are paths into the labyrinth of the city in the same way that they are clues to the riddle of a life (see 1986f: 31–2), but it is buildings more than bodies which impress themselves on memory. People are evoked in wraithlike form, momentarily and vestigially; 'human figures recede before the place itself' (1986f: 24). People are spectral, places and things are not. Benjamin's friend Fritz Heinle, poet, dead by suicide with his girlfriend at the age of nineteen, is evoked for the author via the room he once dwelt in rather than by the 'inner space' of personality marked out by his poetry (1986f: 17). Walking later in the half-remembered spaces of his youth, Benjamin takes each step 'with the same uneasiness that one feels when entering an attic unvisited for years. Valuable things may be lying around, but nobody remembers where' (1986f: 20). Memory, he says, resembles the rooms of a gallery that preserves shards of the past, ruined and out of place, but which contain larger stories within them. These fragments – precious or otherwise – are like snatches of music barely heard, a name or image that comes unbidden to mind. Suddenly they can illuminate memory like a snapshot.

Edward Casey has spoken in a similar manner of the way that places 'gather in' and 'hold' memories. Visiting his own hometown (in this case, Topeka, Kansas, somewhat more prosaically than Berlin), Casey (1996: 25) writes that he 'finds this place more or less securely holding memories for me. In my presence, it releases these memories, which belong as much to the place as to my brain or body.' Memory and space are articulated in slightly different ways in these accounts: to Benjamin, memory is an imaginative act which can be done, as it were, long-distance, while for Casey, memory is an embodied act which depends on its presence in place. Even so, each points to how memory works in and on space, and to the complex ways in which spaces tell time. Certain sites in the city, for instance, might be said to bear not only the scars of the past but traces of the future. Benjamin called the Lichtenstein Gate at Berlin's zoological gardens 'a prophesying place', and went on to suggest that 'just as there are plants that primitive peoples claim confer the power of clairvoyance, so there are places endowed with such power: they may be deserted promenades, or treetops, particularly in towns, seen against walls, railway level-crossings, and above all thresholds that mysteriously divide the districts of a town' (1986f: 25). It may be easy to dismiss this as a sort of occultism but there remains something awful and prophetic in Benjamin's observation, made after all by a Jew in the early 1930s, that Berlin – 'noisy, matter-of-fact Berlin' – possessed more than its share of places where it 'bears witness to the dead, shows itself full of dead' (1986f: 28; see also Ladd 1997).

Reading space

Benjamin, who died at a border, evinced a fascination with crossing-over places, such as those 'thresholds that mysteriously divide the districts of a town'. In his writings Berlin and other cities could be read in terms of the social topographies of different neighbourhoods, of boundaries real and imagined. Some of these translate lines of social power into actual lines on a map, as in those contours that mark out pockets of bourgeois affluence, like a 'ghetto held on lease', from what then appears as 'the exotic world of abject poverty' (1986f: 10, 11). Other borders are less visible, if no less real: for Benjamin, crossing the street to accost a prostitute is also to cross a social boundary of class (1986f: 11). A subject's passages through the city may be traced in the form of social and intimate geographies, as well as in the mundane narratives of subway stops and street-signs. In *One Way Street* Benjamin recalls how 'A highly embroiled quarter, a network of streets that I had avoided for years, was disentangled at a single stroke when one day a person dear to me moved there. It was as if a search-light set up at this person's window dissected the area with pencils of light' (1985a: 69). The streets arrange themselves around this person's presence, giving up their complicated secrets as though every turning now was marked. A strange geography becomes smaller and tamer as part of a personal history. Here again we come to the city as a site of individual memoirs, where spatial stories can be written in numerous ways even as they unfold across the same territory.

The idea of disentangling unfamiliar social space is especially evident in the sketches of foreign cities Benjamin wrote during the 1920s in his essays on Naples, Moscow and Marseilles. In these accounts, social and cultural meanings are embedded in spaces and things, disinterred by the engaging eye. Different metaphors are used to describe the ways one unlocks the strange city – the city appears as a maze, a stage, a book, a ruin. It is as if you can only get at what the city *is* by describing what it is *like*. In Naples, the metaphor is that of the stage: domestic architecture is presented as if a theatre, and street-life offers a variety of performance (Benjamin and Lacis 1986). In Marseilles, the notion of 'reading' that might be applied to the unravelling of buildings, spaces and objects extends to the sense of a whole city. 'In the early morning', Benjamin writes (1985a: 90–1), 'I drove through Marseilles to the station, and as I passed familiar places on my way, and then new, unfamiliar ones or others that I remembered only vaguely, the city became a book in my hands, into which I hurriedly glanced a few last times.' This idea of the city as a kind of 'text' has become very common in recent years (see Donald 1992); in Benjamin it has a freshness that speaks to the experience of being in a place, catching at glimpses through the window of a moving car. Moscow is a cunning maze: Benjamin writes of a capering city that 'turns into a labyrinth for the newcomer . . . the city is on guard against him, masks itself, flees, intrigues, lures him to wander its circles to the point of exhaustion . . . But in the end, maps and plans are victorious: in bed at night, imagination juggles with real buildings, parks, and streets' (1986b: 99). In this note Benjamin gets at the double life of cities – the way they slide between the subjective and the objective – and at the contrast between the mobile life of the streets and the static order of the map.

These imaginative ways of knowing the city are lateral, indirect. One's sense of a place is mediated by the experience of other cities: you come to know better an already familiar territory by getting or failing to know other places. Such detours to knowledge operate across space (seeing Moscow helps you see Berlin more clearly) and across time (recalling Berlin as it appeared in childhood and youth). Remnants of the old are always to be found in the new, just as the past and the future can each be discerned in the present. Knowledge of the city is never fixed as its material forms, its inhabited places and shades of meaning encounter the imagination of the subject in space. The collision of different sightlines, the confusion of metaphors, means that reading Benjamin can sometimes be breathtaking, at others stultifying. His style is at moments beautifully evocative and at others obscure or just clumsy. Amongst his travelogues of foreign cities, for instance, 'Hashish in Marseilles' (1986d) has all the self-absorption and about as much of the plot of any stoner story: Benjamin runs the gamut of themes from wondering why he isn't feeling anything, to delighting in everybody and everything he comes across, to the edge of paranoia, to ravenous hunger.

It can be tempting more generally to think of Benjamin as a sort of trance stylist, but he tells us in his wonderful, headlong essay on surrealism that it is no use to dwell on 'the mysterious side of the mysterious' (Benjamin 1986e: 190). His caution that 'we penetrate the mystery only to the degree that we recognize it in the everyday world, by virtue of a dialectical optic that perceives the everyday as impenetrable, the impenetrable as everyday' could be written for the city as a space that is both enchanted and ordinary. The mundane figures who populate Benjamin's urban scene – 'the loiterer, the *flâneur*', and so on – he claims as 'types of illuminati just as much as the opium eater, the dreamer, the ecstatic' (ibid.). You don't have to be a mystic or a madman to perceive the mysterious realities of the everyday: you could, however, require a kind of double vision that Benjamin calls 'dialectical' and which allows you to see the prosaic as at the same time strange. The piece on surrealism offers an aid to reading Benjamin himself, fellow traveller as he is, particularly the insistence that surrealist writing is concerned 'literally with experiences, not with theories and still less with phantasms' (1986e: 179). However skewed his eye may be at times, Benjamin is dealing in things, places and experiences that are real, strange and familiar.

It was this way of seeing that Adorno would memorably describe as crossing magic with positivism (Adorno 1979: 129–30). He meant it as criticism but it remains one of the best accounts of what Benjamin's work is like. Adorno counselled that only the serious application of theory could save Benjamin from 'wide-eyed presentation of mere facts', but Benjamin was never a great one for theory. Rather, he was taken with a method of 'delicate empiricism' that applied itself carefully, even minutely, to things – a form of enquiry 'which so intimately involves itself with the object that it becomes true theory' (1985b: 252). One place in which Benjamin finds such an intent regard is in the modern photographic eye. Getting in close, enlarging what is tiny, the photograph can reveal those 'visual worlds which dwell in the smallest things, meaningful yet covert enough to find a hiding place in waking dreams' (ibid.: 244). His essay on photography dwells in particular on the work of Eugene Atget, whose look anticipated the surrealists' slant on the world and who, like Benjamin himself, 'looked for what was unremarked, forgotten, cast adrift' (Benjamin 1985b: 250). For Benjamin, Atget's work evinces that mix of strangeness and detail that offers the best vantage onto the city. Atget captures an empty scene – 'the city in these pictures looks cleaned out' – yet while he might pass by Paris' landmarks without notice, 'what he did not pass by was a long row of boot lasts; or the Paris courtyards, where from night to morning the hand-carts stand in serried ranks; or the tables after people have finished eating and left, the dishes not yet cleared away' (ibid.: 250–1). Atget's photographs, he comments, have been likened to crime scenes, and Benjamin finds this a particularly apt way of thinking about the city: its ordinary spaces that are at the same time full of portent, its layers of meaning concealed in what might seem the most innocuous clues or traces. Benjamin's way of seeing seems especially appropriate to one who was himself short-sighted – concerning itself with bits and pieces of detail, with the things that a sweeping eye would miss – but it also can be understood as deeply modern. It is in the cut-up aesthetics of an emerging modern photographic style that it becomes possible, like Atget, to signify Westminster, Lille, Antwerp or Breslau as 'here a piece of balustrade, there a tree-top whose bare branches criss-cross a gas lamp, or a gable wall, or a lamp-post with a life-buoy bearing the name of the town' (ibid.: 250).

In Benjamin's view what is ordinary, unregarded or leftover may give onto larger meanings; the most unexceptional objects or places can disclose flashes of knowledge. He sought to grasp reality in terms of scattered or minor things, found objects, and especially in the form of fragments or ruins – writing of his wish 'to establish . . . the image of history even in its most inconspicuous fixtures of existence, its rejects' (NLB 1979: 35). This concern with 'rejects' extends to the urban characters found in Benjamin's writings, particularly those who pass through his Arcades Project. The prostitute, the bohemian, the poet, the rag-picker or the gambler stand in various relations to the order and the meaning of the modern city. The *flâneur* – the bourgeois man of uncertain standing, little occupation and self-regarding intellect who idles in the spaces of the street, the arcade, the café – is Benjamin's most well-known urban type. He exemplifies an ambivalent mode of being in the modern city which combines immersion with estrangement, consumption with detachment, desire with boredom. He is, always, 'just looking'. Like Benjamin's other urban types, all outsiders or minor characters, the *flâneur* possesses something of the easy exoticism of the margins. This recondite and rather unattractive figure, whom Eagleton (1981: 25) called 'that drifting relic of a decaying petty bourgeoisie', has come to exert a surprising hold on ways of thinking about the subject in the city. Its resonance is partly due to the way the concept of *flânerie* provides a simple if not always very precise shorthand for cruising and perusing the city. While Benjamin placed his *flâneur* in nineteenth-century Paris, the type has translated into other temporal and spatial contexts. Shedding his class and sometimes changing his gender, the idea of the *flâneur* as a moving body and a devouring eye in the city has been used to describe more recent and less dandified urban experience, including that of women (see Amin and Thrift 2002; Friedberg 1993; Munt 1995; Parsons 2000; Tester 1994; Wilson 1992; Wolff 1985). It is slightly intriguing that such an historical 'relic' has been able to speak to very different kinds of urban experience, and even more interesting that the figure which has come to typify the subjective experience of urban space is one whose subjectivity is in fact effaced.

The *flâneur*, if he represents for Benjamin a passing moment in the career of the modern bourgeois, can be more freely translated as a version of subjectivity produced out of the modern city. Distracted by the urban spectacle even as he is estranged from it, the bored desire of the *flâneur* bears a likeness to Simmel's jaded metropolitan, battered to the point of the blasé. This contrasts with Benjamin's accounts of his own relation to various cities, where the self appears less as acted on by the urban scene and as more creative in its engagement with places and things. Still, the matter of subjectivity is never merely a question of the projection of the self onto space. Places and things have a reality – Casey (1996: 35) calls it sheer 'thisness' and I cannot find a better word – that is neither simply given nor fully grasped by the perceptions of the subject. It is in this alterity 'that space becomes a question, ceases to be self-evident, ceases to be incorporated. Space is a doubt: I have constantly to mark it, to designate it. It's never mine, never given to me, I have to conquer it' (Perec 1999: 91). This notion of space as a question captures very deftly Benjamin's attitude to the everyday mysteries of the city. And it anticipates, too, the ideas of Michel de Certeau, for whom the answer to the question posed by urban space was not a solution, but a story.

In the embrace of the street: de Certeau

> I start walking again. Despair does not exist for a walking man.
>
> Reda, *The Ruins of Paris*

Simmel and Benjamin offer different slants on urban subjectivity, but both consider the physical city in relation to the sensory or imaginative responses it elicits. Such an interest in the subject's encounter with the brute fact of the city is central to Michel de Certeau's work in *The Practice of Everyday Life*, from which comes the notion of 'spatial stories'. The routes people take through the city can be likened to stories they tell under their breath, ways of making sense in space that leave no traces behind them, trails which are less lasting even than footprints in sand. This idea of spatial stories turns, then, on the contrast between the solidity and actuality of the material city, and the elusive movements of subjects within it.

In a well-known passage, but one that has come to possess a resonance it didn't previously have, Michel de Certeau begins his account of 'Walking in the city' with a view from the 110th floor of the World Trade Center in downtown

Manhattan. Seen from above, the city is laid out, legible, resolved. One can see how things relate to each other, put certain markers in place, take in distances across the city in a single sweep. This view, de Certeau supposes, is a bit like the mind's eye of the planner, the urbanist, or the master-builder. It suggests a particular logic of seeing in the city, a rationality of urban order that is in thrall to the plan. This is the 'concept city' seen in overview, like one of those urban models encased under glass. De Certeau contrasts such a prospect with the view (which is not a view) from the street. Architectural models of the city will occasionally add tiny figures to the scene, but these are incidental to the shape of the thing and – if they are meant as a humanizing touch – can tend to ruin the lines. They should, in any case, be moving. Buildings stand still, people don't. The rationality of the plan or the model is foreign to the range of barely visible moves that make up everyday spatial practice. To de Certeau, these minor byways through the city represent one of the small freedoms of urban life, a sense in which the everyday escapes from larger patterns of visibility, of order, of design.

The act of walking in the city is central to de Certeau's understanding of the subject in space. It is one of the minor practices of everyday life through which people make room for themselves in the city. The urban environment is conceived here less as a physical structure or a spatial container than as a site of practice. In this emphasis on walking there are, of course, family resemblances to Benjamin's *flâneur*, but de Certeau's pedestrians lack his louche glamour – these 'ordinary practitioners' really are meant to be ordinary. Within the weave of a larger urban design the mundane tactics of walking in the city constitute little practices of resistance, the small coups involved in beating the city at its own game. There is a staple scenario one sees in the movies, where two characters just miss each other: one turns the corner as the other comes along the street; someone pauses to look in a store window and fails to see the other come out of the subway. And much cinematic suspense has been created out of the difficulties of following someone on foot through a crowded city. De Certeau might have written these scripts. His argument opposes the rational order of the city to the range of illegible and unsigned moves that make up everyday urban life. Below the level of visibility ordinary inhabitants enact their own maps of the city. These many passages through the city are the spatial expression of social anonymity: it can be as hard to walk in someone else's tracks as it is to get inside their skin. Following in another's path, the 'merciless separation of space' (Simmel 1997c: 170) reinforces the fact of otherness, the unknowability of a subject in space. Benjamin (1985b: 256) liked the idea that every inch of the modern city was a crime scene, 'every passer-by a culprit', and in de Certeau's account, people are always making their get-away.

In treating walking in the city as an exemplary practice of everyday life, Certeau wants to challenge the notion that the ordinary individual is merely a consumer of urban space, or else its docile subject. People do not, he contends, simply rehearse an established spatial script, nor are the meanings of the city given by material forms and their official instructions for use – as if walking in the city was always to take a guided tour, telling us where to turn, when to look up, what to think. There are no one-way streets when you are on foot. For Certeau, the practice of walking in the city is a matter of telling one's own spatial stories, drawing on a mobile and private language of the streets. This is just the opposite of those tourist paths to be found in some places, where you follow a line of painted footsteps around approved sites of interest. It would be impossible to map out the routes that everyday users take through the city. As Georges Perec (1999: 91) put it, 'Space melts like sand running through one's fingers.' Each spatial story, as the taking of an opportunity in space and time, is unrepeatable and resists representation. One never crosses exactly the same street twice. The many lines of everyday movement through the city cannot be mapped or read; they confound the cartographic impulse and are illegible even to their authors. It is as though different 'bodies follow the thicks and thins of an urban "text" they write without being able to read. . . . These practitioners make use of spaces that cannot be seen; their knowledge of them is as blind as that of lovers in each other's arms' (de Certeau 1984: 93). Moving bodies know but cannot see the text of their wandering, just as one knows but does not wholly see the body of a lover. They are inside their spatial stories as if inside an embrace.

No two actors could tell quite the same spatial story. Benjamin, for instance, gives us plenty of clues, place names and points of references in 'A Berlin chronicle' but we could never really walk in his footsteps (and, anyway, Berlin's Zoo might signify something else to us). The spaces of the city are overlaid by memory, by unbidden associations, by conscious or unconscious plots. All these inform or confuse the cognitive maps we use to navigate in space. How often do you see strangers in a city poring over a map that refuses to make sense, before a local shows them the way by pointing not to the map but to the signs in the street? 'Turn right when you reach the butcher . . . If you come to the cinema you have gone too far.' Mental maps tend to be composed of this mishmash of landmarks, personal haunts, good guesses and routine paths. Sometimes the city helps out, at others it confounds our plans. Simmel, Benjamin and Certeau all speak of the magic, the spell of street names. De Certeau mentions a friend who lives in the region of Sèvres and who finds themself, when in Paris, drawn as if unconsciously to the area on the Left Bank around the rue de Sèvres. But we all have our favourite latitudes, our shortcuts and our blindspots: the city comes to us in bits and pieces.

This is to point to the way that something always escapes from representations of the city, as it does from official attempts to impose order and transparency upon it. Not everything shows up on the map. It has to do with the texture of everyday movement in the city, the chance encounters and cross-cutting paths of the urban crowd, the tricky and momentary ways in which people make space.

> The paths that correspond in this intertwining, unrecognized poems in which each body is an element signed by many others, elude legibility. It is as though the practices organizing a bustling city are characterized by their blindness. The networks of these moving, intersecting writings compose a manifold story that has neither author nor spectator, shaped out of fragments of trajectories and alterations of space: in relation to representations, it remains daily and indefinitely other. (de Certeau 1984: 93)

The 'blindness' of everyday practice – unthinking, routine, minor or private – cuts through the will to see and to represent urban space that is typical of government and police systems, as it is of architects or planners. Where spaces are heavily policed, the desire for transparency becomes very clear; actualized in the curfews, cameras, check-points or barricades that seek to order and make visible people's use of space. Such spaces represent extreme (even if common) versions of what de Certeau calls 'the concept city' and Lefebvre terms 'representations of space'. This scientific, governmental or architectural ordering of space lays out the city to view. Sites of everyday practice, in contrast, do not give themselves up to the consuming eye. Like Lefebvre's representational space, they are 'linked to the clandestine or underground side of social life' (1991: 33). For de Certeau, however, this underside was not the preserve of romantics or insurgents but the normal space of everyday users. While Lefebvre (1991: 56) worried over 'the passivity and silence of the "users" of space', in de Certeau it is precisely this stance that provides cover for the tactics of everyday life. De Certeau can easily be criticized for his tendency to get misty-eyed over the ordinary user, engaged in the commonplace heroics of crossing to walk on the sunny side of the street. There is clearly a kind of bathos in thinking of ordinary inhabitants of a city as 'poets of their own affairs, trailblazers in the jungle of functionalist rationality' (de Certeau 1984: xviii). Hutchinson (2000: 17), for instance, writes more prosaically of the 'unenviably intimate knowledge of the rhythms and cadences of the city's streets' of the poor black women who rely on public transport in Los Angeles. The experience of walking in the city, so central to de Certeau's conception of the everyday, will be very different depending on which city you are walking in, why you are walking, and who you are. Still, there may be more to this everyday version of urban subjectivity than to the marginal poses of the *flâneur*. And in the private routes that you take to get through the city, in the ways that you lose your way, there opens a 'little space of irrationality' (de Certeau 1984: 111) that means no one else lives in exactly the same city.

Conclusion

The distinction between objectivity and subjectivity is one of the most basic frameworks in social theory, and one of its most tenacious dualisms. The city takes this distinction matter-of-factly and also makes it easy. Cities have an 'objectivity' as both physical and social products, they exist and have effects beyond any individual's perception of them, they are real and (quite literally) concrete. And yet the experience of being in the city can blur the line between the objective and the subjective in the most pleasurable or most unnerving ways. People's urban practice is constrained by the social and spatial relations that frame their actions, but it is not only these factors which ensure that everyone's spatial stories turn out differently. The random and fragile connections and disconnections of an everyday life, the shortcuts of memory, the dead-ends and private jokes that steer a subject in space, are like so many maps of the city – written over and folded badly, consigned to routine or made up as you go along.

The urban subject we find in Simmel or Benjamin, their nerves jangled or their dreams haunted, can appear a little punch-drunk from the encounter with the modern city. This has partly to do with the brute fact of urban forms – the rush, the crowd, the scale and density of things. But it also has to do with the 'kind of regimen that cities keep over imagination' (Benjamin 1986f: 30), the ways that material forms impress themselves on consciousness. In Benjamin's account, the shape of the city dogs the contours of thought. It maps out the unconscious paths of the everyday, it conceals stores of meanings, it buries the dead, it gives form to memories. And it is in the stubborn architecture of memory that we discover, as Angela Carter (1992: 126) once remarked, 'how impossible it is to pull down an imaginary city'.

7 Making Space: Urban Cultures, Spatial Tactics

> The space of a tactic is the space of the other.
>
> M. de Certeau, *The Practice of Everyday Life*

Sous les pavés, la plage. The revolutionary slogan of Paris 1968 catches at the idea that transforming social life is also about changing space. *Under the paving-stones, the beach.* In this radical imagination, all that is solid gives way to sand.

Not all subversions of space are so dramatic. If social and political movements seek to alter space in decisive ways, the Paris slogan also implies that there are moments and means of escape to be found in more minor practices, tactics of space which rely on sudden or small gestures. This chapter is concerned with interruptions to the normal run of space. It looks to the city as a site of diversion, a product of quick thinking and clever footwork. It traces some of the ways that spatial order is disrupted through inventive modes of using space, as well as the everyday escape routes that are worked through the fabric of the city. The discussion is developed around the ideas of three thinkers: Michel Foucault, Roland Barthes, and Michel de Certeau. The first section focuses on Foucault's concept of heterotopia. This is a critical notion for thinking about the 'otherness' of certain places: Foucault uses it to describe sites which stand outside a conventional order of space, which are set apart or which operate on their own, different terms. In his account, alterity is an effect of such spaces themselves, a quality of places distinguished by their separation from the usual run of things, by crisis or deviance, by their perfection or subversion of certain spatial designs. The distinctive rationality of these spaces – the barracks or hospital, the colony, carnival or brothel – shapes people's conduct within them. There are rules or codes, whether enforced or unspoken, about how you should act and interact in such sites. While the heterotopia disrupts spatial norms, therefore, it puts into place an alternative order of space.

If these 'other spaces' can be seen to organize behaviour, however, we can in turn think about how social practice organizes space. The second frame for discussion is Roland Barthes's work on the semiology of the city, and particularly his idea that subjects compose space for themselves as if 'speaking' the city. Thinking about the city as a system of signs is also to conceive of a certain ordering of space, but for Barthes the encounter between the subject and the city is an inventive one, as spaces signify and are read in different ways. The signs in the street are open to the play of meaning and to contrary interpretations just as spaces give themselves to different uses. It is this uncertainty at the level of meaning and practice that opens up the erotic dimensions of urban life – the pleasures to be found in making and missing connections, the unsettled nature of what and who the spaces of the city are for. Following Barthes's reading, the city is never quite tamed, never entirely familiar. Even the oldest cities contain the shock of the new.

An emphasis on practice is crucial, third, to Michel de Certeau's account of spatial tactics. The discussion here builds on the treatment of de Certeau's work in the previous chapter, to focus more closely on his analysis of people's tactical use of space. For de Certeau, the order of the city is fragmented as actors 'poach' bits and pieces of space in ways which can be neither programmed nor prevented. The everyday practice of space re-interprets or just ignores official meanings and uses. De Certeau points to how ordinary subjects transform existing spaces through use, even if only in partial, temporary or private ways. The last part of the chapter explores de Certeau's arguments on the tactical seizure of space through the lens of urban cultures of graffiti and skateboarding. These subcultural tactics illustrate the artful or wily means by which actors take space in the city, telling the spatial story in another way.

Of other spaces: Foucault on heterotopia

How might we think about the alterity of certain spaces? A suggestive approach is offered by Michel Foucault's notion of the 'heterotopia'. In his brief and somewhat curious discussion of the concept, Foucault proposes the heterotopia as a site that undoes the usual order of space. Its meaning turns on the contrast with the idea of a utopia – an ideal place which has no actual location, which remains unrealized, imaginary. Like the utopia, the heterotopia runs counter to a conventional spatial order; it puts in place 'counter-sites' in which existing social and spatial arrangements are 'represented, contested and inverted' (Foucault 1986: 24). But unlike utopia, the figure of the heterotopia refers to *real* spaces. Heterotopias exist, Foucault suggests, utopias (by definition) do not. If a utopia is in lexical terms a 'non-place', a heterotopia is an actual place of difference: literally, an 'other place'.

Foucault sketches a number of types of heterotopia which he sees as appearing in different historical and cultural contexts. There is, first, the heterotopia of 'crisis': spaces laid aside for transitions or events that set an individual apart from the larger social group. Foucault sees this kind of heterotopia as typical of 'primitive' societies and is thinking of instances (menstruation, initiation, illness or death) where women, the adolescent or the old might have been confined or separated from social contact. There is a residual sense of these spaces, he thinks, in the modern boarding school – particularly as this enacts certain rites of passage for young men – or in military barracks. While Foucault contends that the heterotopia of crisis survives only in vestigial forms, we might see something of this type in the labour ward (perhaps in the hospital more generally), the old people's home, and quite vividly in those gated retirement villages that secure their residents in a kind of total twilight environment. The modern equivalent of the heterotopia of crisis in Foucault's account, however, is better understood as a heterotopia of *deviance*: represented by those sites, such as asylums or prisons, which remove the abnormal individual from normal social space and which are governed by an internal spatial order. Such places of separation and regulation were to be important in Foucault's own work on how power and discipline were organized through institutional forms, and how modes of power/knowledge played out in particular spaces – in clinics, asylums, prisons, and so on.

The modern heterotopia is not, however, confined to disciplinary spaces. Other sites subvert or escape the commonplace order of space by putting in place their own spatial logic. Foucault cites the quarantine quarter, the brothel, the cinema, the library, the public bath, the sauna, the motel room used for illicit sex. Each of these spaces has a touch of the uncanny. Some involve their own rules of order, divisions of space and regulations of practice. Many are places out of the ordinary, where to enter is to take on a different kind of bearing, to put oneself differently. They involve conventions of noise or of silence, of restraint or abandon, of attention or distraction. And they contain the potential to subvert, to caricature, to distil or to perfect 'real arrangements' of space. Women-only spaces – the bar, the club or the swimming pool – could be seen as heterotopias of separation that escape the eyes and the order of men. We might think, too, of military spaces – the base camp, the field hospital, the command post, or the bunker – and places modelled on them (boot camps or detention centres, say). In these places an often strict spatial order exists together with the essential strangeness of the space. They mimic certain codes for arranging and pacifying space (eating places, offices, spaces for the sick, etc.) while remaining well outside spatial 'normality'. Or again of clubs – a heterotopia of pleasure – with their arrangements of space around different types of music, their sometimes arcane rules of entry (they 'hide curious exclusions', as Foucault might have put it), their spoken and unspoken codes of dress and conduct, their inversions of time.

In addressing contemporary forms of heterotopia Foucault looks to places that remake relations of space and time. There are places, for instance, that toy with space itself, which juxtapose 'in a single real place several spaces, several sites that are in themselves incompatible' (1986: 25). In the theatre un-alike and unlikely spaces coexist, as the stage is at one moment a garden, then a bedroom, then a battlefield. In the cinema the audience orients itself to another three-dimensional space which is in fact a projection onto a depthless screen. Other kinds of heterotopia have a critical relation to time. Libraries, museums, fairgrounds and carnivals are spaces, as Foucault puts it, linked to 'slices in time' (1986: 26). The archive or the museum sediments and encloses time in a unified place, in an ordering attitude to the past which

Foucault sees as deeply modern. Different sites adopt a less curatorial and more capricious approach to time. The carnival or the fair create space in a way that is 'absolutely temporal' (1986: 26). They are momentary translations of everyday places (the park, the street, the city outskirts) that have a singular temporality, which seize bits of time in space. (Cemeteries, meanwhile, have their own relation to both the transitory and the eternal.)

Foucault's discussion of the heterotopia reflects his early structuralist interest in the dividing practices that separated out different categories of persons and things – sick from well, mad from sane, deviant from normal. His efforts to typologize various kinds of heterotopia, and to suggest cross-cultural patterns in the heterotopic ordering of space, betray a concern with classification that tends to disappear from his later work. At the same time, his series of principles for how heterotopias might be analysed (number two: societies may transform the function of a heterotopia over time; number five: heterotopias assume systems of opening and closing) seems to impose quite rigid terms on what kinds of space might qualify while failing – on my reading at least – to make much clearer what he actually means by the concept. It remains an evocative term, however, in signifying spatial otherness or difference, and some of the examples Foucault offers are more suggestive of how the heterotopia might be used to think about spatial alterity than is the checklist he develops for classifying them.

In this sense the idea of heterotopias as 'counter-sites, a kind of effectively enacted utopia' (1986: 24) opens onto a wider engagement with how existing spaces may be altered. In particular, the relation of time and space that Foucault stresses in his treatment of modern heterotopias is crucial to thinking about spatial practice – the ways that these other spaces come to be, precisely, 'enacted'. Transforming space is often linked to stealing moments in time. Think of the protest or demonstration as a form of heterotopia: taking to the streets or the square is both a tactical reworking of space – the embassy or the government building is no longer simply a site of official power, but also a site of protest or resistance – and an enactment in time (the French term, *manifestation*, catches this idea especially well). In that moment, and in that place, it is possible to see the cracks in the edifice of official power, to disrupt the smooth story of political order with the splinter of protest. The demonstration makes very obvious the way that political order is expressed through spatial order, as its policing is so clearly tied to the freedoms and uses of public space, and to those unruly uses of space that qualify as offences of disorder. So too does the protest – if only temporarily – make of itself and its location an 'other space'. This bears comparison with Lefebvre's concept of the 'counter-space' which is imagined in alternative political projects, and realized by oppositional strategies (see Lefebvre 1991: 381–3; see also Cohen 1993; McKay 1998). Such counter-spaces resist the dominant organization of space around the requirements of political order or the interests of economic accumulation. A heterotopia of this kind is visible, momentarily, when anti-capitalist protests in different cities take place against a backdrop of boarded-up McDonald's and Armani stores, making spaces that are – at least for the moment – no good for capital.

Taking the demonstration as an example of heterotopia is to extend Foucault's account beyond its original terms. It highlights the role of practice in remaking space, the potential for social action to produce 'counter-sites' within an established spatial order. In contrast, Foucault's notion of hetero-topia treats alterity as a quality of spaces themselves. Individuals' conduct is to a large extent determined by the organization of a given space, whether we speak of the soldier in the barracks, the patient in the hospital, or the reveller at carnival. Such a capacity for space to shape practice is evident in Foucault's examples of various colonial arrangements (the Puritans in the North American colonies, or Jesuits in South America) which laid out space as a matrix for the organization of social life, and is especially clear in his account of the spatial order of the Panopticon (Foucault 1977). While such sites are, of course, products of social action, the emphasis in Foucault's analysis is on how these spaces serve to form and regulate conduct. With a different emphasis, however, it is possible to think about spatial otherness by starting out from spatial practice. This has less to do with the unusual order of certain peculiar spaces, than with the potential for more everyday spaces to be disordered through tactics of use.

Speaking the city: Barthes

Such an emphasis on the inventive nature of practice is not always associated with structuralist approaches to space, but it is to be found in Roland Barthes's semiology of the city. His urban semiotics takes the city not simply as a text to be read, but as a vivid and mobile language to be spoken. Cities are for Barthes both a kind of writing (and the urban user a 'kind of reader'), and a manner of speaking. 'The city', as he puts it, 'speaks to its inhabitants, we speak our city, the city where we are, simply by living in it, by wandering through it' (Barthes 1997: 168). It is very gratifying, now, to walk along rue Roland Barthes in the east of Paris – to think about Barthes getting a final word in, even if the street itself doesn't seem to have much to say. Walking in the city, people invent their own urban idioms, a local language written in the streets and read as if out loud. A strange city, too, can seem like a language you don't know. Gradually you pick up a few words, recognize certain expressions, try out some turns of phrase. Navigating the city, we compose spatial sentences that begin to make sense, gradually master the intricate grammar of the streets. Slowly, we learn to make the spaces of the city speak.

Barthes is recalling (in more poetic register) the work of Kevin Lynch in *The Image of the City*, arguing that the kinds of physical or visual elements that come into play as people compose their images of the city – paths, edges, nodes, landmarks – are precisely *semantic* terms that make up the city as a language or discourse (cf. Lynch 1960). Language is not used as a metaphor here – Barthes is, after all, a more hard-line semiotician than Lynch; rather he wants to speak of the language of the city in the same way that Freud spoke of the language of dreams. It is not simply that the spaces of the city can be read *as if* they were a language, this urban semiotics makes a stronger claim to grasp 'the city in the same terms as the consciousness perceiving it' (Barthes 1997: 167). The spaces of the city are organized, for the perceiving subject, in the form of a language; urban space derives its sense from relationships of sequence, context and differentiation. Barthes's account, however, while it deals with the grammar of spatial borders, edges and units, is not so wedded to structuralist analysis as one might think. The ways in which different spaces in the city signify are not tied to any single meaning, nor do meanings reside securely in place. There is, in the city as elsewhere, what Derrida terms a 'wandering of the semantic', a play of signification, exchanges and deferrals of meaning. There exists always the potential for wilful or perverse readings as much as for obedient or conventional ones. Even laid out as a system of signs, cities won't rest quiet on the page – finally and exuberantly, the city for Barthes is a kind of poem that he wants 'to grasp and make sing' (1997: 172).

The capacity for odd and pleasurable connections, this creative *joie d'espace*, is a quality not only of spatial experience but also of social life in the city. Urban spatiality and sociality are similarly connective, mercurial – in Barthes's terms, erotic. He is using the concept of Eros in the original sense here: the city is intrinsically erotic as a space of exchange, of vitality and connection. It makes room for the Dionysian dimensions of life – desire, excess, play, violence, risk, transgression (see also Lefebvre 1991: 177–8). This pleasure principle in urban space is always vulnerable to the spatial sway of the reality principle, the dominant rationality of productivity, utility and order in the city. Indeed, such an organizing rationality always threatens to colonize the realm of play. Barthes contrasts the untamed erotic potential of the city with the pedestrian efforts of urban planning to set out approved sites of pleasure: 'the concept of the place of pleasure', as he puts it, 'is one of the most tenacious mystifications of urban functionalism' (1997: 170–1). Lefebvre takes a similarly jaded view of designated leisure spaces – as he has it: 'The case against leisure is quite simply closed – and the verdict is irreversible: leisure is as alienated and alienating as labour' (1991: 383). A functional concept of pleasure, dutifully pursued in the playground or park within the limits set by their catalogue of rules, bye-laws and opening hours, or doggedly consumed in the regimented spaces of 'nightlife', is quite different from a concept of pleasure understood as a play of meanings, of surprising encounters or unexpected delights. A notion of the erotics of the city, that is, goes beyond those pleasures one enjoys while keeping off the grass, avoiding ball-games, committing no nuisance and leaving quietly.

The erotic dimension animates the city as a space of otherness. The semiotic play of the city, the slide of connections between spaces, meanings and things, preserves a sense of strangeness in urban life. Here again, what is true of urban space is true of urban sociality. The city, Barthes writes (he is thinking of Paris), stands as the 'place where the other is and where we ourselves are other, as the place where we play the other' (1997: 171). The eroticism of urban space lies not only – perhaps not even primarily – in the fascination of the other, but in the estrangement of the self. It is not simply that one encounters the city as a place of strangers, but that you experience yourself as a stranger there. There is a mutual strangeness in being together in the city, in a landscape of temporary connections, chance meetings and near misses. This contingency in urban experience is deftly captured by de Certeau's (1984: 103) idea of the city as a 'universe of rented spaces' – a geography of places that are dwelt in momentarily, inhabited for an instant, passed through (see also Sadler 1999). Still, the haphazard pleasures of the city are not obvious, and not so available, to everyone. Barthes suggests that the erotic potential of urban spaces, their possibilities for social encounter and play, are especially apparent to young people – those who have time to make space in the city. (Robert Park, we might recall, thought you needed 'young and fresh nerves' to really relish the 'element of chance and adventure' in city life.) Outside the rationality of the working day and the strictures of official use, the young or the unconscripted are free to experience the centre of a city as 'the space where subversive forces, forces of rupture, ludic forces act and meet' (Barthes 1997: 171).

Barthes's perspective may be a little questionable here. What is imagined as the erotic moment where 'ludic forces act and meet' equally might be seen as the mundane manoeuvres in which young people in the city meet 'others' who are pretty much like themselves, walk knee-deep in tracks well-worn by them and others like them, act out the standard moves of rupture and subversion. It is not clear that the centre of Paris (wherever that might be) is more exciting than any other city in this regard, its young users any more inventive or open to difference – although they have their moments. Urban space, if it contains the potential for play, for desire, for *jouissance*, can also be deeply predictable, stubbornly un-erotic. However, between the romance of endless semantic possibilities and the limits of everyday practice, between the erotic charge enjoyed by the 'cruising grammarian' (Morris 1988: 195) and the blank routine of the ordinary user, Barthes's ideas do make room for the resourceful ways people engage with their city. His account remains open to different ways of reading, writing and speaking urban space. Outside the easy subversions of youth, after all, we all have our moments of truancy.

Urban subcultures, spatial tactics: Michel de Certeau

Barthes might celebrate a banal sort of rapture, but thinking about the encounter between the subject and the city is to think about a point at which the mundane meets the enchanted. In Michel de Certeau's account, spatial tactics involve a kind of ordinary magic that transforms space when nobody is looking. De Certeau uses two sets of metaphors to analyse everyday spatial practice. The first, which he borrows from military thinking, is the distinction between strategic and tactical approaches to space. The second, taken from linguistics, suggests that individuals use space in a way that is comparable to their use of language. Through both devices, de Certeau opposes the over-arching order of the city to the range of invisible moves that make up every-day urban life. Below the level of 'legibility', he suggests, in between the lines on the grid, ordinary users of the city tell spatial stories that do not get writ-ten down. To borrow a notion from Barthes, individuals 'speak' the city by moving through it, enunciating a private language of place and practice. This contrast between the official order of the city and people's colloquial use of it turns on de Certeau's version of a military distinction between 'strategy' and 'tactics'. As in battle, strategy involves a design that extends across and organ-izes space, while tactics work as chancy and sudden plays within the field of engagement. If strategies of urban design operate through the ordering of space and vision – as in Foucault's account of panoptic technologies of power – tactics of urban use are 'non-space', unfixed and unseen. They are skirmishes in the terrain of everyday life.

De Certeau's interest in using this military metaphor is to consider the potential for action possessed by the 'weak' in the order of the 'strong', to explore the inventive range of the ordinary user or prosaic 'practitioner of urban space' (1984: 31). These actors in the everyday do not simply rehearse an established order of the city; rather, they make their own spatial meanings, producing urban space in canny and idiomatic ways. We take different routes through the city, not always the most rational, the quickest or the most well-lit. We don't always cross at the lights. Protean tactics of everyday movement involve passing and clever appropriations of space. They are like the Freudian conception of wit – working through agile juxtapositions, surpris-ing collisions, high relief, tricky inversions (1984: 39). This analogy between spatial tactics and the play of language is the second key metaphor that de Certeau uses to illuminate the everyday practice of space. People's use of spatial tactics can be likened to their use of language. A tactics of the city 'poaches' space for an instant, just as an act of speech – a single utterance – takes just what it needs for the moment from a whole system of grammar, a complex order of language. Tactics of the city might in this way be seen as a kind of spatial slang, a local mode of expression and articulation, an artful way of getting yourself across.

If the tactical use of space is one instance of how the everyday *escapes* (the term is Blanchot's), such escape attempts are only ever temporary – they slip between rather than tear apart the mesh of rational order. To de Certeau, spatial tactics are to be found in the common routines of walking, moving, dwelling in space. It is an image of an 'anthill society' (1984: 1), highly worked and barely visible. These ways of occupying space are means by which people make room for themselves in the city, appropriate space and time to their own design, live in the city as a subjective space (see Jarvis et al. 2001). We might think of the delights that small children will find in the most common-place spaces, the endless play of crawling backwards down stairs, balancing on the edge of walls, disappearing behind corners. De Certeau's argument suggests that we do not entirely lose this pleasurable relation to ordinary spaces, or this facility for transforming the everyday environment into a kind of game. The tactics that take us via certain 'scenic' routes of our own devis-ing, the woman who chooses the same seat on the bus every morning, the places where you glance up to get a felicitous view. Under scrutiny, it is true, some of these can look a little offbeat, but the point is that nobody is really looking. They are ways of playing at space, making yourself at home in the routine passages of everyday life, producing your own version of the city. Sometimes props will help: personal stereos, for instance, allow people to add a soundtrack to their spatial story (see Bull 2000). Such a technique amplifies de Certeau's point about the tactical means by which people occupy and pass through space, but you don't necessarily need the gadgets to do so.

Viewed in this way, spatial tactics could be seen as one of the minor opiates or meagre releases of everyday life, a small strategy for making city life a little more survivable. In more critical mode, Henrietta Moore has argued that such gambits have a capacity to transform space that goes beyond the small diversions of the everyday:

> If meaning is given to the organization of space through practice, it follows that small changes in procedure can provide new interpretations of spatial layouts. Such layouts provide potential commentaries on established ways of doing things and divisions of privilege. Shifting the grounds of meaning, reading against the grain, is often something done through practice, through the day-to-day activities that take place within symbolically structured space. This can involve small things, such as putting something in the wrong place or placing it in relation to something else from which it is normally kept separate. It can include using space in a different way or commandeer-ing space for new uses or invading the space of others. (1994: 83)

Moore is writing, in particular, about gendered divisions of space – some of the most 'symbolically structured' of spatial regimes. But her point bears more broadly on the symbolic and practical weight of conventional space, with its established relations of proximity, hierarchy and sequence. And she alerts us to the minor incursions that can disrupt such spatial order. The last part of the chapter takes up this conception of spatial tactics as unsettling the standard organization of space. It does so by reading Certeau's ideas in rela-tion to urban sub-cultures of graffiti and skateboarding. Such tactics provide illustrations of the way that urban spaces can be rewritten, cut up and put together differently. They also bring into focus the practices of groups of young people in urban spaces (see Skelton and Valentine 1998). They are instances of the way, as Dick Hebdige (1988: 17–18) writes, that 'young people make their presence felt by going "out of bounds", by resisting through rituals, dressing strangely, striking bizarre attitudes, breaking rules . . . issuing rhetorical challenges to the law'. These marginal tactics point to how contests over urban space are not simply ranged between dominant strategies of order and ordinary tactics of space, but involve tensions – often more obvious and more intrusive – between different kinds of 'everyday' user.

'Perfect gestures of violence': urban graffiti

In his emphasis on how users 'speak' their city de Certeau is close to Barthes, but he also refers to one very literal sense in which the spaces of the city get *written*:

> we could mention the fleeting images, yellowish-green and metallic-blue calligraphies that howl without raising their voices and emblazon themselves on the subterranean passages of the city, "embroideries" composed of letters and numbers, perfect gestures of violence painted with a pistol. Shivas made of written characters, dancing graphics whose fleeting apparitions are accompanied by the rumble of subway trains: New York graffiti. (1984: 102)

De Certeau is almost reluctant to cite the example of graffiti as a tactics of space. Graffiti are, paradoxically, *too visible* as an instance of those illegible practices that 'transform the scene, but . . . cannot be fixed in a certain place by images' (1984: 102). The point to be made here, though, is that even if graffiti themselves are fixed in place as images, the *practice* – the act of writing – is not. The image or text left behind is only the trace or tag of a tactic that has already escaped, an author who has slipped back between the lines.

If graffiti can be understood as a form of 'enunciation' in the city (1984: 39), the stories that they tell are diverse. Reading the writing on the walls is to read a social and political geography. Walter Benjamin noticed this: the walls in the centre of Marseilles, he wrote in 1928, are in the pay of the rich and have been bought off by advertisements for various items of consumption, whether the latest aperitif, department store or movie star. 'In the poorer quarters,' however, 'they are politically mobilized and post their spacious red letters as the forerunners of red guards in front of dockyards and arsenals' (Benjamin 1986c: 135). The various uses of graffiti are not always distinct, but it is possible to think about different tactics of writing and the competing claims they make to space. The political use of graffiti, first, takes the surface of the city as a space in which demands might be advanced, identities inscribed, and challenges issued. Outside a formal public sphere of political exchange and reportage, graffiti deals in an economy of slogans and signs – from expressions of solidarity to gestures of refusal to the ciphers of movements and factions. Political discourse is reduced to its barest terms, exhorting us simply to smash the state or eat the rich. Still, in these compressed forms, graffiti offer 'an assertion of something, a criticism of public reality' (Sontag 2001: 148). While the walls of the Marseilles dockyards were, in the 1920s, mobilized by a workerist politics, fifty years or more later feminists would take the fight to the advertisers. The guerrilla tactics of feminist graffiti, aimed at the easy sexism of advertising, both marks and extends the limits of political speech. If feminism has involved a redrawing of the space of politics, feminist graffiti actualize this in rewriting as political sites those images which project women's bodies as passive surfaces of consumption (see Posener 1982). In this sense, feminist graffiti enact the sort of disruption which Moore (1994) described, commandeering space and commenting on the kinds of power expressed in certain spatial 'layouts'.

Another mode of 'political' graffiti, however, has less to do with speaking up to power than with defending place and marking exclusions. Racist and sectarian graffiti seek to make real, by making visible, particular claims to ownership. They aim to convert space into territory, to draw a colour line down the streets of the city. Such uses of graffiti enact all the moves of a tactics of space but have only one spatial story to tell. These gestures of purification imagine that boundaries can be secured, separations can be total, and real presences written over. The racist script is an act of symbolic violence against known or imagined others, in defence of a self-identity that is tied into place. It rejects the notion that there might be more than one form of belonging in the same space. Back et al. (1999) suggest that racist graffiti, even as it makes aggressive claims of belonging and entitlement, can in fact mark the insecurity of identity, the fragility of its hold on place. Statements of exclusion and possession betray the unstable nature of the very divisions they seek to entrench. While these graffiti may draw lines that will not hold, however, they also read as calling-cards of other forms of violence, signatures of more effective modes of exclusion.

The naming and claiming of space are typical of a third form of graffiti, the use of tags, throw-ups and bombing as the marks of individual writers or of crews. Here there is no other message than the name or sign of the artist, the simple statement that says 'I was here'. These assertions of presence by an author who has got away transform blank spaces into the scene of a crime. The more unlikely or risky the site – the undersides of railway bridges or the sides of trains – the greater the claims of the artist as a tactician of space (Ewenstein 2004: 5–6). As de Certeau (1984: 37) has it, a tactical use of space must 'make use of the cracks that particular conjunctions open in the surveillance of the proprietary powers. It poaches in them. It creates surprises in them. It can be where it is least expected.' There are different ways of reading these graffiti, illegible though they often are to the uninitiated. You could say that there are no spaces in the city wholly given over to pure function, no space so alienating that it cannot be inhabited, no places that are strictly forbidden. The act of tagging, moreover, subverts a logic of urban anonymity by declaring a wilful presence and a name. The 'tide of indecipherable signatures of mutinous adolescents which has washed over and bitten into the facades of monuments and the surface of public vehicles' in New York City, writes Sontag (2001: 149), acts as 'an assertion of disrespect, yes, but most of all simply an assertion: the powerless saying, I'm here, too'. Marginal spaces provide sites for declaring refractory identities – although one should be wary of assuming too much about the deprived demographics of the graffiti artist. These 'crimes of style' (Ferrell 1996) involve a tension between the assertive claims of the writer and the often unwilling compulsion of the reader, who has no choice but to take in the texts that scratch across communal spaces. Such statements can be read not simply as the invasion or vandalism of public space, but as a gesture of appropriation that serves to alienate other users of everyday spaces, to show up de Certeau's 'ordinary practitioners' as even more ordinary. In these incursions into public space, the politics of graffiti take the form of an identity politics which insists that nameless others should notice your presence and remember your name (see Sennett 1990: 205–7).

Tags and throw-ups shade into a final way of thinking about graffiti: as a mode of artistic expression. The aesthetics of graffiti mark a shift from a tactics of writing (as in 'political' modes of graffiti) to one of figuration. At this point, graffiti as a fugitive tactics of space can be assimilated back into forms of visual order. There is a slide from treating the surface of the city as canvas to the valorization of graffiti as art, a relocation from the wall of the subway to that of the gallery (see Cresswell 1992; Powers 1999; Stewart 1988; Smith 2000). In this move, graffiti – from realizing illicit use values in stolen spaces – get commodified in terms of exchange value. Such a conversion confounds Benjamin's distinction between walls bought off by the rich and given over to advertising, and walls that are politically mobilized by graffiti tactics. Graffiti can be bought off, too. It may be a mistake to draw too hard a line between the 'pure' form of aerosol or stencil art in the street, and the compromised graffiti art of the gallery. But what makes the latter art rather than graffiti, amongst other things, is the fact that such works are one-offs for particular consumption and exchange, rather than throw-ups that might appear anywhere, be repeated again and again . . . be painted over. The moment at which graffiti stop being graffiti (and become, rather portraits of graffiti) is suggestive of how the city gets signified. Pacified, graffiti art brings the street inside, but still connotes something vaguely outlaw and definitively *urban*.

Tactics of graffiti take the idea of reading and writing urban space almost too literally. After all this is not simply a figurative question of 'writing' the city but a matter of writing *on* the city, remaking its material fabric as text. Graffiti artists embody the metaphors of reading and writing in a 'mobile language' of streets and sites (de Certeau 1984: 5). The practice of writing depends, first, on a good *reading* of space: finding a site, making a reconnoitre of the scene, establishing points of access and getaway, choosing the moment (Ewenstein 2004: 5). A good graffiti artist should also be a good escape artist. Inside spatial knowledge is critical for a tactics that alters space visually, and also disrupts spatial meanings and unsettles claims to ownership. De Certeau (1984: 37) could be describing the manoeuvres of the graffiti artist when he writes that the tactical 'operates in isolated actions, blow by blow. It takes advantage of "opportunities" . . . What it wins it cannot keep.' These are momentary conquests of space in which timing is everything – think of the peculiar bathos of the half-finished graffito. Tactics of graffiti, to borrow from Foucault (1986: 26), go to work in space by stealing 'slices in time'.

De Certeau compared his notion of tactics with Freud's account of wit, and graffiti realize this analogy very well. Like a good joke, graffiti work through 'verbal economy and condensation, double meanings and misinterpretations, displacements and alliteration, multiple uses of the same material' (de Certeau 1984: 39). The comparison of spatial tactics with linguistic expression goes beyond the literal example of graffiti, however: more generally, tactics work in space as tricks of rhetoric work on language. Extending the metaphor of spatial practice as a kind of writing or speaking, de Certeau offers two figures of rhetoric which can be mapped onto the tactical use of space. *Synecdoche*, first, occurs in language when a part is taken to stand for the whole – as when we refer to cars, say, as 'wheels'. It is at play in a spatial imaginary when 'the bicycle or the piece of furniture in a store window stands for a whole street or neighbourhood' (1984: 101). *Asyndeton*, meanwhile, refers to the omission of terms that usually begin or connect sentences; it skips over these linking and composing bits of language. In a spatial context, it is as if 'every walk constantly leaps, or skips like a child, hopping on one foot' from place to fragmentary place.

The grammar of movement: skateboarding as spatial tactics

De Certeau's translations between the verbal and the pedestrian do not always work. The embodied quality of moving through the city, for one, is not entirely captured as a 'rhetoric of walking' (1984: 100), much less the idea that wrong turns can be more dangerous than slips of the tongue. Writing about walking as a kind of speaking is in a circular and very obvious way to privilege language as a form of expression and a mode of practice. De Certeau is caught here in the bind of writing about something that he says evades representation. More simply, if you are writing about doing something, you're usually not doing it. But some of these translations – between language and spatial practice – are very suggestive, including what he does with the recondite figures of *synecdoche* and *asyndeton*. These two concepts refer to the ways, in language, that we magnify parts to stand in for wholes, or hiccup over the rules of composition that keep sentences in order. Translated into space, they point to how you can distort perspective, telescope and foreshorten distances, put together different bits and pieces, skip across boundaries and gaps, play with relationships and juxtapositions.

The idea of synecdoche relates to the ways people remember or imagine space. In memories of places that have been left behind or transformed over time, certain parts (the bicycle in the shop window, the fragmentary memories of childhood) stand in for a whole that may no longer exist. This recalls Benjamin's evocation of different cities as 'here a piece of balustrade, there a tree-top whose bare branches criss-cross a gas lamp, or a gable wall, or a lamp-post with a life-buoy bearing the name of the town' (Benjamin 1985b: 250). It also touches on Lynch's studies in 'imageability', the ways in which people draw their cognitive maps of the city around certain landmarks, whether natural, official or highly personal. As de Certeau (1984: 101) has it, synecdoche 'replaces totalities by fragments', it magnifies details in the place of wholes. It gets things out of proportion as an aid to memory or to familiarity.

Asyndeton works differently. It has less to do with how we symbolize space than with the improvised ways we put it together in practice. It cuts up and skips over spaces, disrupting order and making odd connections. It leaves bits out. It is the shrewd shortcut or the illicit exit. This is a wonderful idea for thinking about the 'grammar' of movement, but it is not immediately clear how it actually works in terms of spatial practice. Not stepping on the cracks in the pavement can seem a kind of escape, maybe, but also a variety of neurosis. De Certeau's notion of opening 'gaps in the spatial continuum' might amount to little more than small subversions en route to the subway (cutting across the park or going over a fence), the minor tactics of jumping the bus queue.

A more suggestive way of imagining a cut-up tactics of space is in the urban subcultures of skateboarders or rollerbladers (see Borden 2001). Each of these involves a tactical use of space, appropriating streets, subways, concourses or bridges for unofficial and inventive practices. The meaning of space is altered as its use is changed, especially as functional spaces (car parks, underpasses) become sites of pleasure, dead spaces are turned into places of expression. Skaters have the knack of taking the blankest spaces, the most mundane features, and making them a stage. In the dank underspaces created by modernist public architecture on the South Bank in London, on the bare pavement over the Bastille metro station in Paris, in empty swimming pools in Los Angeles or parched storm water drains in Melbourne, skateboarding is tactical in poaching sites for uses other than those they were intended for. In doing so, it disrupts any 'proper' logic of function, of transit or bare rationality. These wily uses of space are, surely, 'clever tricks of the "weak" within the order established by the "strong", an art of putting one over on the adversary on his own turf' (Certeau 1984: 40).

Moreover, these are tactical claims to space made through the body. While graffiti leave the *traces* of bodily gestures in space, skating has everything to do with the movement of the body in space and time. It involves a haptical experience of place that disrupts visual order – distorting levels, making unlikely connections, playing with speed and with direction. Skaters, Borden (2000: 227) suggests, reconfigure space as they 'make their own edit of discontinuous building elements and spaces', turning up into down, walls into floors, skirting or jumping obstacles (seating, bollards, kerbs, stairs) that are precisely meant to conduct, impede or direct one's movement. This tactics of space is analogous to the play of asyndeton in language as de Certeau describes it (1984: 101), in that it 'cuts out: it undoes continuity and undercuts its plausibility'. It composes space, like an improvised sentence, in terms of fragments, jumps and deliberate misuses.

Skating, like graffiti, puts into question not only the function of spaces but their ownership. The spatial tactics of the spray can or the skateboard deploy a 'creativity as persistent as it is subtle, tireless, ready for every opportunity, scattered over the terrain of the dominant order and foreign to the rules laid down and imposed by a rationality founded on established rights and property' (de Certeau 1984: 38). Claims are made in taking space for one's own use, creating an 'other space' in which subcultural identities are declared and enacted. Such practices can appear as threatening to those everyday users (older, less agile, simply on their way to work) who then become 'outsiders' in relation to spaces that have been appropriated, inverted and remade. There is something fugitive in skateboarding – suggested by its speed, as well as by its illicit and sometimes illegal use of space – but there is also something possessive. It can be hard, simply, for other users to negotiate the sites occupied by skaters, unless they can read for themselves the vectors that are being opened up across space. In challenging official lines of exclusion drawn around urban spaces, skateboarding asserts alternative but still exclusive claims over the use of certain sites. '[S]katers test the boundaries of the urban environment, using its elements in ways neither practised nor understood by others' (Borden 2000: 227–8), articulating a contrary spatial knowledge and expert bodily practice that shades between heroism and deviance. Skateboarding in this sense represents a marginal tactics of space not only in terms of the liminal spaces it carves out but in the illicit status of the practice itself. What appears as a creative spatial practice – like graffiti – is rationalized and policed in terms of trespass, public order and criminal damage (see Stratford 2002). As with graffiti, the spatial tactics of skateboarding slides between 'crime and art' (Stewart 1988; see also Ferrell 1996). Both offer rich examples of Certeau's conception of spatial tactics, but they also show up the limits to this idea. While subcultural practices, and the less visible everyday practices of ordinary urban users, may open up sites of distraction and dissent, they remain after all subject to the strategies of state and capital in the ordering of urban space. In terms of the way power plays in the city, subcultural tactics can reduce to little more than the 'power to pose' (Hebdige 1988: 18).

Conclusion

In his 1925 essay on the city Robert Park wrote of the way that distinctive 'moral regions' formed in urban space. These were places of encounter between those who shared certain tastes, temperaments or appetites (for vice, politics, art, sport or whatever). Marked out from the regular order of space, they were sites in which 'a divergent moral code prevails', one which was not always obvious to the uninitiated. He writes, more dramatically, of 'detached milieus in which vagrant and suppressed impulses, passions, and ideals emancipate themselves from the moral order'; of untamed zones in the city which are given over to unusual or illicit desires or practices (Park 1967a: 45). The map of moral regions in the city, then, might extend from the racetrack to the gym or the opera house, from the cruising ground to the terrain of various 'scenes', the divided turf of gang rivalry to the geography of drugs. Spaces of otherness are marbled through the surface of the modern city. One might say that cities enclose any number of heterotopias – 'other spaces' which put into place their own order of things.

Such spaces are not simply given by the design of urban forms, but are created through practice. Barthes's notion of writing and speaking the city points to an inventive engagement with urban spaces that can be put together in different ways. It is echoed in Georges Perec's conception of space as 'a form of writing, a *geography* of which we had forgotten that we ourselves are the authors' (1999: 79). The semiotics of the city, like the idea of spatial tactics, plays on the dual nature of urban forms as at once concrete, structural and structuring, and yet also plastic, unfinished, tricky. Tactical interventions can unsettle and disorder space. We might think, for instance, of such tactics as culture jamming or flash mobbing as deliberate moves on the conventional order of everyday space. Posting faked bills on walls and billboards (a favourite tactic of culture jamming) works through sly insertions into the visual spectacle of the city. It plays with Benjamin's distinction between the commodified walls of the advertisers and the politicized surfaces of graffiti, as the viewer is uncertain whether they are seeing a real ad for a real product, a counterfeit ad for a real product, or a complete fake. Of course, they may not even notice the tactical phoney in the gallery of fetish images which surrounds them in the urban scene, but that is all part of the game. Flash mobbing, too, queers the normal run of urban space with sudden and simple acts. A crowd gathers for a quick burst of applause at Grand Central in New York, or stands in silence at Sydney's Central Station, and just as suddenly dissolves. They could be any of a number of things – a performance or a tourist group, a demonstration or a queue (it's not so weird for throngs of people to stand in silence in a railway station, looking at the departure boards) – but in fact they are nothing more than the act itself. The people waiting on the platform are not, actually, waiting at all. These minor gambits possess and alter space in ways which can make the most mundane bits of the city strange.

Under the paving-stones, the beach. Some thirty-five years after the slogan was coined the City of Paris – 'the proprietary powers', as de Certeau (1984: 37) might have put it – laid out a beach on the quays of Paris for the summer.

This official (although not entirely un-erotic) 'place of pleasure' shows how easily co-opted gestures of spatial subversion can be. And it didn't, in any case, turn out to be much of a beach. There is always a fine line to be taken between the wide-eyed celebration of ordinary practices and the downbeat dismissal of docile bodies in space. Urban life is not, sadly, one big flash mob – waiting for a bus is generally only 'play' when you're not really waiting for a bus (see Hutchinson 2000). Yet it still seems right to speak of users, borrowing from Foucault (1986: 22), as 'determined inhabitants of space', whose paths are not always predictable and whose pleasures are not always visible. The pathos of de Certeau's (1984: v) 'common hero' or 'anonymous hero' in the city will not persuade everyone. But, then, how you read him will have something to do with the kinds of urban heroes you expect, and with your own versions of escape.

Conclusion

This is what a city is, bits and pieces.

J. Jacobs, *The Death and Life of Great American Cities*

The preceding chapters have explored urban social forms in relation to critical themes in social analysis – community, difference, politics and public space, class and capital, gender, sexuality and subjectivity. None of these issues are exclusively urban, but my argument has been that cities provide important contexts for thinking about how these social relations are constituted and reproduced. Cities also tend to emphasize the complex ways in which these factors cross-cut each other, the extent to which the carving out of spaces of urban community is underpinned by logics of class and race, or how the subjective experience of the city is conditioned by issues of gender or sexuality. It has not been my intention to give precedence either to spatial forms or to social relations in examining the city as a site of sociation, but rather to explore how the spatial and the social shape each other – how spatial relations, to reiterate Simmel's (2004: 73) point, are both the condition for, and the symbol of, social relations.

Does this mean, though, that the city does not figure as a distinctive or unified space in its own right, but rather merely as 'bits and pieces' of space, sociality and built form? As de Certeau stated, the city – viewed from above – appears as a coherent and a governable field. The view from below, however, only ever provides partial sightlines and situated knowledge (see also Thrift 2000). The question of whether 'the city' constituted a real theoretical and analytical object animated debates in urban sociology in the 1970s and 1980s (see Castells 1977; Logan and Molotch 1987; Saunders 1995). It was questionable whether any social processes could be identified which were typically or solely 'urban', particularly given the way that modern logics of capital accumulation and rationalization tended to homogenize space across any conventional urban – rural divide. These are important arguments and in their own terms they are hard to contest, but they also tend to dismiss as a kind of ideological 'common sense' the categories which have structured urban social analysis – such as community, neighbourhood or diversity – as well as underplaying the meanings that different spaces have for social actors, the modes of consciousness and related practices that constitute urbanism as a way of life.

More recent arguments put the coherence of the city into question not in terms of logics of rationalization or capitalist development, but in terms of a more open system of socio-spatial networks and connectivity (see Amin and Thrift 2002; Castells 1989, 1996; Graham and Marvin 2001; Smith, M. P. 2001; Thrift 2000). In a speeded-up and wired world, urban space appears more 'porous', urban agents (whether people, technical actors or symbolic forms) more mobile. Cities, like the social actors moving through them, do not stand still as objects of study. Such accounts tend to divide between those which stress a macro-level analysis, in which networks and flows operate beyond the grasp and the control of ordinary social actors (Castells 1989, 1996), and those which emphasize questions of practice, the 'performative' aspects of actors' engagement with urban space (Amin and Thrift 2002; Thrift 2000).

This is not simply to rehearse the structure–agency split which has vexed sociological thinking throughout its development. But it is to point to the problems of scale which confront urban social analysis, the gap between the city as a kind of 'machine' for organizing social life and the ways in which subjects make space for themselves in the city. This problematic is especially well put in Michel de Certeau's work, with its reminder that people live in cities as *local* spaces composed out of routine practices and private connections, and of the incompleteness of schemes to know and to order urban space. Amin and Thrift (2002: 4) are right to caution against 'a romanticism of the everyday and of action for itself', but it is also too easy to suggest that the perceptual experience of the city sketched by Benjamin or the ordinary diversions detailed by de Certeau are merely the preserve of the well-protected or the better-off – as if only the relatively privileged get to have a subjective life in the city. To be 'lost' in the city, as Benjamin put it, will only be a source of pleasure when one has the certainty of being found; just as Barthes's relish in the chance to 'play the other' works rather differently as a kind of urban erotic game than as an index of the stark divisions and discriminations that can disfigure urban space. The freedoms of the city are uneven and insecure. The poor or the socially marginal, women and sexual minorities, racial, ethnic and cultural minorities may have less room for manoeuvre in the city, more limited command over the use and the meanings of urban space. At the same time, cities have provided critical sites for challenging structures of social, sexual and racial inequality. Nor do cities simply reproduce – uniformly, always and everywhere – relations of social power or contours of social injustice. The heterogeneity that is typical of city life also provides sites of encounter and local spaces of solidarity, the refuge of privacy and common claims to publicity. A primary challenge for urban social analysis is to hold in balance the larger social and economic processes that shape cities with the 'micro-networks of social action that people create, move in, and act upon in their daily lives' (Smith 2001: 6). Within the 'cramped spaces' afforded by dominant social, economic and political arrangements, in the 'little territories of the everyday', these minor urban practices 'seek to engender a small reworking of their own spaces of action' (Rose 1999: 280).

Not all of this will be visible. De Certeau's and Benjamin's emphasis on the illegible or non-rational nature of how subjects encounter the city has been taken up in recent approaches to the 'non-representational' aspects of urban life. Subjects engage with and act upon urban space in ways which do not always lend themselves to narrative or representation. Social action in the city is largely composed of the kinds of 'embodied non-cognitive activity which is the mainstay of how we go on' (Thrift 2000: 234). Language – even the words running through the commentary or conversation in your own head – moves only slowly to capture the mess of perceptions, unthinking reactions and routine gestures that steer actors through space. The discussions developed above in this sense have traced a movement from programmatic attempts to make the modern city legible, to place people within it and track their movements across it, to accounts which suggest that something always escapes efforts to map urban space – just as it does from projects to engineer or control it. This is not intended to mean that more subjective approaches should trump objective forms of analysis, but that cities will appear differently as socio-spatial facts than as sites of experience.

The relation between the stubborn materiality of urban forms and the subjective experience of urban space touches very clearly on the notion that cities and their problems are both real and constructed. In thinking, then, about the senses in which urban spaces are produced, it is necessary to work on different levels: to think about systematic patterns of division and segregation in modern cities; and to think about the way that culture, identity and territory are imagined in urban sites. Of course, these two categories leak into each other – 'imagined' spaces are realized in concrete forms and embedded in social practices. In considering how urban space is socially produced and reproduced, we are concerned with the ways that spatial arrangements and social action condition each other. But we are also concerned with the elusive or minor ways that social actors make space for themselves, to their own fit if not exactly to their own design. Maps of social and economic division, after all, do not say it all about the territory of everyday life.

Bibliography

Abel-Smith, P. and Townsend, P. (1965) *The Poorest of the Poor*. London: Bell.

Abrahamson, M. (1996) *Urban Enclaves: Identity and Place in America*. New York: St Martin's Press.

Adler, S. and Brenner, J. (1992) 'Gender and space: lesbians and gay men in the city', *International Journal of Urban and Regional Research* 16/1: 24–34.

Adorno, T. (1979) *Aesthetics and Politics*. London: New Left Books.

Ahmed, S. and Fortier, A.-M. (2003) 'Re-imagining communities', *International Journal of Cultural Studies* 6/3: 251–9.

Ainley, R. (1998) 'Watching the detectors: control and the panopticon', in R. Ainley (ed.) *New Frontiers of Space, Bodies and Gender*. London and New York: Routledge, pp. 88–100.

Amin, A. and Thrift, N. (2002) *Cities: Reimagining the Urban*. Cambridge: Polity.

Amin, A., Massey, D. and Thrift, N. (2000) *Cities for the Many Not the Few*. Bristol: Policy Press.

Anderson, E. (1990) *Streetwise: Race, Class and Change in an Urban Community*. Chicago: University of Chicago Press.

Anderson, E. (1999) *Code of the Street: Decency, Violence and the Moral Life of the Inner City*. New York and London: W. W. Norton.

Ankum, K. von. (ed.) (1997) *Women in the Metropolis: Gender and Modernity in Modern Culture*. Berkeley: University of California Press.

Antonopoulos, G. A. (2003) 'Ethnic and racial minorities and the police: a review of the literature', *Police Journal* 76/3: 222–45.

Atkinson, R. (2000) 'Measuring gentrification and displacement in central London', *Urban Studies* 37/1: 149–65.

Atkinson, R. and Moon, G. (1994) *Urban Policy in Britain: The City, the State and the Market*. Basingstoke: Macmillan.

Augé, M. (1995) *Non-Places: Introduction to the Anthropology of Supermodernity*. London: Verso.

Back, L. (2004) 'Inside out: racism, class and masculinity in the "inner city" and the English suburbs', in C. Jenks (ed.) *Urban Culture: Critical Concepts in Literary and Cultural Studies*. London and New York: Routledge, vol. III, pp. 118–37.

Back, L., Keith, M. and Solomos, J. (1999) 'Reading the writing on the walls: graffiti in the racialised city', in D. Slyden and R. Whillock (eds) *Soundbite Culture: The Death of Discourse in a Wired World*. London and Newbury Park: Sage, pp. 69–101.

Bailey, R. W. (1998) *Gay Politics, Urban Politics: Identity and Economics in the Urban Setting*. New York: Columbia University Press.

Bannister, J. and Fyfe, N. (2001) 'Introduction: fear and the city', *Urban Studies* 38/5–6: 807–13.

Barthes, R. (1997) 'Semiology and the urban', in N. Leach (ed.) *Rethinking Architecture: A Reader in Cultural Theory*. London and New York: Routledge, pp. 166–72.

Bartley, P. (2000) *Prostitution: Prevention and Reform in England, 1860–1914*. London and New York: Routledge.

151

Bassett, C. (2003) 'How many movements?' in M. Bull and L. Back (eds) *The Auditory Culture Reader*. Oxford and New York: Berg, pp. 343–55.

Bauman, Z. (1990) 'Effacing the face: on the social management of moral proximity', *Theory, Culture and Society* 7/1: 5–38.

Bauman, Z. (1999) *In Search of Politics*. Cambridge: Polity.

Bauman, Z. (2000) *Community: Seeking Safety in an Insecure World*. Cambridge: Polity.

Bell, D. (1991) 'Insignificant others: lesbian and gay geographies', *Area* 23/4: 323–9.

Bell, D. (1995a) 'Pleasure and danger: the paradoxical spaces of sexual citizenship', *Political Geography* 14/2: 139–53.

Bell, D. (1995b) 'Perverse dynamics, sexual citizenship and the transformation of intimacy', in D. Bell and G. Valentine (eds) *Mapping Desire: Geographies of Sexualities*. London and New York: Routledge, pp. 304–17.

Bell, D. (2001) 'Fragments for a queer city', in D. Bell, J. Binnie, R. Holliday, R. Longhurst and R. Peace (eds) *Pleasure Zones: Bodies, Cities, Spaces*. Syracuse, NY: Syracuse University Press, pp. 84–102.

Bell, D., Binnie, J., Cream, J. and Valentine, G. (1994) 'All hyped up and no place to go', *Gender, Place and Culture* 1/1: 31–47.

Bell, D. and Valentine, G. (eds) (1995a) *Mapping Desire: Geographies of Sexualities*. London and New York: Routledge.

Bell, D. and Valentine, G. (1995b) 'Introduction: orientations', in D. Bell and G. Valentine (eds) *Mapping Desire: Geographies of Sexualities*. London and New York: Routledge, pp. 1–27.

Benhabib, S. (ed.) (1996) *Democracy and Difference: Contesting the Boundaries of the Political*. Princeton, NJ: Princeton University Press.

Benjamin, W. (1977 [1928]) *The Origin of German Tragic Drama*. London: New Left Books.

Benjamin, W. (1983) *Charles Baudelaire: A Lyric Poet in the Era of High Capitalism*. London: Verso.

Benjamin, W. (1985a [1925–6]) 'One way street', in *One Way Street and Other Writings*. London: Verso, pp. 45–104.

Benjamin, W. (1985b [1931]) 'A small history of photography', in *One Way Street and Other Writings*. London: Verso, pp. 240–57.

Benjamin, W. (1986a [1916]) 'On language as such and the language of man', in P. Demetz (ed.) *Reflections: Essays, Aphorisms, Autobiographical Writings*. New York: Schocken, pp. 314–32.

Benjamin, W. (1986b [1927]) 'Moscow', in P. Demetz (ed.) *Reflections: Essays, Aphorisms, Autobiographical Writings*. New York: Schocken, pp. 97–130.

Benjamin, W. (1986c [1928]) 'Marseilles', in P. Demetz (ed.) *Reflections: Essays, Aphorisms, Autobiographical Writings*. New York: Schocken, pp. 131–6.

Benjamin, W. (1986d [1928]) 'Hashish in Marseilles', in P. Demetz (ed.) *Reflections: Essays, Aphorisms, Autobiographical Writings*. New York: Schocken, pp. 137–45.

Benjamin, W. (1986e [1929]) 'Surrealism: the last snapshot of the European intelligentsia', in P. Demetz (ed.) *Reflections: Essays, Aphorisms, Autobiographical Writings*. New York: Schocken, pp. 177–92.

Benjamin, W. (1986f [1932]) 'A Berlin chronicle', in P. Demetz (ed.) *Reflections: Essays, Aphorisms, Autobiographical Writings*. New York: Schocken, pp. 3–60.

Benjamin, W. (1986g [1935]) 'Paris, capital of the nineteenth century', in P. Demetz (ed.) *Reflections: Essays, Aphorisms, Autobiographical Writings*. New York: Schocken, pp. 146–62.

Benjamin, W. (1999) *The Arcades Project*. Cambridge, MA: Harvard University Press.

Benjamin, W. and Lacis, A. (1986 [1924]) 'Naples', in P. Demetz (ed.) *Reflections: Essays, Aphorisms, Autobiographical Writings*. New York: Schocken, pp. 163–73.

Berry, B. L. and Kasarda, J. D. (1977) *Contemporary Urban Ecology*. New York: Macmillan.

Bhabha, H. (1994) *The Location of Culture*. London and New York: Routledge.

Binnie, J. (1995) 'Trading places: consumption, sexuality and the production of queer space', in D. Bell and G. Valentine (eds) *Mapping Desire: Geographies of Sexualities*. London and New York: Routledge, pp. 182–99.

Binnie, J. and Skeggs, B. (2004) 'Cosmopolitan knowledge and the production and consumption of sexualized space: Manchester's "Gay Village" ', *The Sociological Review* 52/1: 39–61.

Blackman, T. (1995) *Urban Policy in Britain*. London and New York: Routledge.

Blakeley, E. J. and Snyder, M. G. (1997) *Fortress America: Gated Communities in the United States*. Washington, DC: Brookings Institute.

Blokland, T. and Savage, M. (2001) 'Networks, class and place', *International Journal of Urban and Regional Studies* 25/2: 222–5.

Body-Gendrot, S. (2000) *The Social Control of Cities? A Comparative Perspective*. Oxford: Blackwell.

Bondi, L. (1991) 'Gender divisions and gentrification: a critique', *Transactions of the Institute of British Geographers* 16/2: 190–8.

Bondi, L. (1999) 'Gender, class and gentrification: enriching the debates', *Environment and Planning D: Society and Space* 17/3: 261–82.

Bondi, L. and Christie, H. (2000) 'Working out the urban: gender relations and the city', in G. Bridge and S. Watson (eds) *A Companion to the City*. Oxford: Blackwell, pp. 292–306.

Borden, I. (2000) 'Skateboarding', in S. Pile and N. Thrift (eds) *City, A–Z*. London and New York: Routledge, pp. 226–8.

Borden, I. (2001) *Skateboarding, Space and the City: Architecture and the Body*. Oxford and New York: Berg.

Bourdieu, P. (1977) *Outline of a Theory of Practice*. Cambridge: Cambridge University Press.

Bourdieu, P. (1990) *The Logic of Practice*. Cambridge: Polity.

Bouthillette, A.-M. (1994) 'Gentrification by gay male communities: a case study of Toronto's Cabbagetown', in S. Whittle (ed.) *The Margins of the City*. Aldershot: Arena, pp. 65–83.

Bowling, B. (1999) *Violent Racism: Victimisation, Policing and Social Context*. Oxford: Oxford University Press.

Boys, J. (1998) 'Beyond maps and metaphors? Re-thinking the relationships between architecture and gender', in R. Ainley (ed.) *New Frontiers of Space, Bodies and Gender*. London and New York: Routledge, pp. 203–17.

Bridge, G. (2005) *Reason in the City of Difference*. London and New York: Routledge.

Brown, M. (1995) 'Sex, scale and the new urban politics: HIV-prevention strategies from Yaletown, Vancouver', in D. Bell and G. Valentine (eds) *Mapping Desire: Geographies of Sexualities*. London and New York: Routledge, pp. 245–63.

Brown, M. P. (2000) *Closet Space: Geographies of Metaphor from the Body to the Globe*. London and New York: Routledge.

Bull, M. (2000) *Sounding Out the City: Personal Stereos and the Management of Everyday Life*. Oxford and New York: Berg.

Burgess. E. W. (1967 [1925]) 'The growth of the city: an introduction to a research project', in R. E. Park et al. (eds) *The City*. Chicago: University of Chicago Press, pp. 47–62.

Burgess, J. (1998) 'But is it worth taking the risk? How women negotiate access to urban woodlands: a case study', in R. Ainley (ed.) *New Frontiers of Space, Bodies and Gender*. London and New York: Routledge, pp. 115–28.

Burskik, R. J. (1988) 'Social disorganization and theories of crime and delinquency: problems and prospects', *Criminology* 26/4: 519–51.

Burskik, R. J. and Grasmick, H. G. (1993) *Neighborhoods and Crime: The Dimensions of Effective Community Control*. New York: Lexington Books.

Butler, T. (1997) *Gentrification and the Middle Classes*. Aldershot: Ashgate.

Butler, T. and Robson, G. (2001) 'Social capital, gentrification and neighbourhood change in London: a comparison of three South London neighbourhoods', *Urban Studies* 38/12: 2145–62.

Caldeira, T. (1996) 'Fortified enclaves: the new urban segregation', *Public Culture* 8/2: 329–54.

Caldeira, T. (2000) *City of Walls: Crime, Segregation and Citizenship in São Paulo*. Berkeley, CA: University of California Press.

Canavan, P. (1988) 'The gay community at Jacob Riis Park', in V. Boggs, G. Handel and S. Fava (eds) *The Apple Sliced: Sociological Studies of New York City*. Prospect Heights, IL: Waveland, pp. 67–82.

Carpenter, J. and Lees, L. (1995) 'Gentrification in New York, London and Paris: an international comparison', *International Journal of Urban and Regional Research* 19/2: 286–303.

Carter, A. (1992) *Expletives Deleted*. London: Chatto and Windus.

Casey, E. S. (1996) 'How to get from space to place in a fairly short stretch of time: phenomenological prolegomena', in S. Feld and K. H. Basso (eds) *Senses of Place*. Santa Fe, NM: School of American Research Press, pp. 13–52.

Castells, M. (1977) *The Urban Question*. London: Arnold.

Castells, M. (1983) *The City and the Grassroots: A Cross-Cultural Theory of Urban Social Movements*. Berkeley, CA: University of California Press.

Castells, M. (1989) *The Informational City*. Oxford: Blackwell.

Castells, M. (1996) *The Rise of the Network Society*. Oxford: Blackwell.

Castells, M. (2004) *The Power of Identity*. Second edition. Oxford: Blackwell.

Castells, M. and Murphy, K. (1982) 'Cultural identity and urban structure: the spatial organization of San Francisco's gay community', in N. Fainstein and S. Fainstein (eds) *Urban Policy under Capitalism*. Los Angeles: Sage, pp. 237–59.

Caulfield, J. (1994) *City Form and Everyday Life: Toronto's Gentrification and Critical Social Practice*. Toronto: University of Toronto Press.

Chambliss, W. J. (1994) 'Policing the ghetto underclass: the politics of law and law enforcement', *Social Problems* 41/2: 177–94.

Chauncey, G. (1995) *Gay New York: Gender, Urban Culture, and the Making of the Gay Male World, 1890–1940*. London: Flamingo.

Chiricos, T., Hogan, M. and Gertz, M. (1997) 'Racial composition of neighbourhood and fear of crime', *Criminology* 35/1: 107–31.

Christopherson, S. (1994) 'The fortress city: privatized spaces, consumer citizenship', in A. Amin (ed.) *Post-Fordism: A Reader*. Oxford: Blackwell, pp. 409–27.

Clark, K. B. (1989) *Dark Ghetto: Dilemmas of Social Power*. Second edition. Hanover, NH: Wesleyan University Press.

Cohen, A. (1985) *The Symbolic Construction of Community*. London and New York: Routledge.

Cohen, A. (1993) *Masquerade Politics: Explorations in the Structure of Urban Cultural Movements*. Oxford: Berg.

Conrad, P. (2000) *The Hitchcock Murders*. London: Faber.

Crang, P. (2000) 'Public space, urban space and electronic space', *Urban Studies* 37/2: 301–17.

Cresswell, T. (1992) 'The crucial "where" of graffiti: a geographical analysis of reactions to graffiti in New York', *Environment and Planning D: Society and Space* 10/3: 329–44.

Cunneen, C. (1999) 'Zero Tolerance policing and the experience of New York City', *Current Issues in Criminal Justice* 10/3: 299–313.

Dahl, R. (1961) *Who Governs?* New Haven, CT: Yale University Press.

Davis, M. (1990) *City of Quartz: Excavating the Future in Los Angeles.* London: Verso.

Davis, M. (1998) *Ecology of Fear: Los Angeles and the Imagination of Disaster.* New York: Metropolitan.

Davis, T. (1995) 'The diversity of queer politics and the redefinition of sexual identity and community in urban spaces', in D. Bell and G. Valentine (eds) *Mapping Desire: Geographies of Sexualities.* London and New York: Routledge, pp. 284–303.

Day, K. (1999) 'Embassies and sanctuaries: women's experience of race and fear in public space', *Environment and Planning D: Society and Space* 17/3: 307–28.

De Certeau, M. (1984) *The Practice of Everyday Life.* Berkeley, CA: University of California Press.

Demetz, P. (1986) 'Introduction', in P. Demetz (ed.) *Reflections: Essays, Aphorisms, Autobiographical Writings.* New York: Schocken, pp. vii–xiii.

D'Emilio, J. (1983) *Sexual Politics, Sexual Communities: The Making of a Homosexual Minority in the United States, 1940–1970.* Chicago: University of Chicago Press.

Devine, J. A. and Wright, J. D. (1993) *The Greatest of Evils: Urban Poverty and the American Underclass.* New York: Aldine de Gruyter.

Domosh, M. (1999) 'Sexing feminist geographies', *Progress in Human Geography* 23/3: 429–36.

Donald, J. (1992) 'Metropolis: the city as text', in R. Bocock and K. Thompson (eds) *Social and Cultural Forms of Modernity.* Cambridge: Polity, pp. 417–61.

Dowling, R. (1998) 'Suburban stories, gendered lives: thinking through difference', in R. Fincher and J. M. Jacobs (eds) *Cities of Difference.* New York: Guilford Press, pp. 69–88.

Duncan, N. (ed.) (1996) *BodySpace: Destabilizing Geographies of Gender and Sexuality.* London and New York: Routledge.

Dunleavy, P. (1980) *Urban Political Analysis.* London: Macmillan.

Durning, L. and Wigley, R. (eds) (2000) *Gender and Architecture.* Chichester: Wiley.

Eagleton, T. (1981) *Walter Benjamin, or Towards a Revolutionary Criticism.* London: Verso.

England, K. (1993) 'Suburban pink-collar ghettos: the spatial entrapment of women', *Annals of the Association of American Geographers* 83/2: 225–42.

Epstein Nord, D. (1995) *Walking the Victorian Streets: Women, Representation and the City.* Ithaca, NY: Cornell University Press.

Evans, D. J. (1995) *Crime and Policing: Spatial Approaches.* Aldershot: Avebury Press.

Ewenstein, B. (2004) *Spatial Stories of Graffiti.* London: Goldsmiths College.

Fainstein, N. and Fainstein, S. (eds) (1982) *Urban Policy under Capitalism.* Los Angeles: Sage.

Fanon, F. (1986) *Black Skin, White Masks.* London: Pluto.

Ferraro, K. F. (1996) 'Women's fear of victimization: shadow of sexual assault?' *Social Forces* 75/2: 667–90.

Ferrell, J. (1996) *Crimes of Style: Urban Graffiti and the Politics of Criminality.* Boston: Northeastern University Press.

Fischer, C. S (1982) *To Dwell Among Friends: Personal Networks in Town and City.* Chicago: University of Chicago Press.

Fiske, J. (1998) 'Surveilling the city: whiteness, the black man and democratic totalitarianism', *Theory, Culture and Society* 15/2: 67–88.

Fleischacker, S. (1998) 'Insignificant communities', in A. Gutmann (ed.) *Freedom of Association.* Princeton, NJ: Princeton University Press, pp. 273–313.

Forest, B. (1995) 'West Hollywood as symbol: the significance of place in the construction of gay identity', *Environment and Planning D: Society and Space* 13/2: 133–57.

Forrest, D. (1994) ' "We're here, we're queer, and we're not going shopping": changing gay male identities in contemporary Britain', in A. Cornwall and N. Lindisfarne (eds) *Dislocating Masculinity: Comparative Ethnographies.* London and New York: Routledge, pp. 97–110.

Forrest, R. and Kearns, A. (2001) 'Social cohesion, social capital and the neighbourhood', *Urban Studies* 38/12: 2125–43.

Foster, J. (1997) *Docklands: Cultures in Conflict, Worlds in Collision*. London: UCL Press.

Foucault, M. (1977) 'Panopticism', in *Discipline and Punish*. London: Penguin, pp. 195–228.

Foucault, M. (1986) 'Of other spaces', *Diacritics* 16/1: 22–7.

Fraser, N. (1991) 'Rethinking the public sphere: a contribution to the critique of actually existing democracy', in C. Calhoun (ed.) *Habermas and the Public Sphere*. Cambridge, MA: MIT Press, pp. 109–42.

Friedberg, A. (1993) 'The mobilized and virtual gaze in modernity: *flâneur/flâneuse*', in *Window Shopping: Cinema and the Postmodern*. Berkeley, CA: University of California Press, pp. 15–38.

Fukuyama, F. (1995) *Trust: The Social Virtues and the Creation of Prosperity*. London: Penguin.

Fyfe, N. and Bannister, J. (1996) 'City watching: closed circuit television surveillance in public spaces', *Area* 28/1: 37–46.

Gardner, C. B. (1995) *Passing By: Gender and Public Harassment*. Berkeley, CA: University of California Press.

Gans, H. T. (1982 [1962]) *The Urban Villagers: Group and Class in the Life of Italian-Americans*. Revised edition. New York: Free Press.

Gans, H. T. (1996) *The War Against the Poor: The Underclass and Antipoverty Policy*. New York: Basic Books.

Geltmaker, T. (1992) 'The queer nation acts up: health care, politics, and sexual politics in the city of angels', *Environment and Planning D: Society and Space* 10/6: 609–50.

Giddens, A. (1991) *Modernity and Self-Identity*. Cambridge: Polity.

Giddens, A. (2000) *The Third Way and its Critics*. Cambridge: Polity.

Gilchrist, E., Bannister, J., Ditton, J. and Farrall, S. (1998) 'Women and the "fear of crime": challenging the accepted stereotype', *British Journal of Criminology* 38/2: 283–98.

Gilfoyle, T. J. (1992) *City of Eros: New York City, Prostitution and the Commercialization of Sex, 1790–1920*. New York: W. W. Norton.

Gilroy, P. (2003) 'Between the blues and the blues dance: some soundscapes of the Black Atlantic', in M. Bull and L. Back (eds) *A Reader in Auditory Culture*. Oxford and New York: Berg, pp. 381–95.

Ginzburg, C. (1990) 'Clues: roots of an evidential paradigm', in *Myths, Emblems, Clues*. London: Hutchinson Radius, pp. 96–125.

Goffman, E. (1963) *Behavior in Public Places*. New York: Free Press.

Goffman, E. (1973) *Relations in Public*. New York: Harper and Row.

Goldberg, D. T. (1993) ' "Polluting the body politic": racist discourse and urban location', in M. Cross and M. Keith (eds) *Racism, the City and the State*. London and New York: Routledge, pp. 45–60.

Goodey, J. (1997) 'Boys don't cry: masculinity, fear of crime and fearlessness', *British Journal of Sociology* 37/3: 401–17.

Gornick, V. (1996) *Approaching Eye Level*. Boston: Beacon Press.

Graham, S. and Marvin, S. (2001) *Splintering Urbanism: Networked Infrastructures, Technological Mobilities, and the Urban Condition*. London and New York: Routledge.

Granovetter, M. (1973) 'The strength of weak ties', *American Journal of Sociology* 78/6: 1360–80.

Green, B. (1994) 'From visible *flâneuse* to spectacular suffragette? The prison, the street, and the sites of suffrage', *Discourse* 17/2: 67–97.

Greene, J. A. (1999) 'Zero Tolerance: a case study of police policies and practices in New York City', *Crime and Delinquency* 45/2: 171–87.

Grosz, E. (1992) 'Bodies-cities', in B. Colomina (ed.) *Sexuality and Space*. Princeton, NJ: Princeton Architectural Press, pp. 241–53.

Gufler, J. (ed.) (1997) *Cities in the Developing World: Issues, Theory, Politics*. Oxford: Oxford University Press.

Gutmann, A. (ed.) (1994) *Multiculturalism: Examining the Politics of Recognition*. Princeton, NJ: Princeton University Press.

Habermas, J. (1974) 'The public sphere: an encyclopedia article', *New German Critique* 1/3: 49–55.

Habermas, J. (1989) *The Structural Transformation of the Public Sphere*. Cambridge, MA: MIT Press.

Halpern, R. (1995) *Rebuilding the Inner City: A History of Initiatives to Address Poverty in the United States*. New York: Columbia University Press.

Harvey, D. (1973) *Social Justice and the City*. London: Edward Arnold.

Harvey, D. (1989) *The Condition of Postmodernity*. Oxford: Basil Blackwell.

Harvey, D. (2003) *The New Imperialism*. Oxford: Oxford University Press.

Hawley, A. (1950) *Human Ecology: A Theory of Urban Structure*. New York: Ronald Press.

Hayden, D. (2000) 'What would a non-sexist city be like?' in R. T. Le Gates and F. Stout (eds) *The City Reader*. London and New York: Routledge, pp. 503–18.

Hayden, D. (2003) *Building Suburbia: Green Fields and Urban Growth*. New York: Pantheon.

Hebdige, D. (1988) 'Hiding in the light: youth surveillance and display', in *Hiding in the Light: On Images and the Things*. London and New York: Routledge, pp. 17–36.

Hemmings, C. (2002) *Bisexual Spaces*. London and New York: Routledge.

Herbert, S. (1997) *Policing Space: Territoriality and the Los Angeles Police Department*. Minneapolis: University of Minnesota Press.

Herek, G. M. and Berrill, K. T. (eds) (1992) *Hate Crimes: Confronting Violence against Lesbians and Gay Men*. London and Newbury Park, CA: Sage.

Herek, G. M., Corgan, J. C. and Gillis, J. R. (2002) 'Victim experiences in hate crimes based on sexual orientation', *Journal of Social Issues* 58/2: 319–39.

hooks, b. (1991) *Yearning: Race, Gender and Cultural Politics*. London: Turnaround.

Humphries, L. (1970) *Tearoom Trade: Impersonal Sex in Public Places*. Chicago: Aldine.

Hutchinson, S. (2000) 'Waiting for the bus', *Social Text* 18/2: 107–20.

Ingram, G., Bouthillette, A.-M. and Retter, Y. (1997) *Queers in Space*. Seattle: Bay Press.

Jackson, P. (1987) *Race and Racism: Essays in Social Geography*. London: Allen and Unwin.

Jacobs, J. (1964 [1961]) *The Death and Life of Great American Cities: The Failure of Town Planning*. Harmondsworth: Penguin.

Jacobs, J. M. (1998) 'Staging difference: aestheticization and the politics of difference in contemporary cities', in R. Fincher and J. M. Jacobs (eds) *Cities of Difference*. New York: Guilford Press, pp. 257–78.

Jargowsky, P. A. (1997) *Poverty and Place: Ghettos, Barrios and the American City*. New York: Russell Sage Foundation.

Jarman, N. and Tennant, A. (2003) *An Acceptable Prejudice? Homophobic Violence and Harassment in Northern Ireland*. Belfast: Institute for Conflict Research.

Jarvis, H., Pratt, A. C. and Wu, P. C.-C. (2001) *The Secret Life of Cities: The Social Reproduction of Everyday Life*. London: Prentice Hall.

Jencks, C. (1993) *Rethinking Social Policy: Race, Poverty and the Underclass*. New York: HarperCollins.

Jordan, T. and Lent, A. (1998) *Storming the Millennium: The New Politics of Change*. London: Lawrence and Wishart.

Judge, D., Stoker, G. and Wolman, H. (1995) *Theories of Urban Politics*. London and Newbury Park, CA: Sage.

Katz, M. (1989) *The Undeserving Poor.* New York: Pantheon Books.

Katz, M. (1993) *The Underclass Debate: The View from History.* Princeton, NJ: Princeton University Press.

Katznelson, I. (1981) *City Trenches.* New York: Pantheon.

Kearns, G. and Philo, C. (eds) (1993) *Selling Places: The City as Cultural Capital, Past and Present.* Oxford: Pergamon Press.

Keating, M. (1993) *Comparative Urban Politics: Power and the City in the United States, Canada, Britain and France.* Aldershot: Edward Elgar.

Keith, M. (1993) *Race, Riots and Policing.* London: UCL Press.

Keith, M. (2000) 'Identity and the spaces of authenticity', in L. Back and J. Solomos (eds) *Theories of Race and Racism: A Reader.* London and New York: Routledge, pp. 521–38.

Keith, M. (2005) *After the Cosmopolitan? Multicultural Cities and the Future of Racism.* London and New York: Routledge.

Keith, M. and Pile, S. (eds) (1993) *Place and the Politics of Identity.* London and New York: Routledge.

Keith, M. and Rogers, A. (eds) (1991) *Hollow Promises: Rhetoric and Reality in the Inner City.* London: Mansell.

Kitchin, R. (2002) 'Sexing the city: the sexual production of space in Belfast, Manchester and San Francisco', *City* 6/2: 205–18.

Kleinberg, B. (1995) *Urban America in Transformation: Perspectives on Urban Policy and Development.* London and Newbury Park, CA: Sage.

Knopp, L. (1987) 'Social theory, social movements and public policy: recent accomplishments of the gay and lesbian movements in Minneapolis, Minnesota', *International Journal of Urban and Regional Research* 11/2: 243–61.

Knopp, L. (1992) 'Sexuality and the spatial dynamics of capitalism', *Environment and Planning D: Society and Space* 10/6: 651–69.

Knopp, L. (1998) 'Sexuality and urban space: gay male identities, communities and cultures in the US, UK and Australia', in R. Fincher and J. M. Jacobs (eds) *Cities of Difference.* New York: Guilford, pp. 149–76.

Knox, P. L. and Taylor, P. (eds) (1995) *World Cities in a World System.* Cambridge: Cambridge University Press.

Koskela, H. (1997) 'Bold walks and breakings: women's spatial confidence versus fear of violence', *Gender, Place and Culture* 4/3: 301–14.

Koskela, H. and Pain, R. (2000) 'Revisiting fear and place: women's fear of attack and the built environment', *Geoforum* 31/2: 269–80.

Ladd, B. (1997) *The Ghosts of Berlin: Confronting German History in the Urban Landscape.* Chicago: University of Chicago Press.

Lane, J. and Meeker, J. W. (2000) 'Subcultural diversity and the fear of crime and gangs', *Crime and Delinquency* 46/4: 497–521.

Lapovsky Kennedy, E. and Davis, M. D. (1993) *Boots of Leather, Slippers of Gold: The History of a Lesbian Community.* London and New York: Routledge.

Larana, E., Johnston, H. and Gusfield, J. R. (eds) (1994) *New Social Movements: From Ideology to Identity*, Philadelphia, PA: Temple University Press.

Lash, S. and Urry, J. (1994) *Economies of Signs and Space.* London and Newbury Park, CA: Sage.

Lauria, M. and Knopp, L. (1985) 'Towards an analysis of the role of gay communities in the urban renaissance', *Urban Geography* 6/2: 152–69.

Lee, J. (2002) *Civility in the City: Blacks, Jews, and Koreans in Urban Areas.* Cambridge, MA: Harvard University Press.

Lefebvre, H. (1991 [1974]) *The Production of Space.* Oxford: Basil Blackwell.

Lewis, O. (1959) *Five Families: Mexican Case Studies in the Culture of Poverty.* New York: Basic Books.

Lewis, O. (1966) *La Vida: A Puerto Rican Family in the Culture of Poverty – San Juan and New York.* New York: Random House.

Lewis, O. (1996 [1966]) 'The culture of poverty', in R. T. Le Gates and F. Stout (eds) *The City Reader.* London and New York: Routledge, pp. 218–224.

Levinas, E. (1987) *Time and the Other and Additional Essays.* Pittsburgh, PA: Duquesne University Press.

Levine, M. (1979) 'Gay ghetto', *Journal of Homosexuality* 4/4: 363–77.

Ley, D. (1994) 'Gentrification and the politics of the new middle class', *Environment and Planning D: Society and Space* 12/1: 53–74.

Ley, D. (1996) *The New Middle Class and the Remaking of the Central City.* Oxford: Oxford University Press.

Lippard, L. (2000) 'Home in the weeds', in M. Miles and T. Hall (eds) *The City Cultures Reader.* London and New York: Routledge, pp. 269–76.

Little, J., Peake, L. and Richardson, P. (eds) (1988) *Women in Cities: Gender and the Urban Environment.* London: Macmillan.

Lofland, L. H. (1973) *A World of Strangers: Order and Action in Urban Public Space.* New York: Basic Books.

Lofland, L. H. (1998) *The Public Realm: Exploring the City's Quintessential Social Territory.* Hawthorne, NY: Aldine de Gruyter.

Logan, M. and Molotch, H. (1987) *Urban Fortunes: The Political Economy of Place.* Berkeley, CA: University of California Press.

Low, S. (2001) 'The edge and the center: gated communities and the discourse of urban fear', *American Anthropologist* 103/1: 45–59.

Low, S. (2003) *Behind the Gates: Life, Security and the Pursuit of Happiness in Fortress America.* London and New York: Routledge.

Lowe, S. (1986) *Urban Social Movements: The City after Castells.* London: Palgrave Macmillan.

Lynch, F. (1987) 'Non-ghetto gays: a sociological study of suburban homosexuals', *Journal of Homosexuality* 13/4: 13–42.

Lynch, K. (1960) *The Image of the City.* Cambridge, MA: MIT Press.

Lynch, K. (1972) *What Time is This Place?* Cambridge, MA: MIT Press.

Lyod, B. and Rowntree, L. (1978) 'Radical feminists and gay men in San Francisco: social space in dispersed communities', in D. Lanegran and R. Palm (eds) *An Invitation to Geography.* New York: McGraw-Hill, pp. 78–88.

MacGregor, S. and Pimlott, B. (1990) *Tackling the Inner Cities.* Oxford: Clarendon Press.

Marcuse, P. and van Kempen, R. (eds) (2002) *Of States and Cities: The Partitioning of Urban Space.* Oxford: Oxford University Press.

Mason, A. and Palmer, A. (1996) *Queer Bashing: A National Survey of Hate Crimes Against Lesbians and Gay Men.* London: Stonewall.

Mason, G. and Tomsen, S. (eds) (1997) *Homophobic Violence.* Annandale: Federation Press.

Massey, D. (1994) *Space, Place and Gender.* Cambridge: Polity.

Massey, D. S. and Denton, N. (1993) *American Apartheid: Segregation and the Making of an Underclass.* Cambridge, MA: Harvard University Press.

MATRIX (1984) *Making Space: Women and the Man-Made Environment.* London: Pluto.

Mayer, M. (1999) 'Urban movements and urban theory in the late twentieth century city', in R. A. Beauregard and S. Body-Gendrot (eds) *The Urban Moment: Cosmopolitan Essays on the Late Twentieth Century City.* London and Newbury Park, CA: Sage, pp. 209–38.

Mayer, M. (ed.) (2000) *Urban Movements in a Globalised World.* London and New York: Routledge.

McArdle, M. and Erzen, T. (eds) (2001) *Zero Tolerance: Quality of Life and the New Police Brutality in New York City*. New York: New York University Press.

McDowell, L. (1999a) 'In and out of place: bodies and embodiment', in *Gender, Identity and Place: Understanding Feminist Geographies*. Minneapolis: University of Minnesota Press, pp. 34–70.

McDowell, L. (1999b) 'In public: the street and spaces of pleasure', in *Gender, Identity and Place: Understanding Feminist Geographies*. Minneapolis: University of Minnesota Press, pp. 148–69.

McGarrell, E. F., Giacomazzi, A. L. and Thurman, Q. C. (1997) 'Neighbourhood disorder, integration and the fear of crime', *Justice Quarterly* 14/3: 479–500.

McKay, G. (ed.) (1998) *DiY Culture: Party and Protest in Nineties Britain*. London: Verso.

McKenzie, R. D. (1967 [1925]) 'The ecological approach to the study of the human community', in R. E. Park et al. (eds) *The City*. Chicago: University of Chicago Press, pp. 63–79.

McLaughlin, E. and Muncie, J. (1999) 'Walled cities: surveillance, regulation and segregation', in S. Pile, C. Brook and G. Mooney (eds) *Unruly Cities? Order/Disorder*. London and New York: Routledge, pp. 104–38.

Melucci, A. (1989) *Nomads of the Present: Social Movements and Individual Needs in Contemporary Society*. London: Hutchinson Radius.

Melucci, A. (1996) *Challenging Codes: Collective Action in the Information Age*. Cambridge: Cambridge University Press.

Mingeone, E. (ed.) (1996) *Urban Poverty and the 'Underclass'*. Oxford: Blackwell.

Mitchell, D. (1997) 'The annihilation of space by law: the roots and implications of anti-homeless laws in the United States', *Antipode* 29/3: 303–35.

Mitchell, D. (2003) *The Right to the City: Social Justice and the Right for Public Space*. New York: Guilford Press.

Mollenkopf, J. H. (1983) *The Contested City*. Princeton, NJ: Princeton University Press.

Mooney, G. (1999) 'Urban "disorders" ', in S. Pile, C. Brook and G. Mooney (eds) *Unruly Cities? Order/Disorder*. London and New York: Routledge, pp. 53–92.

Moore, H. (1994) 'Bodies on the move: gender, power and material culture', in *A Passion for Difference*. Bloomington, IN: Indiana University Press, pp. 71–85.

Moran, L. (2000) 'Homophobic violence', in S. Munt (ed.) *Cultural Studies and the Working Class*. London: Cassell, pp. 206–18.

Morris, M. (1988) 'Things to do with shopping centres', in S. Sheridan (ed.) *Grafts: Feminist Cultural Criticism*. London: Verso, pp. 193–225.

Morrison, C. and McKay, A. (2000) *The Experience of Violence and Harassment of Gay Men in Edinburgh*. Edinburgh: Scottish Executive Central Research Unit.

Mort, F. (1998) 'Cityscapes, consumption, masculinities and the mapping of London since 1950', *Urban Studies* 35/5: 889–907.

Mort, F. (1999) 'Mapping sexual London: The Wolfenden Committee on Homosexual Offences and Prostitution 1954–57', in F. Mort and L. Nead (eds) *Sexual Geographies*. London: Lawrence and Wishart, pp. 92–113.

Mort, F. (2000a) *Dangerous Sexualities: Medico-Moral Politics in England since 1830*. London and New York: Routledge.

Mort, F. (2000b) 'The sexual geography of the city', in G. Bridge and S. Watson (eds) *A Companion to the City*. Oxford: Blackwell, pp. 307–15.

Mort, F. and Nead, L. (eds) (1999) *Sexual Geographies*. London: Lawrence and Wishart.

Moynihan, D. P. (ed.) (1969) *On Understanding Poverty: Perspectives from the Social Sciences*. New York: Basic Books.

Moynihan, D. P. (ed.) (1970) *Toward a National Urban Policy*. New York: Basic Books.

Munt, S. (1995) 'The lesbian *flâneur*', in D. Bell and G. Valentine (eds) *Mapping Desire: Geographies of Sexualities*. London and New York: Routledge, pp. 114–25.

Murray, C. (1994) *Losing Ground: American Social Policy, 1950–1980*. Second edition. New York: Basic Books.

Myslik, W. (1996) 'Renegotiating the social/sexual identities of places: gay communities as sites of resistance', in N. Duncan (ed.) *BodySpace: Destabilizing Geographies of Gender and Sexuality*. London and New York: Routledge, pp. 156–69.

Nash, K. (2000) *Contemporary Political Sociology: Globalization, Politics and Power*. Oxford: Blackwell.

Nast, H. and Pile, S. (eds) (1998) *Places Through the Body*. London and New York: Routledge.

Nead, L. (1988) *Myths of Sexuality: Representations of Women in Victorian Britain*. Oxford: Basil Blackwell.

Nead, L. (1997) 'Mapping the self: gender, space and modernity in mid-Victorian London', in R. Porter (ed.) *Rewriting the Self: Histories from the Renaissance to the Present*. London and New York: Routledge, pp. 167–85.

Nead, L. (1999) 'From alleys to courts: obscenity and the mapping of mid-Victorian London', in F. Mort and L. Nead (eds) *Sexual Geographies*. London: Lawrence and Wishart.

Nead, L. (2000) *Victorian Babylon: People, Streets and Images in Nineteenth-Century London*. New Haven, CT: Yale University Press.

Neal, P. (ed.) (2003) *Urban Villages and the Making of Communities*. London: Spon Press.

Negt, O. and Kluge, A. (1993) *Public Sphere and Experience: Analysis of the Bourgeois and Proletarian Public Sphere*. Minneapolis, MN: University of Minnesota Press.

Newman, O. (1972) *Defensible Space: Crime Prevention through Urban Design*. New York: Macmillan.

Nisbet, R. (1953) *The Quest for Community*. Oxford: Oxford University Press.

NLB (1979) 'Publisher's note', in W. Benjamin (1985) *One Way Street and Other Writings*. London: Verso.

Nochlin, L. (1992) 'Lost and found: once more the fallen woman', in N. Broude and M. D. Garrard (eds) *The Expanding Discourse: Feminism and Art History*. New York: HarperCollins, pp. 221–46.

Nochlin, L. (1999) *Representing Women*. London: Thames and Hudson.

Nochlin, L. and Bolloch, J. (1998) *Women in the Nineteenth Century*. New York: The New Press.

O'Connor, A. (2001) *Poverty Knowledge: Social Science, Social Policy and the Poor in Twentieth-Century US History*. Princeton, NJ: Princeton University Press.

Ogborn, M. (1992) 'Love-state-ego: "centres" and "margins" in nineteenth-century Britain', *Environment and Planning D: Society and Space* 10/3: 287–305.

Osofsky, F. (1971) *Harlem: The Making of a Ghetto*. New York: Harper and Row.

Pain, R. (1991) 'Space, sexual violence and social control: integrating geographical and feminist analyses of women's fear', *Progress in Human Geography* 15/4: 415–31.

Pain, R. (1997) 'Social geographies of women's fear of crime', *Transactions of the Institute of British Geographers* 22/2: 231–44.

Pain, R. (2000) 'Place, social relations and the fear of crime: a review', *Progress in Human Geography* 24/3: 365–87.

Pain, R. (2001) 'Gender, race, age and fear in the city', *Urban Studies* 38/5–6: 899–913.

Parenti, C. (2003) *The Soft Cage: Surveillance in America from Slavery to the War on Terror*. New York: Basic Books.

Park, R. E. (1928) 'Foreword', in L. Wirth, *The Ghetto*. Chicago: University of Chicago Press, pp. vii–ix.

Park, R. E. (1967a [1925]) 'The city: suggestions for the investigation of human behavior in the urban environment', in R. E. Park et al. (eds) *The City*. Chicago: University of Chicago Press, pp. 1–46.

Park, R. E. (1967b [1925]) 'Community organization and juvenile delinquency', in R. E. Park et al. (eds) *The City*. Chicago: University of Chicago Press, pp. 99–112.

Park, R. E. (1967c [1925]) 'Community organization and the romantic temper', in R. E. Park et al. (eds) *The City*. Chicago: University of Chicago Press, pp. 113–122.

Park, R. E. (1967d [1925]) 'Magic, mentality, and mental life', in R. E. Park et al. (eds) *The City*. Chicago: University of Chicago Press, pp. 123–41.

Park. R. E., Burgess, E. W. and McKenzie, R. D. (eds) (1967 [1925]) *The City*. Chicago: University of Chicago Press.

Parker, K. D. (2001) 'Black–white differences in perceptions of fear of crime', *Journal of Social Psychology* 128/4: 487–94.

Parsons, D. (2000) *Streetwalking the Metropolis*. Oxford: Oxford University Press.

Patterson, J. (2000) *America's Struggle against Poverty in the Twentieth Century*. Cambridge, MA: Harvard University Press.

Peake, L. (1993) ' "Race" and sexuality: challenging the patriarchal structuring of urban social space', *Environment and Planning D: Society and Space* 11/6: 415–32.

Perec, G. (1999 [1974]) *Species of Spaces and Other Pieces*. Harmondsworth: Penguin.

Phillips, R., Watt, D. and Shuttledon, D. (eds) (2000) *De-centring Sexualities: Politics and Representation Beyond the Metropolis*. London and New York: Routledge.

Pickvance, C. (1995) 'Where have urban movements gone?' in D. Sadler and C. Hadjimichaels (eds) *Europe at the Margins: New Mosaic of Inequality*. Chichester: Wiley, pp. 197–217.

Pile, S. (1996) *The Body and the City: Psychoanalysis, Space and Subjectivity*. London and New York: Routledge.

Pile, S. (1999) 'The heterogeneity of cities', in S. Pile, C. Brook and G. Mooney (eds) *Unruly Cities? Order/Disorder*. London and New York: Routledge, pp. 7–41.

Pile, S., Brook, C. and Mooney, G. (eds) (1999) *Unruly Cities: Order/Disorder*. London and New York: Routledge.

Pile, S. and Keith, M. (eds) (1997) *Geographies of Resistance*. London and New York: Routledge.

Pile, S. and Thrift, N. (eds) (1995) *Mapping the Subject: Geographies of Cultural Transformation*. London and New York: Routledge.

Pollock, G. (1988) 'Modernity and the spaces of femininity', in *Vision and Difference*. London and New York: Routledge, pp. 50–90.

Portes, A. and Landolt, P. (1996) 'The downside of social capital', *The American Prospect* 26 (May–June): 18–21.

Posener, J. (1982) *Spray It Loud*. London: Routledge and Kegan Paul.

Potter, S. and Lloyd-Evans, S. (1998) *The City in the Developing World*. Harlow: Longman.

Powers, S. (1999) *The Art of Getting Over: Graffiti at the Millennium*. New York: St Martin's Press.

Putnam, R. (2000) *Bowling Alone*. New York: Simon and Schuster.

Quilley, S. (1997) 'Constructing Manchester's "New Urban Village": gay space in the entrepreneurial city', in G. Ingram et al. (eds) *Queers in Space*. Seattle: Bay Press, pp. 275–95.

Radner, H. (1999) 'Roaming the city: proper women in improper places', in M. Featherstone and S. Lash (eds) *Spaces of Culture: City–Nation–World*. London and Newbury Park, CA: Sage, pp. 86–100.

Reda, J. (1996) *The Ruins of Paris*. London: Reaktion.

Riley, D. (2002) 'The right to be lonely', *differences* 13/1: 1–13.

Robbins, B. (ed.) (1993) *The Phantom Public Sphere.* Minneapolis, MN: University of Minnesota Press.

Robinson, J. (1999) 'Divisive cities: power and segregation in cities', in S. Pile, C. Brook and G. Mooney (eds) *Unruly Cities? Order/Disorder.* London and New York: Routledge, pp. 149–91.

Robinson, J. (2005) *Ordinary Cities: Between Modernity and Development.* London and New York: Routledge.

Rodaway, P. (1994) *Sensuous Geographies: Body, Sense and Place.* London and New York: Routledge.

Rose, N. (1999) *Powers of Freedom: Reframing Political Thought.* Cambridge: Cambridge University Press.

Rothblum, E. D. and Bond, L. A. (eds) (1996) *Preventing Heterosexism and Homophobia.* London and Newbury Park, CA: Sage.

Rothenberg, T. (1995) ' "And she told two friends": lesbians creating urban social space', in D. Bell and G. Valentine (eds) *Mapping Desire: Geographies of Sexualities.* London and New York: Routledge, pp. 165–81.

Ryan, M. P. (1990) *Women in Public: Between Banners and Ballots 1825–1880.* Baltimore, MD: Johns Hopkins University Press.

Ryan, W. (1971) *Blaming the Victim.* New York: Pantheon Books.

Rybczynski, W. (1995) *City Life: Urban Expectations in a New World.* New York: Scribner.

Sadler, S. (1999) *The Situationist City.* Cambridge, MA: MIT Press.

Sassen, S. (2001) *The Global City.* Second edition. Princeton, NJ: Princeton University Press.

Sassen, S. (ed.) (2002) *Global Networks, Linked Cities.* London and New York: Routledge.

Saunders, P. (1995) *Social Theory and the Urban Question.* Second edition. London and New York: Routledge.

Saunders, P. (2001) 'Urban ecology', in R. Paddison (ed.) *Handbook of Urban Studies.* London and Newbury Park, CA: Sage, pp. 36–51.

Savage, M., Warde, A. and Ward, K. (2003) *Urban Sociology, Capitalism and Modernity.* Basingstoke: Palgrave Macmillan.

Self, W. (1999) 'Big Dome', in *London: The Lives of the City. Granta* 65 (Spring): 116–25.

Seligman, A. (2000) 'Trust and civil society', in F. Tonkiss and A. Passey (eds) *Trust and Civil Society.* Basingstoke: Macmillan, pp. 12–30.

Sennett, R. (1974) *The Fall of Public Man.* New York: W. W. Norton.

Sennett, R. (1990) *The Conscience of the Eye: The Design and Social Life of Cities.* New York: Alfred A. Knopf.

Sennett, R. (1994) *Flesh and Stone: The Body and the City in Western Civilization.* New York: W. W. Norton.

Shaw, C. R. and McKay, H. D. (1942) *Juvenile Delinquency and Urban Areas.* Chicago: University of Chicago Press.

Shevky, E. and Bell, W. (1955) *Social Area Analysis.* Stanford, CA: Stanford University Press.

Showalter, E. (1990) *Sexual Anarchy: Gender and Culture at the Fin de Siècle.* New York: Viking.

Sibley, D. (1995) *Geographies of Exclusion.* London and New York: Routledge.

Simmel, G. (1997a [1903]) 'The sociology of space', in D. Frisby and M. Featherstone (eds) *Simmel on Culture.* London and Newbury Park, CA: Sage, pp. 137–70.

Simmel, G. (1997b [1903]) 'The metropolis and mental life', in D. Frisby and M. Featherstone (eds) *Simmel on Culture.* London and Newbury Park, CA: Sage, pp. 174–85.

Simmel, G. (1997c [1909]) 'Bridge and door', in D. Frisby and M. Featherstone (eds) *Simmel on Culture.* London and Newbury Park, CA: Sage, pp. 170–4.

Simmel, G. (2004 [1908]) 'The stranger', in C. Jenks (ed.) *Urban Culture: Critical Concepts in Literary and Cultural Studies.* London and New York: Routledge, vol. III, pp. 73–7.

Skelton, T. and Valentine, G. (eds) (1998) *Cool Places: Geographies of Youth Cultures*. London and New York: Routledge.

Skogan, W.G. (1990) *Disorder and Decline: Crime and the Spiral of Decay in American Neighborhoods*. New York: Free Press.

Smith, M. P. (1980) *The City and Social Theory*. Oxford: Basil Blackwell.

Smith, M. P. (2001) *Transnational Urbanism: Locating Globalization*. Oxford: Blackwell.

Smith, M. P. and Feagin, J. R. (eds) (1987) *The Capitalist City*. Oxford: Basil Blackwell.

Smith, N. (1986) 'Gentrification, the frontier, and the restructuring of urban space', in N. Smith and P. Williams (eds) *Gentrification of the City*. London: Allen and Unwin, pp. 15–34.

Smith, N. (1987) 'Of yuppies and housing: gentrification, social restructuring and the urban dream', *Environment and Planning D: Society and Space* 5/2: 151–72.

Smith, N. (1991) 'Mapping the gentrification frontier', in M. Keith and A. Rogers (eds) *Hollow Promises: Rhetoric and Reality in the Inner City*. London: Mansell, pp. 85–109.

Smith, N. (1992) 'New city, new frontier', in M. Sorkin (ed.) *Variations on a Theme Park: The New American City and the End of Public Space*. New York: Hill and Wang, pp. 61–93.

Smith, N. (1996a) 'After Tompkins Square Park: degentrification and the revanchist city', in A. D. King (ed.) *Re-Presenting the City: Ethnicity, Capital and Culture in the 21st Century Metropolis*. London: Macmillan, pp. 93–107.

Smith, N. (1996b) *The New Urban Frontier: Gentrification and the Revanchist City*. London and New York: Routledge.

Smith, N. (2001) 'Global social cleansing, postliberalism, revanchism and the export of Zero Tolerance', *Social Justice* 28/3: 68–74.

Smith, N. (2002) 'New globalism, new urbanism: gentrification as global urban strategy', *Antipode* 34/3: 427–50.

Smith, N. and Williams, P. (eds) (1986) *Gentrification of the City*. London: Allen and Unwin.

Smith, S. (1987) 'Residential segregation: a geography of English racism?' in P. Jackson (ed.) *Race and Racism: Essays in Social Geography*. London: Allen and Unwin.

Smith, S. J. (2000) 'Graffiti', in S. Pile and N. Thrift (eds) *City, A–Z*. London and New York: Routledge, pp. 86–9.

Soja, E. (1995) *Thirdspace*. Oxford: Blackwell.

Soja, E. (2000) *Postmetropolis: Critical Studies of Cities and Regions*. Oxford: Blackwell.

Solomos, J. (1988) *Black Youth, Racism and the State*. Cambridge: Cambridge University Press.

Sontag, S. (1982) 'Unguided tour', in *A Susan Sontag Reader*. Harmondsworth: Penguin.

Sontag, S. (2001 [1987]) 'The pleasure of the image', in *Where the Stress Falls*. New York: Farrar, Straus and Giroux, pp. 142–50.

Sorkin, M. (1991) *Exquisite Corpse: Writing on Buildings*. London: Verso.

Sorkin, M. (ed.) (1992) *Variations on a Theme Park: The American City and the End of Public Space*. New York: Hill and Wang.

Spear, A. H. (1967) *Black Chicago: The Making of a Negro Ghetto, 1890–1920*. Chicago: University of Chicago Press.

Staeheli, L. (1996) 'Publicity, privacy and women's political action', *Environment and Planning D: Society and Space* 14/5: 601–19.

Stallybrass, P. and White, A. (1986) *The Politics and Poetics of Transgression*. London: Methuen.

Stanko, E. A. (1995) 'Women, crime and fear', *Annals of the American Association of Social and Political Science* 539: 46–58.

Stanko, E. A. (1996) 'Warnings to women: police advice and women's safety in Britain', *Violence against Women* 2/1: 5–24.

Stein, A. (2001) *The Stranger Next Door: The Story of a Small Community's Battle over Sex, Faith and Civil Rights*. Boston: Beacon Press.

Stewart, S. (1988) 'Ceci tuera cela: graffiti as crime and art', in J. Fekete (ed.) *Life after Postmodernism*. London: Macmillan.

St. John, C. and Heald-Moore, T. (1995) 'Fear of black strangers', *Social Science Research* 24/3: 262–80.

St. John, C. and Heald-Moore, T. (1996) 'Racial prejudice and fear of criminal victimization by strangers in public settings', *Sociological Inquiry* 66/2: 267–84.

Stratford, E. (2002) 'On the edge: a tale of skaters and urban governance', *Social and Cultural Geography* 3/2: 193–206.

Sugrue, T. (1996) *The Origins of the Urban Crisis: Race and Inequality in Post-War Detroit*. Princeton, NJ: Princeton University Press.

Suttles, G. (1968) *The Social Order of the Slum*. Chicago: University of Chicago Press.

Suttles, G. (1972) *The Social Construction of Communities*. Chicago: University of Chicago Press.

Taylor, C. (1992) *Multiculturalism and 'The Politics of Recognition'*. Princeton, NJ: Princeton University Press.

Tester, K. (ed.) (1994) *The Flâneur*. London and New York: Routledge.

Thibaud, J.-P. (2003) 'The sonic composition of the city', in M. Bull and L. Back (eds) *The Auditory Culture Reader*. Oxford and New York: Berg, pp. 329–41.

Thrasher, F. (1963) *The Gang*. Abridged edition. Chicago: University of Chicago Press.

Thrift, N. (2000) 'Not a straight line but a curve, or, cities are not mirrors of modernity', in D. Bell and A. Haddour (eds) *City Visions*. London: Longman, pp. 233–63.

Tönnies, F. (1955) *Community and Society*. London: Routledge and Kegan Paul.

Touraine, A. (1981) *The Voice and the Eye: An Analysis of Social Movements*. Cambridge: Cambridge University Press.

Urry, J. (1995) *Consuming Places*. London and New York: Routledge.

Valentine, G. (1989) 'The geography of women's fear', *Area* 21/4: 385–90.

Valentine, G. (1991) 'Women's fear and the design of public space', *Built Environment* 18/4: 288–303.

Valentine, G. (1992) 'Images of danger: women's sources of information about the spatial distribution of male violence', *Area* 24/1: 22–9.

Valentine, G. (1993) '(Hetero)sexing space: lesbian perceptions and experiences of everyday spaces', *Environment and Planning D: Society and Space* 11/4: 395–413.

Valentine, G. (1995) 'Out and about: geographies of lesbian landscapes', *International Journal of Urban and Regional Research* 19/1: 96–111.

Valentine, G. (1996) '(Re)negotiating the heterosexual street: lesbian productions of space', in N. Duncan (ed.) *BodySpace: Destabilizing Geographies of Gender and Sexuality*. London and New York: Routledge, pp. 146–55.

Valentine, G. (2000) *From Nowhere to Everywhere: Lesbian Geographies*. Binghamton, NY: Harrington Park Press.

Valentine, G. and Skelton, T. (2003) 'Finding oneself, losing oneself: the lesbian and gay "scene" as a paradoxical space', *International Journal of Urban and Regional Research* 27/4: 849–67.

Wacquant, L. (1993) 'Urban outcasts: stigma and division in the Black American ghetto and the French urban periphery', *International Journal of Urban and Regional Research* 17/3: 366–83.

Wacquant, L. (1994) 'The new urban color line: the state and fate of the ghetto in Postfordist America', in C. J. Calhoun (ed.) *Social Theory and the Politics of Identity*. Oxford: Basil Blackwell, pp. 231–76.

Wacquant, L. (1996) 'Red Belt, Black Belt: racial division, class inequality, and the state in the French urban periphery and the American ghetto', in E. Mingeone (ed.) *Urban Poverty and the 'Underclass': A Reader*. Oxford: Basil Blackwell.

Wacquant, L. (2002) 'The rise of advanced marginality: notes on its nature and implications', in P. Marcuse and R. van Kempen (eds) *Of States and Cities: The Partitioning of Urban Space*. Oxford: Oxford University Press, pp. 221–39.

Walker, L. (1998) 'Home and away: the feminist remapping of private and public space in Victorian London', in R. Ainley (ed.) *New Frontiers of Space, Bodies and Gender*. London and New York: Routledge, pp. 65–75.

Walklate, S. and Evans, K. (1999) *Zero Tolerance or Community Tolerance? Managing Crime in High Crime Areas*. Aldershot: Ashgate.

Walkowitz, J. R. (1980) *Prostitution and Victorian Society: Women, Class and the State*. Cambridge: Cambridge University Press.

Walkowitz, J. R. (1992) *City of Dreadful Delight: Narratives of Sexual Danger in Late Victorian London*. London: Virago.

Walkowitz, J. R. (1998) 'Going public: shopping, street harassment, and streetwalking in late Victorian London', *Representations* 62 (Spring): 1–30.

Walton, J. (1987) 'Urban protest and the global political economy: the IMF riots', in M. P. Smith and J. R. Feagin (eds) *The Capitalist City*. Oxford: Blackwell, pp. 354–86.

Walzer, M. (1997) *On Toleration*. New Haven, CT: Yale University Press.

Warde, A. (1991) 'Gentrification as consumption: issues of class and gender', *Environment and Planning D: Society and Space* 9/2: 223–32.

Warner, M. (2002) 'Publics and counter-publics', *Public Culture* 14/10: 49–90.

Warr, M. (1984) 'Fear of victimization: why are women and the elderly more afraid?' *Social Science Quarterly* 65: 681–702.

Warr, M. (1985) 'Fear of rape among urban women', *Social Problems* 32/3: 238–50.

Watson, S. (1999) 'City politics', in S. Pile, C. Brook and G. Mooney (eds) *Unruly Cities? Order/Disorder*. London and New York: Routledge, pp. 201–39.

Weisman, L. K. (1992) *Discrimination by Design: A Feminist Critique of the Man-Made Environment*. Urbana, IL: University of Illinois Press.

White, E. B. (1999 [1949]) *Here is New York*. New York: The Little Bookroom.

Whyte, W. (1943) *Street Corner Society: The Social Structure of an Italian Slum*. Chicago: University of Chicago Press.

Whyte, W. (1988) *City: Rediscovering the Center*. New York: Doubleday.

Willmott, P. (1966) *Adolescent Boys in East London*. London: Routledge and Kegan Paul.

Willmott, P. and Young, M. (1960) *Family and Class in a London Suburb*. London: Routledge and Kegan Paul.

Wilson, E. (1991) *The Sphinx in the City: Urban Life, Control and the Disorder of Women*. London: Virago.

Wilson, E. (1992) 'The invisible *flâneur*', *New Left Review* 195: 90–110.

Wilson, J. Q. and Kelling, G. L. (1982) 'Broken windows: the police and neighborhood safety', *The Atlantic Monthly* 249/3: 29–38.

Wilson, W. J. (1978) *The Declining Significance of Race: Blacks and Changing American Institutions*. Chicago: University of Chicago Press.

Wilson, W. J. (1987) *The Truly Disadvantaged: The Inner City, the Underclass, and Public Policy*. Chicago: University of Chicago Press.

Wilson, W. J. (1996) *When Work Disappears: The World of the New Urban Poor*. New York: Vintage.

Winchester, H. and White, P. (1988) 'The location of marginalised groups in the inner city', *Environment and Planning D: Society and Space* 6/1: 37–54.

Wirth, L. (1928) *The Ghetto*. Chicago: University of Chicago Press.

Wirth, L. (1967 [1925]) 'A bibliography of the urban community', in R. E. Park et al. (eds) *The City*. Chicago: University of Chicago Press, pp. 161–228.

Wirth, L. (1995 [1938]) 'Urbanism as a way of life', in P. Kasinitz (ed.) *Metropolis: Centre and Symbol of Our Time*. Basingstoke: Macmillan, pp. 58–82.

Wolf, D. G. (1979) *The Lesbian Community*. Berkeley, CA: University of California Press.

Wolff, J. (1985) 'The invisible *flâneuse*: women and the literature of modernity', *Theory, Culture and Society* 2/3: 37–46.

Wolff, J. (1990) 'The culture of separate spheres: the role of culture in nineteenth-century public and private life', in *Feminine Sentences*. Berkeley, CA: University of California Press, pp. 12–33.

Wolman, H. and Agius, E. (eds) (1996) *National Urban Policy*. Detroit, IL: Wayne State University Press.

Worpole, K. (1992) 'Safety in numbers: towards women-friendly cities', in *Towns for People*. Buckingham: Open University Press, pp. 50–65.

Young, I. M. (1990a) *Justice and the Politics of Difference*. Princeton, NJ: Princeton University Press.

Young, I. M. (1990b) 'The ideal of community and the politics of difference', in L. Nicholson (ed.) *Feminism/Postmodernism*. London and New York: Routledge, pp. 300–23.

Young, M. and Willmott, P. (1957) *Family and Kinship in East London*. London: Routledge and Kegan Paul.

Zukin, S. (1982) *Loft Living: Culture and Capital in Urban Change*. Baltimore, MD: Johns Hopkins University Press.

Zukin, S. (1993) *Landscapes of Power: From Detroit to Disneyworld*. Berkeley, CA: University of California Press.

Zukin, S. (1996) 'Space and symbols in an age of decline', in A. D. King (ed.) *Re-presenting the City: Ethnicity, Capital and Culture in the 21st-Century Metropolis*. Basingstoke: Macmillan, pp. 43–59.

Zukin, S. (1998) 'Urban lifestyles: diversity and standardization in spaces of consumption', *Urban Studies* 35/5–6: 825–39.

Index

Adorno, T. 124
Amin, A. 2, 59, 66, 126, 149
Anderson, E. 4, 53–4, 69–72, 76, 91–2
anonymity 8–9, 13, 23–4, 27–9, 57, 95, 107,
    111, 118–19, 127, 141
anti-Semitism 41–4
architecture 60, 87–9, 93
assimilation 39–40
asyndeton 143–5
Atget, E. 124–5

Back, L. 46, 141
Barthes, R. 4, 7, 102, 131–2, 135–8, 140,
    146, 149
Bauman, Z. 25, 79
begging 74, 77–9
Bell, D. 96, 106, 110–11
belonging 12, 15–17, 20–1, 25–7, 67–8, 73,
    79, 141
Benjamin, W. 1, 4, 6, 11, 81, 113–15, 117,
    119–30, 140, 141, 144, 146, 149–50
Berlin 3–4, 81, 114–24, 128
Bhabha, H. 9
'Black Belt' 39, 45
blasé attitude 116–17, 126
bodies 23, 59, 94–100, 128, 141, 144–5
Borden, I. 144–5
borders 30-2, 46, 57–8, 122, 141, 143
Boston 10, 17–18, 83, 109
boundaries *see* borders
Bourdieu, P. 97
Burgess, E. 30, 33–40, 45–6, 49, 82, 84–5

Carter, A. 130
Casey, E. 122, 126
Castells, M. 36, 61–3, 66, 82, 87, 91, 107–9,
    148–9
CCTV 76, 104
Chicago 3, 35–6, 40–2, 45–6, 51, 56, 84
Chicago School 1–2, 4, 8, 11–16, 30, 32–47,
    49, 52, 54, 70, 80–1, 85, 107
children 20, 54, 86, 103, 139
Chinatown 39, 44–5
Chinese communities 41, 45
Christopherson, S. 57, 74, 76, 90, 92
class 9, 18–22, 33–9, 51, 53–5, 57, 61, 67–73,
    78, 80, 84–7, 106–9
cognitive maps *see* mental maps
collective consumption 54–5, 61–2, 91
community 8–10, 12, 14–22, 24–9, 34, 40–3,
    78, 95, 106–9

definition 15–16, 24–5, 44
politics 24–9, 65–8, 108
community studies 18–20
consciousness 30, 113–19, 130, 148
consumption 54, 72–4, 81–2, 87–8, 93, 96,
    109–10, 140
    see also collective consumption
control 14, 36–7, 72–5, 101–2
counter-spaces 64, 68, 107, 134–5
    see also heterotopia
crime 30, 34, 46–7, 49–51, 55, 77
criminals 38–9, 74
cultural capital 55, 110
culture jamming 146
culture of poverty 52–3, 56, 84

danger 95, 102–5, 112
Davis, M. 36–7, 56–7, 74–5
de Certeau, M. 3–4, 6–7, 63, 87, 89, 113–15,
    120, 126–9, 131–2, 137–50
deindustrialization 48, 51, 69, 82
delinquency 39–40, 46, 49–50
demonstrations *see* protest
deprivation 30, 45, 47–8, 53, 70, 81, 84, 92
Derrida, J. 136
development 17, 19–20, 63, 73, 81, 86, 88
deviance 50, 133
difference 9, 11, 15, 17, 23–58, 63, 68, 90,
    94, 107, 111, 118–19, 134
disorganization 30, 33, 40, 49–56, 70
distinction 75, 78–9, 86–9, 93
diversity 15, 25, 32–3, 58, 89–93
    see also heterogeneity; social mix
Durkheim, É. 12–13, 119

'ecology of fear' (Davis) 36–7
economic restructuring 51, 70, 85
elderly people 102–3
erotics of space 132, 135–7, 149
ethnicity 8–9, 15, 18–19, 22, 25, 33–4,
    38–40, 45–8, 83
    see also minorities
exclusion 26, 28, 30–1, 38–9, 43, 48, 52,
    55–6, 58, 63, 66, 68, 72–9, 96, 141, 145

family ties 12–13, 18–19, 24, 41
fear 102–5
feminism 68, 95, 97, 100–1, 131, 141
Fischer, C. 106–8
flâneur 124–9
flash mobs 146–7

168